DANIEL DAY-LEWIS

DANIEL DAY-LEWIS

The Fire Within

GARRY JENKINS

St. Martin's Press
New York

DANIEL DAY-LEWIS: THE FIRE WITHIN. Copyright © 1994
by Garry Jenkins. All rights reserved. Printed in the
United States of America. No part of this book may
be used or reproduced in any manner whatsoever without
written permission except in the case of brief quotations
embodied in critical articles or reviews.
For information, address St. Martin's Press,
175 Fifth Avenue, New York, N.Y. 10010.

Library of Congress Cataloging-in-Publication Data

Jenkins, Garry.
Daniel Day-Lewis : the fire within / Garry Jenkins.
        p.   cm.
        ISBN 0-312-13044-9
1. Day-Lewis, Daniel. 2. Actors—Great Britain—Biography.
                I. Title.
        PN2598.D323J46   1995
        791.43'028'092—dc20
        [B]   95-12418   CIP

First published in Great Britain by Sidgwick & Jackson

First U.S. Edition: July 1995
10   9   8   7   6   5   4   3   2   1

To Eric and Jean – simply for everything.

CONTENTS

'You cannot create experience. You must undergo it.'
ALBERT CAMUS

PROLOGUE

DUBLIN, December, and the dead of night. The River Liffey runs cold and Stygian black, a callous wind knifes its way down O'Connell Street, there is snow in the air, the snow of James Joyce's *Dubliners*, 'falling faintly through the universe and faintly falling'.

If the body-language of another of Ireland's artist-heroes is to be believed, the faintest of flakes are settling somewhere in the soul of Daniel Day-Lewis. In the Donnybrook studios of Radio Telefis Eireann his slow-breaking smile is dissolving, his chiselled features are fretting themselves into cruel contortions. Under the table his long, slender fingers are nervously knotting and unknotting themselves, his limpid eyes are riveting a stare into the ground.

It is many months since he was freed from the shackles of a jail called Gerry Conlon. The pain of his incarceration in the cells of Dublin's Ardmore film studios and Kilmainham Prison has passed. 'Like a toothache.' Yet once more, as a questioning world closes in around him, he carries the look of a caged man.

It should not be this way. In Dublin he should feel warmer and safer than anywhere else in the world. On this weekend of all weekends.

The 'hooley' started last night, with the premiere of the movie about Conlon and the Guildford Four, *In the Name of the Father*. The 'crack' had been great, the Guinness flowed freely, it had been another fine feather in the cap for the auld country.

Twenty-four hours after the screening at the Savoy Cinema on O'Connell Street all the talk is still of Gerry and Guiseppe,

1

Daniel and Pete, the unbreakable bond of father and son. No one should be feeling the cold, only the ember afterglow.

Daniel Day-Lewis is in Donnybrook to appear on Ireland's best-loved TV programme, *The Late, Late Show*. He is surrounded by faces familiar and familial. On his right shoulder there is 'Shay', Jim Sheridan to the rest of the gathering, but 'Shay' to his adopted brother and son, collaborator on two movies and sharer of a million more harebrained ideas. To his left there is Pete Postlethwaite, a friend and mentor since distant drama school days. Elsewhere sit Emma Thompson, Paddy Armstrong, Terry George and Arthur Lappin. Each is a friend, a protector, a doctor in the 'hospital of the spirits' that is Ireland.

Even his inquisitor wears a filial face. Gay Byrne, 'Gaybo' to the man on the Killarney omnibus, shares a passion for football and fast motor-cycles. He speaks in a blarney-blessed patter and smiles leprechaun smiles. He too is friend not foe.

For most of the hour-long show he had seemed a seamless part of it. 'Gaybo' had shown clips from the film: Daniel as Gerry Conlon fleeing the Brits, Pete as his father Guiseppe in a cell with his son, Emma as Gareth Pierce, the lawyer fighting to quash their convictions for IRA bombings.

Between the clips had come questions, each of the assembly, faces still nicely coloured from the night before, taking turns. Shay had defended the accuracy of a film that had caused predictable fury in Great Britain. 'We took a little bit of poetic licence, but nothing compared to what the English policemen took.' Emma Thompson landed a laugh, eulogizing on Sheridan's uniqueness. 'He is the only director to have punched me on the dance-floor!' Postlethwaite topped it with a memory from his Bristol Old Vic days with Daniel. His teacher had described Pete as having 'a face like a fucking stone archway'.

Daniel Day-Lewis had sat, laughing, clapping, smiling at it all, party to it all. Now, though, the time for his question has come. And now a million fellow-Irishmen watch him descend deep into his mists. The snow of *Dubliners*, 'flakes silver and dark', starts falling.

As usual, the question is about the Method, the madness

2

therein. The stories about the extraordinary lengths he had gone to in immersing himself in the role of the rapscallion Conlon had flown around Dublin and then the world during filming. There had been abuse, interrogations, pails of cold water and porridge. He had spent two days and nights in a cell.

'Daniel, would you speak to us about that?' Gaybo asks. 'Absolutely not,' he replies.

The fingers knot and unknot themselves, the eyes fix themselves on the floor, the fine features warp themselves with worry. Nervous laughter, then silence. A deafening one.

A few beats later and it breaks. The reassuring looks of friends encourage him. But Gaybo and the rest know he will not yield an answer. In the end Daniel Day-Lewis says something. But only by way of explaining nothing.

'I have never felt able to describe it in such a way that I thought was an accurate reflection or an accurate description of the way I work,' he says, his forehead creased in concentration. 'So I thought it was pointless talking about it.

'People choose to speak about it on my behalf. These strange rumours go about and through Chinese whispers they become more and more flamboyant and perverse. I do nothing to stop them, perhaps I should.'

He smiles a charming smile, shrugs his hunched shoulders and sighs. Like Byron's Prisoner of Chillon, he finds freedom with a sigh. Moments later he is released.

It is the enigma in microcosm, a life in a moment. Private in his publicity, eloquent in his inarticulacy, civil in his disobedience, somehow lost in the place he now calls home. Free one moment, imprisoned the next, free again after that, but never truly so.

Soon it will be ten years since the conundrum was set, since two belief-beggaring roles announced his arrival to the world. Since then his stock has climbed, a ceiling nowhere in sight. Today he stands acknowledged: the most accomplished actor of his generation.

In that time, just as he has on this night, he has talked a little and told us even less. In the jagged void, the whispers have become a roar, the most confused roar in cinema.

3

For every answer there is another question. It is a Churchillian puzzle, a riddle wrapped in a mystery inside an enigma. Is he the man in the Byronic mask or Hamlet in hiding? Is he cracked actor or cool chameleon, the first British hunk or the Last of the Method Mohicans? Is he Disparate Dan, Dan Juan, or simply Dan yer man the Anglo-Irishman?

It is time to find out.

CHAPTER ONE

AWKWARD CUSTOMERS

'Deep in the cavern of the infant's breast,
The father's nature lurks and lives anew.'

HORACE, *Odes*

THE PRINCE emerged, aquiline and ashen, fierce-boned, fire-eyed, a mask of nobility concealing a mass of anxiety. Daniel Day-Lewis will always remember Prince Florizel, son of Polixenes, King of Bohemia, an heir burdened by the expectations of an eminent father. That night, in December 1971, he somehow shared his pain.

He was a 'morose and spotty' fourteen-year-old when he first stepped from darkness to light, from the wings to the stage at Bedales School, in Hampshire. It was his debut as a serious actor: Shakespeare, *The Winter's Tale*, Prince Florizel.

Art imitated his young life in an instant. The words of his opening scene, Act Four, Scene Four, resonated with echoes. Polixenes, angered at not having been consulted over his son's choice of a shepherd girl, Perdita, for a bride, rejected the Prince.

> Thou art too base
> To be acknowledged.
> Thou a sceptre's heir,
> That thus affects a sheep-hook?

Moments later Florizel mourned the loss of his King's love:

> Should I now meet my father
> He would not call me son.

In his troubled mind, Daniel Day-Lewis too had imagined his father might think him unworthy, that somehow he too

5

would not call him son. Like Florizel, he yearned for a father's acceptance. That December night, however, acceptance was a mere few yards away. There the Poet Laureate Cecil Day-Lewis sat, dying, delighted.

Every day Daniel Day-Lewis regrets his father did not live to witness other, wiser performances. He wishes he had stayed to see him flourish into the wonder of his acting age, be as dedicated to his own art as he was to his, pick up the poet's torch. Cecil Day-Lewis saw Daniel act seriously only once. That night he was proud to call him son.

Cecil Day-Lewis wrote of the sentimental and the sinister, lyric celebrations of life stained with the certain knowledge of death.

He spoke, mostly, in a soft, sing-song brogue made even more seductive by a gentle lisping on his final rs and the affectation of a thoroughbred Irishness that was not quite his to claim. When he did not, the words flew out in a banshee of fury, as short as it was shocking. His words echoed around the enchanted sites of a childhood. Hanging in the brute, Atlantic winds on holidays off Old Head, County Mayo, at home in the thick tobacco smoke of a book-stacked, Greenwich study and in the Christmas morning quiet of a favourite rectory in snow-drifted Dorset. There were so many and yet so few.

His father, Poet Laureate, classicist, translator and detective novelist, was the most potent formative force in the early life of Daniel Day-Lewis. His mother, Jill Balcon, Day-Lewis's second wife, has remained to guide him. Her bequests have been formidable too.

But, in leaving long before Daniel emerged even embryonically as a shining star, Cecil left a tantalizing legacy, a weight his son has found immense, sometimes unbearably so. By his own admission, his feelings for his father have grown rather than diminished. His father's indelible ink underlines every aspect of his life. He provided 'the sack of genes I did not choose, though finally of which I am immensely proud'.

Daniel Day-Lewis has been imprisoned by many forces.

The words and wisdom of his father captivated him first. They are shackles he will never wish to be free of. The story of Daniel Day-Lewis starts with the story of his father.

Cecil Day-Lewis was born on 27 April 1904 in the village of Ballintubbert, County Laois, Ireland. His mother was Kathleen Day-Lewis, his father, the Reverend Frank Day-Lewis, a Church of Ireland clergyman. Both were born in Dublin, the children of English-born fathers drawn to the then second capital of Great Britain, members of that historical half-breed, the Anglo-Irish.

The family name had been born, forty years or so before Cecil's birth, in Dublin. His paternal grandfather, Frank Day of Berkhamsted, Hertfordshire, had travelled to Ireland to join the country's biggest soap-refining business. Its proprietor was one Frank Lewis. In 1863, Frank Day changed his name by deed poll to Frank Day-Lewis.

Within a year of his birth, however, with the Church of Ireland in decline, Cecil's father moved back across to England. Frank and Kathleen moved to Malvern, Worcestershire and, three years later, on to Ealing in west London. Kathleen Day-Lewis died of cancer there when her only child was four years old. Years later the only image of his mother Cecil could summon up was of his coldness at her deathbed. 'I can remember no pain, no perturbation, no sense of parting,' he wrote once. A rootlessness and an inescapable sense of decay took hold at that deathbed, never to leave him.

Cecil was raised by his father and an aunt, Agnes 'Knos' Squires. Frank Day-Lewis continued his peripatetic good works in London and later Nottinghamshire. He was devoted to Cecil, too much so in his son's eyes. He said in later years that he felt suffocated by his affection. Human nature sets us all in rebellion against the experiences of our pasts. So it was to prove when Cecil became a father himself.

Cecil was sent to school at Sherborne in Dorset, a straw-boatered bastion of traditional English education. At school he excelled at sport, playing rugby for the second XV and cricket for his house. He also joined in Sherborne's theatrical society, his most notable venture on to the boards playing Florizel in *A Winter's Tale*.

The performance was memorable not merely for its promise of acting excellence. Cecil, already a dashingly attractive young man with an eye for the opposite sex, had a passionate affair with the girl who played the Prince's love Perdita.

In the classroom he performed well enough to win an exhibition to Wadham College, Oxford. Ambitious and studious, he opted for a degree in 'Greats', Ancient History and Classical Philosophy. '"Mods" teach you to dot your i's, "Greats" teach you to open your i's,' the undergraduate gag went.

A life-long love of literature truly took root at Oxford. Cecil arrived in the dreaming spired citadel during a golden age. It was the time of Graham Greene, Evelyn Waugh and Kenneth Clark. It was also an era of unashamed decadence, orchestrated most flamboyantly by Harold Acton, arch-aesthete prototype for the foppish Anthony Blanche in Waugh's *Brideshead Revisited*.

At school at Eton, Acton's mother had sent him white truffles for tea each day. At varsity it was plovers' eggs. His elegance and style seemed to affect everyone, not just at his college, Christ Church, but all over Oxford. Cecil, something of a dandy even at Sherborne, seems to have been no exception. Until his dying day he retained a dilettantish passion for life's fineries. Good food and chocolate, stylish clothes and cars. His best friend was Rex Warner, a giant of a man. The two shared digs, duets, student pub crawls and a love of rugby and poetry.

Cecil had begun to write poetry long before he went up to university. Throughout his undergraduate years he continued to write prodigiously. In his fourth and final year as an under-graduate he forged the most important literary relationship of his time at Oxford. He and the University's outstanding poet, the Yorkshire-born Wystan (W. H.) Auden remained friends, off and on, for the rest of his life. Together, the two men edited the University's annual publication, *Oxford Poetry*. Two other young writers, Stephen Spender and Louis MacNeice, joined their loose circle. The common thread in their work was to win notoriety.

The Cecil of those Oxford days was a maddening collection of contradictions. He was handsome, charming, witty and always impeccably well-dressed. Then, and throughout his life, his easy manner and genuine warmth inspired affection in almost everyone who met him. Yet, by his own admission, there was another side to him. His solitary childhood had made him a loner, he could be consumed by dark clouds of depression, he also possessed a spectacular short fuse, a temper that normally manifested itself in withering one-line put-downs. Spender once said of him: 'Cecil had a very conscious sense of his intellectual superiority. Malice as well as affection towards others, razorlike contempt, especially for women, perhaps even for those he loved.' Later in his life, in his autobiography, *The Buried Day*, Cecil hoodedly admitted his moodiness and rudeness made him 'an awkward customer'.

As a young man who had already suffered the loss of a parent he had been determined to fly with the winds. His guiding principle at Oxford was 'travel light, unencumbered by your past'. Women were mesmerized by him. The way he looked and talked, the way he dressed and even walked, seemed to stir them. 'He had this very stylish way of holding himself, and dressing, even when he was a schoolboy at Sherborne. The housemaster's daughters used to notice him as he walked with his head held slightly to one side, something he kept up,' his son Sean Day-Lewis remembered. And far from discouraging his admirers, his elusive moodiness made him all the more fascinating.

He had met Mary King at a reading of Shakespeare's *A Midsummer Night's Dream* at Sherborne in 1922. She was the daughter of one of the school's housemasters, Henry King. He fell for her 'beautifully cool voice' and 'the grace of her movements', he later recalled. Their courtship continued throughout his time at Oxford.

Cecil had grown bored with academic study by the second half of his undergraduate years. He admitted later that he spent two years working and two years staring out of the lecture-room windows – at women, clouds, anything. It was typical of a man who, throughout his life, saw many passions peter out. He graduated in 1927 with a disappointing degree, a fourth. In the aspic-set society of England, little has really changed since those times. Then, as now, the natural career for a lower-division graduate was teaching.

He did not enter the profession instantly, however. There was a brief, but disastrous, flirtation with journalism. 'I was offered a book to review. I read it twice, thought about it for three weeks and then found I had nothing to say!' he recalled once.

Cecil took up a post at Summer Fields School, Oxford, and then in Scotland, at Larchfield School in Helensburgh, Dumbartonshire. He was succeeded at the latter by Auden, whose job Cecil fixed for him as a favour. It was during his time in Scotland that he eventually married Mary, two days after Christmas, in 1928. From Larchfield he moved on to a £300-a-year teaching post at Cheltenham preparatory school.

During this period Cecil and Mary had two children. Sean was born in 1931, Nicholas arrived three years later. The arrival of his young family did not deflect Cecil from his ambitions to be a successful writer. By a stroke of luck that is what he became.

Teaching by day and writing by night, Cecil had continued to produce his poetry. It was published in modest print-runs and each volume sold 200 or so copies.

One of Cecil's ten-score followers was T. E. Lawrence, Lawrence of Arabia. In 1934 a newspaper reported that Lawrence had told Winston Churchill the future of British poetry was 'in the hands of Cecil Day-Lewis'. The unsold stock of his back editions, used as a makeshift sofa by his publishers, was sold that morning.

Cecil's sudden rise to celebrity coincided with a new-found political awareness in his life. Britain between the wars, particularly during the 1930s, was a nation in turmoil. Elsewhere in Europe the forces of Communism and Fascism were deconstructing old orders that had stood untouched for centuries. Britain, still a class-riven society but slowly waking up to its waning status as a world super-power and ravaged by the effects of the Depression, viewed events on the Continent with a mixture of fear and hope.

Cecil had witnessed at first hand the misery of the dole queues in his father's parish in rural Nottinghamshire. He had sat and watched coal-miners coughing themselves to death in appalling housing conditions, their children with little hope of a better fate. He had been a staunch socialist for some time, writing for the *Left Review*. By the mid-1930s, however, he had begun to believe that Communism was Western society's salvation.

In 1936 Cecil officially joined the Communist Party and contributed to its mouthpiece, the *Daily Worker* newspaper. He dropped the hyphen from his unproletarian-sounding surname and even stood on street corners selling the paper. He also wrote poems glorifying the ordinary working man. One of them was used as a Communist Christmas card.

His new celebrity and the controversy that his writing aroused again brought him into association with his old Oxford friends, Auden, Spender and MacNeice. They too had all become established poets. Their writing was reflecting a similar political view of the world. Once more they were philosophical fellow-travellers.

The notion of this group of privileged, Oxford-educated swells becoming soul brothers of the revolutionary working classes riled many in Establishment Britain. Their poetry, by now dubbed 'the new poetry' by literary critics, was lampooned as much as it was lauded. Enemies derisively dubbed the quartet's work and its radical message 'McSpaunday' – a mix of all four members' names.

The four fought their corner and continued to argue for socialism. Cecil took on Aldous Huxley, a pacifist, in a public debate on the need to fight Fascism. 'We shall expect no birth hour without blood,' he declared at the time.

World events were soon to render the Utopian dream redundant, however. The rise of Hitler in Germany concentrated Britain's minds on the preservation of its old order. Communism's influence faded, never realistically to return.

Throughout his political period Cecil had continued to write less controversial material. He had even tried his hand at novels and had three published. By his own admission, however, they were not a great success. While school-mastering continued to pay his family's rent, finances were stretched. His predicament was not helped by the fact that his poetry, some of which was becoming defiantly exotic in its language, brought him into conflict with his conservative employers. Once, at Cheltenham, when the headmaster spotted a rather explicit poem of his in a local bookshop, Cecil was summoned to his study. The head thought the verse too 'sexual' and questioned Cecil's fitness to be teaching young boys.

Times were tight and the Cotswold cottage the family was then living in fell into disrepair. Cecil badly needed £100 to fix the roof. After reading scores of the detective novels that were popular at the time, he decided to try his hand in that genre. Writing under the pseudonym of Nicholas Blake, he set himself up as a rival to Dorothy Sayers, H.C. Bailey, and Father Ronald Knox, the leading "mystery" writers in England at the time.

Basing his sleuth, Nigel Strangeways, on his friend Auden, and crashing the book out in three months during a family summer holiday, he produced his first mystery. *Question of Proof* was accepted by Collins in 1935. It went on to earn him £1000 and his agent's blessing to devote himself to full-time writing. Nicholas Blake was to remain Cecil's alter ego for the rest of his life.

For a while he remained an active member of the Communist Party. But by 1938 his flirtation with active politics was over. He resigned from the Party and concentrated on his writing. In later years, he admitted that Communism never helped his writing. Some of his revolutionary rhyming, he conceded, veered dangerously towards doggerel.

By this time he, Mary and their two boys had moved to Musbury in Devon, in the heart of the romantic countryside that inspired Thomas Hardy, Cecil's earliest and most endur-ing literary hero. The verdant West Country landscape remained a welcoming, spiritual place for Cecil throughout his life.

He was a supportive, but strangely distant father to Nick and Sean. 'I think he was conscious of the need not to repeat his father's mistakes in the way of emotional smothering,' Sean said years later in his biography of his father, C. *Day-Lewis: An English Literary Life*. Sean admitted that he suffered a 'disturbed' childhood as a result. 'I was a sleep-walker, fire raiser, nightmare dreamer, bed-wetter.' He attributed his traumas to Cecil's 'parental inhibitions about physical displays of love for a son'. 'There was not much touching in our family,' he recalled.

Despite Cecil's distance, however, there were happy times at Musbury. Sean produced a family newspaper, the *Brimclose News*, after the name of the family's thatched cottage. The journal carried all the family's news, with headlines like 'General Has Kittens', announcing a cat called General de Gaulle's new arrivals. Cecil played cricket in the garden with his boys. 'He was quite good at getting down on all-fours and mucking around and he loved cricket, he was very competitive about it,' says Sean. He remembers a quiet harmony to life. 'He very rarely lost his temper, when he did it made it all the more impressive. He did get depressed and became very quiet but it really was only once in a blue moon that he blew up.'

The peace was destroyed by the outbreak of the Second World War. Cecil served first in the Home Guard in Devon and then in London at the Ministry of Information. Afterwards, while Nicholas Blake earned him a comfortable living, he became, if anything, more passionately committed to poetry. As his former comrades-in-arms, Auden, Spender and Mac-Neice, faded in the eyes of critics in later years, Cecil's verse matured and improved as he grew older.

Politics remained a life-long interest, but there became less and less room for it within his poetry. Instead he wrote about the simpler human issues that moved him. And despite the quintessential Englishness of his education and career – Sherborne and Oxford, prep school teacher turned detective novelist – his admirers began to see a lyrical quality to his writing that was somehow suffused with the melancholy and mysticism of the great Irish writers, Yeats and Joyce.

Such comparisons always pleased him and as his life progressed he was drawn more and more to his Irish lineage. Later in life he wrote a collection of poetry inspired by Ireland called

The Whispering Roots. Thanks to what his son Sean called 'selective knowledge', he contrived family connections to such famous sons of the 'Auld Sod' as Yeats, the writer Oliver Goldsmith and Nicholas the Black, a Welsh pirate who became a Galway wine merchant! A Hibernian softening of his ts and rs became a feature of his readings.

As his poetry matured, love, death, decay and betrayal became familiar themes. And his own life began to provide him with a new wealth of inspirational material.

In the late 1940s he became something of an Establishment figure, giving the prestigious Clark Lecture in poetry at Cambridge University in 1946 and travelling the country reciting, broadcasting, judging competitions and sitting on august bodies like the Book Society Committee. It was during this period that his marriage to Mary broke down.

Women were drawn more than ever to Cecil at this time. His self-effacing wit, his wickedly winning smile and debonair deportment had always been a formidably disarming combination. His by now widespread fame as the most charismatic poet in the country only added to his attraction.

The writer Elizabeth Jane Howard first met him at a cocktail party for the launch of her debut novel. Years later she described him as 'one of the most beautiful men I have ever seen in my life, a marvellous forehead creased or mapped like the tributaries of some river, blue eyes, the head and face a lovely shape, and this extraordinarily captivating voice, at once both soft and pedantic'.

There were times when the poet found temptation impossible to resist. Long afterwards Sean told how he discovered a letter in which his father confessed to having seven mistresses in his life. 'It wasn't the sex that mattered so much as the love affair,' he said in an interview with the London *Evening News*. 'He felt that the love affairs were very good for the poetry.'

One affair outlasted the others, however. The novelist Rosamond Lehmann was one of the most prominent women writers of her generation. Her first novel, *Dusty Answer*, published when she was just twenty-six, was a powerful piece of writing about a woman suffocated by love. She and Cecil were drawn together by the tight-knit world of the London literati. They conducted a long-running romance.

For years, however, Cecil lived a double life, dividing his time between Lehmann, in London, and his wife Mary in Devon. In his book Sean recounted how the situation reached crisis point one weekend in 1947, when he was still at boarding school. That weekend Cecil confessed his adultery to his wife and told her he was leaving her for Lehmann.

'They were going to the station in the car and my mother was pleading with him. Halfway there my father found he didn't have the ruthlessness to go ahead with it and turned back,' Sean said many years afterwards. It was only then, while reading his father's diaries, that he learned himself of the anguish his parents went through.

In the end, however, Cecil was to summon up the strength to leave Mary. He left Lehmann at the same time. It was another woman who provided him with the strength to walk away.

Cecil had met Jill Balcon at the BBC's radio studios at Alexandra Palace one evening in January 1948. There they read selections of poetry by Robert Browning together. Cecil had spoken in his famously smooth, faintly Irish brogue. The twenty-three-year-old actress, already a veteran radio voice, had delivered her pieces in a calm, controlled, thoroughly unruffled BBC English. Inside, however, she had been a maelstrom of emotions. 'She recognized their love at first sight,' her best friend, Elizabeth Jane Howard, recalled years later.

Cecil had been under the impression that it was their first encounter. But he was wrong. Ten years earlier he had travelled to Roedean School to judge a drama competition. At the back of the hall where the competition was held, a determined twelve-year-old had slotted herself into a position from where she could get a clear view of the eminent poet. The young Jill Balcon was already a passionate poetry fan, and an admirer of Cecil Day-Lewis in particular. She was not disappointed by her first glimpse of the writer in person, and once recalled how sales of his books soared afterwards. 'I bullied all my friends into buying his books and his sales went rocketing up,' she said.

Her artistic enterprise was an inheritance from her father. Jill Balcon had been born in 1924, the daughter of the man who even then was becoming the most influential figure in British cinema. Sir Michael Balcon, born in Birmingham but of Lithuanian–Jewish descent, had almost single-handedly engineered the boom in the country's film-making industry.

Balcon made his first movie in 1923, the year before Jill was born. His debut as producer could not have been more remarkable. Working out of a studio that was little more than a glorified shed and with an unknown director called Alfred Hitchcock in charge of filming, he made the movie *Woman to Woman*, starring the equally anonymous Clive Brook, on a shoestring. The film was a runaway success, generating substantial profits for Balcon.

The next year he formed his first company, Gainsborough Pictures. There he produced silent films and early 'talkies'. In 1932 Balcon's business merged with Gaumont British and produced a major box-office success when it cast American star Robert Taylor in *A Yank at Oxford*.

Four years later Balcon became chief producer for the powerful MGM studio's British operation. He produced a succession of hits, from *The Blue Lamp* with Jack Warner and *The Cruel Sea* with Jack Hawkins, to *The Thirty-nine Steps* and *Goodbye Mr Chips* with Robert Donat. *Mr Chips*, for all its fustiness, still an irresistible tear-jerker, won Donat an Oscar in 1939.

But it was Balcon's elevation to head of Ealing Studios, in 1938, that was to ensure his place in movie-making legend. Ealing had been opened in 1907 and within five years was the country's largest studio. Under Balcon's shrewd stewardship it became internationally known.

Despite his Eastern European origins, Balcon presented himself as passionately British. He believed British cinema, and British comedy in particular, had something to offer the world and pursued that vision. He defined a British film as one that 'projected Britain and the British character'. 'I want to make comedies about ordinary people with the stray eccentric among them. Films about day dreamers, mild anarchists, little men who long to kick the boss in the teeth,' he said.

Over the following two decades, discovering talents as diverse as Alec Guinness, Peter Sellers, Margaret Rutherford and Stanley Holloway, Ealing comedy charmed the world. Films like *Kind Hearts and Coronets, Whisky Galore* and *Passport to Pimlico* remain among the most enduringly popular British movies ever made. Michael Balcon was knighted for his contribution to the nation's film industry in 1948.

Balcon combined a common touch – he worked out of modest offices and preferred people to call him Mick or Mickey rather than Sir Michael – with a high-combustion temperament. Before taking over at Ealing he suffered a serious nervous breakdown. 'He is extremely nervous, smokes cigarettes with a furious determination and bounds restlessly from chair to chair,' the journalist Milton Shulman described him in an interview in the 1960s.

His only daughter had been hopelessly stage-struck since she was five years old, and she had left Roedean determined to forge a career in acting. Her father had counselled against her joining his profession. Instead he wanted her to go to university to study modern languages. When she refused to be swayed, Balcon told her she could expect no help from him. A self-made man, he abhorred the clubbishness of much of the entertainment world. He expected people to make their way on merit.

Jill enrolled at the Central School of Speech and Drama when she was sixteen. She moved out of the Balcons' lavish London home and set herself up in a flat in Clarendon Road, Pimlico. 'I left home because I did not want to run the risk of picking up jobs the easy way,' she explained once.

Her first job came during the war, working for ENSA. She got the lead in two productions, *Saloon Bar* and *When We Are Married*, and set off on a national tour that took her from the Shetland to the Scilly Isles. She went on from there to become one of the most familiar voices on wartime radio. For two years she worked on the General Forces Overseas programme, doing everything from announcing and playing small parts in radio plays to being a disc jockey.

Throughout her early career Jill admitted she was dogged by accusations of nepotism. Despite her exquisite reading voice and exotic beauty, her peers never quite believed she was cast purely on her talent. 'Being a Balcon is not such an advantage as you might think,' she protested early on. 'It can be the opposite. Lots of people smile knowingly when I got these parts without my father's help.'

In 1946, after a spell in repertory and then at the Bristol Old Vic, where she was befriended by the theatre school's charismatic tutor, Rudi Shelley, Jill was finally beginning to make a breakthrough into television and radio drama. That year she made her screen debut, in *Nicholas Nickleby*, starring alongside such established names as Sybil Thorndike, Cedric Hardwick and Stanley Holloway in the Alberto Cavalcanti-directed version of the Dickens classic.

Her star in the ascendant, she once more found herself in the orbit of the celestial Cecil Day-Lewis. A decade after she had boosted his royalties at Roedean, as they chatted after the end of their BBC broadcast, Cecil and Jill quickly discovered that their tastes in poetry were remarkably similar. 'When Cecil and I met, we discovered we shared a mutual love of Hardy and Robert Frost who were already part of my fabric,' Jill revealed. When they next met, a year after that first meeting, it became apparent that they shared another mutual interest.

Cecil's heart was still riven between Mary and Rosamond Lehmann. But Jill, with her darkly exciting, gypsy-like Eastern European looks, exuded intensity and an infectious exuberance. He was fascinated by her.

He made sure he listened to Jill's next BBC radio reading, when she again read from Browning. Afterwards he sent her a fan letter and they agreed to meet. During that meeting Jill explained why the reading might have drawn such extravagant praise from her new admirer. As she got ready to go on air, she told him, she had been overcome by a brainwave. 'One really should read this in one's brassiere,' she had announced to the studio staff. And that is precisely what she had done! 'I fell in love with young Jill then,' Cecil confided to friends later.

She had always been a highly emotional young woman

embodying many of her father's complexities. By some accounts she too could be an awkward customer. Her father in his autobiography remarked that she was, like him, 'given to the dramatization of minor events'. Elizabeth Jane Howard described, too, how receiving a present could move Jill to floods of tears. 'Jill has one skin less than the rest of us,' another friend said of her.

Today their illicit affair would have been the stuff of celebrity scandal. An extra-marital romance between an eminent poet and the daughter of the most powerful man in the British film industry – a woman twenty years his junior – would have blazed a trail across the front pages. Every twist and turn would have been publicly scrutinized, every member of the dramatis personae pursued for their slice of the story.

In the 1950s, however, Britain's newspapers were not the scandal-sheets they were to become in later decades. Human mores were no different, society simply tended to turn a blind eye to the misbehaviour of its most prominent members. Members of the Royal Family, MPs, film and TV stars were all able to lead their lives in relative anonymity.

Cecil and Jill's relationship was a closely kept secret for some time. After the initial passion of their first meetings, they also went through a three-month 'cooling off' period when they did not see each other at all. Elizabeth Jane Howard acted as an unofficial go-between, lunching at fashionable restaurants like Antoine's with Cecil and reporting back to her friend in Pimlico afterwards. The separation was designed to discover whether their feelings for each other were as intense as they suspected. Both knew they were.

In 1950, after years of agonizing, Cecil summoned the strength to leave Mary, ending his affair with Lehmann at the same time. He set himself up in a flat in Bedford Gardens, Kensington and committed himself to Jill.

The first – and last – the newspapers made of the situation was when Mary sued Cecil for divorce on the grounds of his adultery, citing Jill and her Clarendon Road flat in the court papers. Single-column court reports faithfully recorded that Cecil did not defend the action, heard at Southampton County

Court in February 1951, and that Judge Alfred Taylor granted Mary a decree nisi, awarding undisclosed costs against her ex-husband.

Cecil and Jill were now free to marry. Within nine weeks they did so. On 27 April, Cecil's forty-seventh birthday, under headlines of 'Film chief's actress daughter marries a poet', London newspapers carried photographs of the newly-weds on the steps of London's Kensington Register Office. Cecil, in double-breasted pin-stripe, bow-tied and with a crested Irish ring on his wedding finger, smiled warmly. His bride, in a fashionable, salmon-pink shantung jacket, proudly displaying a pair of aquamarine earrings her new husband had given her, looked serenely happy.

They began married life together in Cecil's studio flat in Bedford Gardens. Friends who visited them there remember the room as bright and airy, filled with books and pictures but little furniture. Cecil and Jill slept in a gallery above the living room and cooked in a small, cramped kitchen at the back.

During those heady early days of marriage both their careers blossomed. That year Cecil, who had been made an OBE for his services to literature in 1950, was made Professor of Poetry at Oxford. He became the first poet of prominence to be given the post since Matthew Arnold in 1857.

The University authorities, whose time-trapped morality had still not embraced the idea of mixed colleges, took a dim view of divorce. When the distinguished historian A. J. P. Taylor was standing for re-election as a Fellow, some opposed it on the grounds that he was 'a fornicator'. He had remarried after the breakdown of his first marriage.

In February 1951, while Cecil's divorce papers were being processed by the courts, he had been a candidate in the election for a successor to the retiring Professor of Poetry, Dr Maurice Bowra. His main rival was the writer C. S. Lewis, ironically another who had scandalized Oxford, in his case over his romance with a married American woman, Joy Gresham.

Such was Cecil's popularity and so widespread was his reputation as the finest reader of poetry in the country by now, however, that when the Convocation met, his personal problems were ignored. C. S. Lewis polled 173 votes and Cecil polled 194. For the next five years he was the most popular Professor of Poetry in living memory at Oxford. Drawn by his beautiful voice and his matinee idol looks, undergraduates fought for seats at his lectures. 'It was amazing, people sat on the floor and clung to the window-sills,' was how one student explained the phenomenon at the time. 'Everybody gazed at him with adoration. It was more like a film star's appearance.'

Away from Oxford Cecil combined his Professorship with writing poetry, Nicholas Blake novels and his role as a director of the publishers Chatto & Windus. Meanwhile, Jill had become one of the most sought-after actresses in the country. The year before she had made a breakthrough performance on television in a play called *Promise of Tomorrow*. The role of a young actress struggling to make it on the grim repertory circuit in the provinces could have been autobiographical. Jill helped make writer Michael Barry's play more authentic by chipping in with some of her own memories of the relentless slog she went through during the early days of her career.

She starred with Robert Shaw in a highly successful production of *A Midsummer Night's Dream* at the Old Vic Theatre in 1951 and 1952. Throughout that time, however, she tried to maintain her reputation as one of the finest of radio actresses and worked regularly at the BBC.

Early in 1953 Jill announced she was pregnant. In anticipation of the new arrival she and Cecil moved from their studio apartment to a slightly more spacious, though still modest, one-bedroom house around the corner in Campden Hill Road, Kensington.

Jill carried on working until the end of her pregnancy. On Friday, 11 September she spent all day at the BBC recording five ten-minute readings called *Daughters of Confucius*. Six days later she gave birth to a baby daughter at Queen Charlotte's Hospital, Fulham.

Jill's joy was made complete by the fact that she had given Cecil a girl. 'I hoped to have a daughter because Cecil had two sons from his previous marriage,' she confided later in life. Cecil and Jill decided to call their first child Lydia Tamasin.

Cecil said the name 'sprang from the air' but then explained that Tamasin was a blend of two famous literary characters. 'It's a mixture. We love Thomas Hardy, so part of it is after him. There is a Thomasin in *The Return of the Native*. And we love Ivy Compton-Burnett's writing – one of her characters is called Tamsin,' the proud father proclaimed. Lydia, he went on, was 'a sound classical name'. Their daughter would be free to choose whichever of the names she preferred, he said. 'She can call herself Lydia if she grows up to be statuesque!'

In a purely literal sense of the word, Tamasin, as she soon became known, became statuesque almost immediately. Cecil asked Jacob Epstein to sculpt a bust of both his wife and daughter. Their baby's bronze image was given pride of place in the living room, where a bust of Cecil already stood proudly on the piano.

The statue of Jill, however, never arrived at Campden Hill Road. Cecil did not like the sculpture although Jill still wanted to own it. The cost of raising a child, however, meant she could not afford it.

During the earliest days of their marriage finances had not been a factor in Jill and Cecil's life. Now, however, matters were different. During Tamasin's first year Cecil became the principal bread-winner. He travelled abroad on lecture tours to earn extra money.

He and Jill had agreed initially that she would remain at home with Tamasin until she was three. But within a year, with Cecil's alimony payments to Mary and his sons eating deep into his pocket, there was no option: Jill would have to return to work. She summed up the situation in a newspaper interview at the time. 'Poets, you know, don't earn a great deal of money,' she told the *Evening Standard* in London. 'When I argued with the butcher about the price of a chicken he said to me, "What are you grumping about? Your father made *The Cruel Sea*, didn't he?" They all seem to think that because you are the daughter of a famous producer you are bound to be fabulously rich. Oh, how wrong they are!'

Jill began to put out feelers for work, but she quickly realized the fickle cruelty of her business. While the lead in a

TV production of *Troilus and Cressida* went to a newcomer called Mary Watson, Jill, despite her pedigree and experience, was given a much smaller part.

At the age of twenty-nine she began to accept that motherhood might have to be her greatest role in life. 'I've been at it too long to become a star now,' she said philosophically in an interview with the *Evening Standard* in September 1954. 'If one is really first class one is given the chance when one starts out. If one isn't then one hasn't got the goods. I don't think I've got the looks to be a star – I'm not photogenic,' she added.

Out of necessity, however, she continued putting herself up for roles. For the following two years she worked predominantly in radio. In the autumn of 1956, however, she told a newspaper that she had won a starring role in a new, untitled West End play.

But by Christmas she had to announce that her return to London's theatreland was off. She had visited the doctor and he had confirmed her suspicions. She was pregnant again . . .

CHAPTER TWO

A LOOSE LEASH

'Fetters of gold are still fetters, and silken cords pinch.'
English Proverb

D ANIEL MICHAEL Blake Day-Lewis would come to intrigue and inspire the world with such counterfeit faces. He would, with a wolfish arch of his eyebrows, declare himself a devil, 'Beelzebub incarnate', for doing so.

For the first eleven years of the life that began on 29 April 1957, however, he presented all but a very few members of that world with one face. It was that of an angel, and it was fixed with a permanent, perfect smile. Often it too was a deceit. The smile, submissively sweet, unbendingly polite, was the first mask behind which the child who was to become the most chameleonic actor of his generation hid his real self.

He entered the world in the front room of his parents' house at 96 Campden Hill Road, Kensington. His shock of lustrous, gypsy jet-black hair was an obvious inheritance from his mother. The slow-breaking smile, yet to be polished into the seraph grin of later, was the earliest evidence of his father. Within hours of his delivery his now famous enigmatic persona was being born too.

Cecil and Jill were determined their son's name would keep both sides of the family happy. So, depending on which side of the Balcon–Day-Lewis divide you sat, their second child became Daniel, son of the 'Auld Sod', heir to the spirit of Daniel O'Connell, Catholic emancipator of Ireland and, in his father's more fanciful moments, a descendant of William Butler Yeats, Oliver Goldsmith and Nicholas the Black of Galway. Or he was Daniel, from the Jewish Old Testament prophet, latest in a line leading back, through East European tributaries, to the children of Israel themselves. His middle names kept both sides of his ancestry happy too: Michael in honour of his grandfather Balcon, Blake from Cecil's Irish mother's family.

His arrival had the most immediate impact on his father. Outside it was a typical, English April day: cloudy with intermittent rain. The Monday morning newspapers were full of the latest developments in the Suez crisis. Nearer home, the actors' union Equity was warning parents that only two-thirds of its members made a living. 'These facts should be blazoned among all those mums who persist in putting their daughters on the stage.'

While one struggling actress recovered her strength and nursed her new son through his first few hours, Cecil retreated from the world and took to his desk. By now fifty-three years of age, he was euphoric at the arrival of another son. Like any father, his mind was alive with thoughts of what his child might become. But as an older parent, a witness to life at its most bitter-sweet, the sense of renewal was all the greater.

He enshrined his thoughts in a poem, 'The Newborn', a very personal welcome to his world. Its verses encapsulated the infinite possibilities soon to be spread out before his son, the child Cecil described as a 'mannikin', newly freed from its wombed prison, a speck of raw clay ready to be shaped into human form, to take on its own unique identity. But, as there was in so much of Cecil's poetry, there was an underlying caution, a warning that, as he put it, truth can blow cold and that love can betray.

Daniel was christened a few weeks later at the church of St Martin-in-the-Fields, in Trafalgar Square. The Reverend Austen Williams, a friend of Cecil and Jill's, officiated. Ursula Vaughan Williams, daughter of the composer, publishers Ian Parsons and Peter Cochrane, and Julia Gaitskell, widow of the Labour Party leader, Hugh Gaitskell, became godparents.

Daniel was, by all accounts, a healthy, hearty baby. His development presented his parents with a headache, however. Their expanding family had once more outgrown their home.

Before their son had arrived Cecil and Jill had hired help to care for Tamasin. Minny Bowler was a Londoner and known to all as Nanny Bowler. She was a child-minder of the old school, starchy, strict, always impeccably uniformed. As if her authoritarian air was not intimidating enough, her grey hair was emblazoned with a streak of yellow. Years later the baby now entrusted to her would wear his own in a similar, badger-striped style. Her only vice was that she chain-smoked. The streak was tinged with a nicotine ochre. But in a house in which both Cecil and Jill puffed away like chimneys, this was hardly a mortal sin. The redoubtable Nanny Bowler brought order and discipline to the turmoil of the nursery.

For the first four months, Cecil, Jill, three-year-old Tamasin and Nanny Bowler somehow survived under one roof with baby Daniel. Jill's parents' spacious London town house was always available as a refuge for mother and children. But in the autumn of 1957 Jill and Cecil agreed to move to a larger house. And this time they began looking for a home in which Tamasin and Daniel could spend the rest of their childhood.

They had first come to hear of Croom's Hill, Greenwich through a friend, the poet Jon Silkin. He knew of a splendid Georgian property for sale there and recommended they travel across from the west to the south-east of London to view it.

Cecil was well versed in Greenwich and neighbouring Deptford's literary associations. When London's docks were the engine-room of Empire the area was home to the city's rowdiest pubs and bordellos. William Shakespeare and Christopher Marlowe could not resist the area's notoriety. Marlowe, famously, died in a pub brawl there. Writers from Daniel Defoe to Charles Dickens found inspiration alongside the mud-died waters of the Thames. Defoe heard tall, ale-house tales of a seaman named Alexander Selkirk, who had run off to sea in 1704, been cast away on the uninhabited Juan Fernandez Islands, and spent five years alone before returning to England. Defoe distilled the drinking tale into the story of Robinson Crusoe. Dickens was a regular drinker at the Trafalgar Tavern. Then known as the George Tavern, the pub featured in his novel *Our Mutual Friend*.

Since Georgian times, the elegant houses of Croom's Hill had been colonized by the maritime middle class. Senior naval officers, explorers and merchants settled on the fringe of

Greenwich Park. Cecil and Jill fell in love with the area instantly and were equally overwhelmed by the house, number 32. Such was the area's burgeoning vogue, however, that they were beaten in the race to buy it by Nicholas Tomalin, one of the most prominent journalists in London at the time. Tomalin once defined his archetypal fellow professional as the owner of 'a plausible manner, a little literary ability and rat-like cunning'. The radar-equipped rodent in him was clearly at its sharpest as he arrived just a few hours ahead of the Day-Lewises to make an acceptable offer.

Daniel's parents' anguish was short-lived, however. Within three months or so another house came up for sale. Number 6, a spacious town house, stood impressively at the foot of Croom's Hill, on the edge of the centre of what locals called 'the village' and opposite a pub called The Rose and Crown and a former music hall. The house arrived on the market after the death of its owner, the local GP, a Dr Elliott. This time Cecil and Jill wasted no time and dashed from Kensington to Greenwich, intent on securing the property. Undoubtedly influenced by having lost out once before and despite the fact that the house was in a sad state of repair and he had not even organized a mortgage, Cecil made Dr Elliott's widow an offer of £5990. It was accepted.

The property included what had been a greenhouse but had years earlier been converted by Dr Elliott into the surgery from where he ran his practice. The practice was taken over by a formidably feisty Scot, Dr Margot Gair. She and her dentist husband John lived in nearby Blackheath. Dr Gair wanted to continue working from 6 Croom's Hill, and reached agreement with her new landlords, the Day-Lewises, for a fair rent for the use of the premises.

The house needed a radical overhaul and was unfit for Tamasin and baby Daniel to live in immediately. While Cecil and Jill energetically and enthusiastically set about imposing their interior design ideas, the children stayed with Jill's parents at their country home in North Parrock, Sussex. The house, set on a hilltop with a small farm attached to it, was a sanctuary for Sir Michael Balcon. There, he remembered late in his life, he enjoyed nothing more than sitting in the garden on a summer's night, a favourite piece of music on his record-player, his family around him.

Cecil and Jill celebrated New Year's Eve 1957 amidst the chaos of half-emptied tea-chests, bare walls and book-shelves. But they could not have been happier. They had found a home where their life together could be complete. Over the next fifteen years the house was to be the scene for what another writer enchanted by Greenwich, Dickens, might have called 'the best of times and the worst of times'.

A few weeks into the New Year, Daniel and Tamasin, along with Nanny Bowler, joined their parents at 6 Croom's Hill. The lower half of the house was devoted to Cecil, Jill and the family's functional priorities. The wainscotted kitchen and dining room were on the ground floor at the back, while the grand study at the front of the house, with its view over bustling Croom's Hill and the fringes of Greenwich Park, was requisitioned by Cecil. It became the poet's inner sanctum.

The first floor was divided between a beautiful drawing room and Cecil and Jill's bedroom. The upper floors of the house were primarily the domain of the junior Day-Lewises. Daniel, Tamasin and Nanny Bowler had rooms on the third floor, while the bedrooms on the fourth floor, ostensibly guest rooms, became an extension of the children's territory.

Soon the Day-Lewises had become a celebrated addition to society on the southerly banks of the Thames. W. H. Auden grandiloquently defined the poet as 'before anything else, a person who is passionately in love with language'. Since his Oxford days Cecil had fitted his friend's description unwaveringly. In his love affair with language and the literary way of life there was total fidelity. Croom's Hill provided him with a home where he could indulge that passion to the hilt. His lust for life rejuvenated by his new surroundings, Cecil entertained extravagantly and with a generosity that was his hallmark. Jill, always an exceptional cook, revelled in organizing dinner and lunch parties. Sunday lunches, in particular, were an institution, Jill's roast beef the acknowledged culinary highlight among visitors to the house, who included Auden, Spender, Edith Sitwell, Elizabeth Jane Howard and other London literati. Politics always had its place at the dinner table too. The Labour Party leader Hugh Gaitskell was a close friend of the former Communist and his wife. Aneurin Bevan's widow, Jennie Lee, was another regular visitor.

If those who journeyed to Greenwich represented a dazzling cross-section of London's intelligentsia, the Day-Lewises' neighbours were no less stimulating, and an equally catholic collection of personalities. Croom's Hill's other residents ranged from journalists – Tomalin – to career diplomats – Sir Julian Bullard, a future British Ambassador to Bonn – to the heirs of one of Greenwich's most famous explorers, Francis Young-husband.

Whilst Cecil's circle tended towards work associations, Jill, as the mother of a young family, made friendships that were often based on mutual maternal instincts. Younghusband's grand-daughter, Ann Broadbent, who lived four houses along from the Day-Lewises, at number 14, had read English at Oxford while Cecil was Professor of Poetry there. She had been one of the star-struck undergraduates who clung to the window-sills of his lecture halls for a glimpse of the great man. She met Jill in August 1960, when her son Tom was born. Her neighbour was taken aback when Ann began quoting her husband's poetry.

'The day after my son Tom was born here Jill came to call on me and the room was full of people. She looked at Tom's face and said, "Just imagine, his whole future is in that face,"' she recalled. 'I quoted a line from "The Newborn". Jill was delighted and we became friends from that moment on.' After that she visited the Day-Lewises' house with her son. 'My first memory of Daniel was when he was very, very small, just a little boy of two or three and he could say helicopter,' she remembered.

By then Daniel had developed into an angelically pretty little boy. 'They were both beautiful people but I think he took more after his mother than his father. He had those dark looks of Jill's,' said Ann Broadbent.

He had also begun to smile that beatific smile. Dr Gair

remembered him that way too. 'We loved him dearly, he was a very sweet boy with a lovely sense of humour. He loved climbing our apple tree, he would always fall off and go home with terribly torn clothes,' she recalled. Her son Frank and Daniel played together, remaining friends for years. Daniel was always a guest at birthday parties. 'A friend of ours, Clifford Davis, was a magician. The boys used to love him. He would produce oranges out of Daniel's ears.'

In 1960 Cecil's son Sean came to live at Croom's Hill for six months. His career as a journalist, begun years earlier as editor of the Day-Lewis family rag, the *Brimclose News*, was blossoming. He had landed his first job on Fleet Street, alongside the son of another eminent man of letters, Auberon Waugh, on the Peterborough column at the *Daily Telegraph*. It was to be the beginning of a shining career in journalism, one which delighted his failed-scribe father. 'He was a terrific encourager. If I got a job in Fleet Street he would be over the moon that I had not actually fallen in a ditch or something. He really loved honours, and we Irish love feathers in our cap,' Sean remembered.

While he adjusted to life in the capital and prepared to marry his fiancée Anna Mott, Sean lived at the top the house, above the nursery. Below him Nanny Bowler was instilling the 'three P' principles of politeness, punctuality and presentation in young Daniel and Tamasin.

Sean recalled a clear division between the life of the children and the nursery and the adult life downstairs. 'Pappa's' study in particular was off limits for the children, or anyone else for that matter, while his door remained closed and he was at work. Cecil's study reflected his innate good taste, his habits and his heroes. A portrait of Thomas Hardy held pride of place on one wall, a Renoir lithograph dominated another. A tankard packed with an assortment of favourite pipes sat on his desk, and books lined every inch of the walls. Here Cecil sat and worked every morning and afternoon, usually with a break for lunch of cornflakes and fruit and a brisk, ninety-minute walk by the river when he needed to induce the 'self-hypnosis' required for writing poetry. Cecil formed an abiding love for the Greenwich riverfront, with its *Cutty Sark* clipper and its Christopher Wren skyline, immortalized by Canaletto.

'Although he was a fairly remote figure in that he spent a lot of time in his study and he liked to walk alone around Greenwich in the afternoon, it didn't appear to me that Jill was any less so,' Sean recalled. 'They had their lives and the children had theirs.' The children came downstairs, usually to the drawing room, for early evening readings by their parents. 'They had their floor and they were presented by Nanny Bowler at a certain time of the day to have stories read to them,' Sean said. 'They always looked terribly spick and span.'

The sight of the Day-Lewis children, always immaculately dressed, usually in white gloves and white socks, became a familiar sight along the banks of the Thames. Outwardly they seemed the perfect children of a perfect household. As Tamasin and Daniel reached schooling age, however, life behind the heavily lacquered white front door revealed itself as less than perfect.

Tamasin had been attending prep school in nearby Blackheath. At eleven she moved up to Blackheath High, a predominantly middle-class school with a reputation for academic excellence. When, in 1962, the time arrived for Daniel to begin his education, it was decided to send him to the local state school. Cecil and Jill decided to entrust their son to the sort of school their socialist lunch guests believed offered Britain egalitarian hope for its future. Daniel was enrolled at Invicta School, a London County Council primary school almost a mile away. On 10 January 1962, Cecil took him to see the headmistress, Mrs Mary Smith. He produced his son's birth certificate and Daniel became the first member of his family to be entrusted to the state school system. Every day for the next six years, he would leave the civilized surroundings of Croom's Hill and head across Greenwich Park to Invicta Road, on the edge of working-class Charlton. At the age of seven, in September 1964, he transferred from Invicta to its sister school, Sherington Junior Boys.

The angelic smile is still remembered at his first school. 'He was a lovely little boy, very polite. I remember taking him home early once because he had been taken ill. As he went in through the front door he said, "Thanks very much for bringing me home,"' remembered one of the school staff then, Mrs Dolly Lyddall.

Soon after Daniel had joined Invicta, Nanny Bowler left the Day-Lewises. Now that the children were of school age, such a formal nanny was no longer thought necessary. Cecil had also begun to be irritated by her presence, Sean recalled. 'I can remember my father getting very bored with Nanny Bowler. She was terribly repetitive. My father used to eat Penguin chocolate biscuits for lunch, she would always make quips about it,' he said.

The departure of the woman who had assumed second-mother status to them came as a body blow to both Tamasin and Daniel. One close friend of the family recalled: 'I think it was a tremendous moment in their lives because these two never pictured her leaving the house. They came back from school one day, asked where Nanny was and were told "She's gone."' According to Jill they lay down beating their hands on the floor saying they couldn't face it. 'A lot of other families kept their nannies in the attic darning socks, but this was one day she was everything the next day nothing.'

Jill, combining acting with poetry readings, often with Cecil, seemed to have been unable to devote all her time to her children. She also wanted to monopolize their father's attentions, she came to admit. Her love for her husband was so overwhelming, she said once, that 'maybe I was guilty of excluding the children from my relationship with Cecil'. So Jenny Dormer, a jolly young nanny who had been working for the Broadbents at number 14 Croom's Hill and who lived nearby with her mother in Croom's Hill Grove, became Nanny Bowler's replacement. On a wage of £8 10s. a week she was to be a part of daily life at Croom's Hill for almost three years.

Jenny Dormer discovered an unmistakable 'upstairs–downstairs' dimension to life at Croom's Hill. For all the libertarian philosophy flung eloquently around the dinner table every Sunday, there was a pronounced air of almost Victorian conservatism as far as the children were concerned. Their nanny found herself working in a home of rigid routine. 'They had both been brought up by Nanny Bowler. Her rules were very, very structured,' she recalled.

The incoming and the outgoing nannies had a brief meeting before Daniel and Tamasin were entrusted to a new pair of hands. 'I was very different from Nanny Bowler and I don't think she approved of me,' remembered the replacement nanny, now a happily married grandmother, still living in Greenwich.

Nanny Bowler's instructions were military in their precision. Jenny was to walk Daniel to and from school, prepare his tea and get him ready for bed. 'After he had come home from school, Daniel had to be bathed and then dried in the nursery, where there always had to be a fire. Both of them used to have lunch at school and then I would cook them tea. Around four-thirty p.m. Jill used to come up and read to them, but they did not go down for a meal in the evening. I used to finish at six o'clock, Daniel had to be in his pyjamas and dressing-gown by that time. They used to get very angry if Daniel stayed up and I was five minutes late. Punctuality was very important in the house.'

Daniel was six years old when Jenny began work at Croom's Hill, nine when she left. His early-evening routine did not change during that time. 'I used to think it was a bit sad. Even in summertime his bath, even at that age, was at half past five. I used to leave and he would be there with his dressing-gown and slippers on. I used to think it was a form of imprisonment.'

Show me the child of seven and I will show you the man. Jenny Dormer's immediate impressions of Daniel, then approaching his seventh birthday, were of a precocious, occasionally arrogant but essentially lonely little boy. 'He was obviously very intelligent, quite complex. Daniel used to say, "You are my servant." He would order me to run his bath and dry him properly. He would sit on my knee. I had to dress him in his pyjamas.

'I think he needed a lot of love, hugs and kisses. He would get them from his mother when she visited the nursery, but it never seemed to be spontaneous,' she remembered.

33

She also recalled Cecil as a remote figure. 'There was a great distance between Cecil and the children. I did not like that. They were very much in awe of him, if we heard him coming up the stair towards the nursery it was very tense. If we had sweets or something we would quickly hide them, even though he probably would not have minded.

'I think he was preoccupied with other things. I can't ever remember him doing anything in a fatherly way.'

The house's adults had their regimens too. 'In the evenings when I was leaving for the day there was this rather lovely ritual. He would pour me a glass of Teacher's whisky, give me a Senior Service cigarette and we would sit and listen to some music or talk,' the former nanny recalled.

It was to Jill rather than Cecil, however, that Jenny had to answer as far as the children were concerned. Jill had very clear ideas about every aspect of her children's upbringing. She was fastidious in every detail, from the clothes they wore and the food they ate, to the music they listened to and the company they kept. If those standards were not met, her temper, sometimes volcanic, would display itself.

'The children's clothes were always absolutely immaculate. They wore beautiful, beautiful clothes. And there was a lot of time spent dressing the children up,' Jenny recalled. For Tamasin it was pretty dresses, for Daniel starchy shirts, perfectly pressed trousers and always – always – a tie. 'Daniel always used to wear these flowery ties. He would not even go out of the nursery without his tie on.'

One of the first 'mistakes' Jenny made was to take Daniel and Tamasin out for a walk in incorrect clothing. Nanny Bowler had always presented the children to the world at their most sparklingly pristine. Jenny saw things differently. 'I remember taking Daniel and Tamasin out in sweater and jeans and really getting hauled over the coals by Jill when I got back. Tamasin should have been wearing a pretty dress and Daniel should have had a coat and a hat. She was furious.'

On other occasions Jenny was chastised for not ironing the children's clothes properly. If a dress of Tamasin's appeared creased or crumpled, Jill would snap: 'That's from her godmother, and it is not pressed, how do you think my daughter is going to look in that dress?'

It was apparent to Jenny early on that Daniel could do no wrong in the eyes of his mother. When Jenny first visited the family to discuss working at number 6, she had found Daniel in his mother's arms. 'When I had my first meeting with them Daniel was cradled on his mother's lap by the fire. In Jill's eyes Daniel was always perfect,' she recalled. Transgressions were inevitably Jenny or Tamasin's fault, it seemed to the nanny. 'When I took Daniel down to the river for the first time, with just a jumper on, it was Tamasin who got the wrath of it: "How could you let her go out with my child in a jumper?"'

Daniel appeared a solitary child. During his years at Invicta Jenny cannot remember him bringing another child home. Mixing with other nannies on Croom's Hill was also frowned on. 'He was a very sheltered little boy when I started there. Jill never approved if I took them out to tea with other nannies and their children. There were quite a lot of nannies on Croom's Hill then. They did not socialize at all with other children,' she recalled. 'I was confused because he was going to a state school yet he was not really allowed to fraternize with other children. It must have been confusing for him too.'

Instead, the children were encouraged to mix with the grand guests their parents invited to Croom's Hill. Even though she was employed on a Monday to Friday basis, Jenny was regularly invited round for Sunday lunch at number 6.

Acting friends of Jill's like Vanessa Redgrave and Peggy Ashcroft were invited, but the atmosphere was invariably bookish. Auden came to visit on two or three occasions. The ageing genius, his face and neck lined with thick folds of wrinkled flesh, his weakening body bent, terrified Daniel. Behind Auden's back the children called him 'the creeping walnut'. 'We were both frightened by him, but Tamasin was not, she used to say, "Oh, they are only people,"' remembered Jenny.

Downstairs Daniel projected an angelic aura to all who came to Croom's Hill and its literary lunches. 'I smiled at everybody and got away with murder,' he admitted in later years. Jenny and Tamasin saw the face behind the mask first.

'There were certainly two sides to him and he used to get me and Tamasin into trouble a lot. He was suppressed. When they went out he used to whack Tamasin and me,' remembered Jenny. 'He used to kick us around the nursery and tell us what he was going to do to us. He was so angelic when his mother was around, he wore that fixed, Cheshire cat grin, and then as we went into the nursery he would really hang on to Tamasin's hair.'

At Invicta the son of the eminent poet was performing his own exploration of the language and its infinite forms of expression. Greenwich and Blackheath – then as now – were oases of middle-class gentility in a desert of inner-city mundanity. Invicta and Sherington schools had a catchment area extending into the working-class estates of Charlton and Deptford. Daniel's less well-to-do classmates taught him much. Jenny Dormer remembers him as the owner of a witheringly wicked and colourful tongue.

'He used to swear like a trooper and could be quite cutting. We used to go swimming at Danson Park, a few miles away, he would be very nice and when his mother was gone he'd say to me, "You've got really fat legs, cover them up." When Jill was there he would smile and say, "Oh, she's so nice,"' she recalled.

He would pick up words and use them endlessly. Guttersnipe was a favourite. Tamasin teased him. 'You want your nanny to cuddle you, don't you?' she would say. 'Shut up, fucking guttersnipe,' he would reply. All the children at Invicta, at one point, were 'guttersnipes'.

Despite their sibling squabbles, there was complicity between Daniel and Tamasin. Acts of rebellion against the autocratic rule of their parents were a team effort. When Cecil and Jill were out for the evening they would sneak to the kitchen with Jenny for illicit meals.

'The emphasis was very much on food in the house, there were very strict rules on what they would eat, even to the point where I remember there being a menu,' Jenny remembered. 'I never used to argue because the food was so wonderful, Jill was a great cook.'

She recalled how one of the two cleaners employed by Jill used to make Daniel a birthday cake every year. 'It was a sponge covered in butter icing and covered with smarties. Jill would say it was "wonderful", and then when she had gone put it away. "Bad ingredients," she would say. She had gone to all the effort to make the cake, I thought it was unkind.'

Daniel's favourite treat was fillet steak, but he had a huge appetite for virtually everything placed in front on him. 'He used to have quite a lot of tummy troubles because he over-indulged so much on food. But he had so much energy that he was never fat.'

In their parents' absence, however, the children would sneak downstairs and cook less grand meals than those on the official bill of fare. 'I would tell them how at the Broadbents' we made pancakes, and Tamasin would say, "Oh, can't we make them?" Because everything was so precise and had to be done perfectly it had to be crêpes rather than soggy pancakes for them. Once or twice if their parents went out in the evening we used to make a plan that we would not eat the tea. Daniel used to whisper to me, "When they go out shall we go downstairs and make chips and fishcakes?" Once we were all caught and Jill was furious.'

Often Daniel and Tamasin seemed children of the 1860s growing up in the 1960s. Outside the swinging decade was at its pendulum peak, the Beatles were conquering the world, every adolescent was glued to Cathy McGowan and *Ready, Steady, Go*. At Croom's Hill life moved to a different beat.

'The children loved the Beatles. Daniel used to strum to an imaginary guitar. Once I let him put pictures of them on the nursery wall and Jill was livid,' Jenny recalled. 'I remember her saying one lunch-time there was a beautiful piece of music playing, I think it was Vaughan Williams, and I said how wonderful it was. Jill said, "You would be far more interested in the Beatles, and encouraging my children to listen to the Beatles."

'Cecil stuck up for me, he said, "Isn't it wonderful that we have someone in the household to encourage the children." Tamasin in particular was elated.'

The children's fashions slowly began to change too. Jenny's first change was to give Daniel a less formal hair-cut. She decided to bring him in line with virtually every other little boy in England and give him the mop-top look of John, Paul, George and Ringo.

'Nanny Bowler had always taken Daniel to have his hair cut at Harrods. He had this beautiful, black, shiny hair. I started taking him to a barber's on Deptford Broadway. Jill was appalled by the idea but Cecil was in full approval of that. It cost two and six. Jill actually liked the Beatle haircut.'

Not all the rituals of life at Croom's Hill were suffocating, however. Far from it. Events like birthdays, Christmas and summer holidays were all the more exciting for their predictability. On birthdays Nanny Bowler would usually visit, bringing chocolate cornflake cakes. The highlight of the day, however, was invariably a trip to Lyons Corner House, a then famous restaurant opposite London's Charing Cross Station. Cecil would pack the family into the back of his car – at this time a hugely stylish Citroën, compensation for the fact that he was never allowed toy cars as a child, according to his son Sean – and indulge everyone with a lavish meal. Few children were invited, however. 'Daniel, like his father, was always dressed immaculately. Birthdays were very grown-up affairs, I can't remember any children apart from Frankie Gair, the doctor's son, a lovely chubby cuddly little boy,' remembered Jenny.

When the family was gathered together, Cecil's wit always shone through. He was a great story-teller, often spinning tales against himself. He would often tell of how, during a passionate poetry reading, his dental plate had flown out of his mouth. He was forced to rely on his old cricket skills, springing like a slip fielder to catch it before it landed in the front row of his audience. It mattered little how true the stories were and often they were worked up considerably. Both Cecil and Jill admitted to spinning yarns, once telling the *Tatler* in unison: 'Being Irish, I exaggerate.' 'And being Jewish, I do the same.'

Cecil also delighted his children by pulling funny faces. Years later Daniel would imitate his party piece, blowing up his face 'like a King Edward potato'.

Jenny once travelled to France for a short break while the family was preparing for a holiday together. Cecil wrote her a letter of introduction. 'Cecil said, "I will write you a French letter." It was very, very humorous. It was for me to apply for a job in France. And it was a joke for months, they used to say, "Pappa's given Jenny a French letter,"' she remembered.

There was also an extreme generosity. 'They were incredibly generous present-givers. They once gave me this beautiful gold fob-watch, it was really lovely and was inscribed with love from Jill, Cecil, Tamasin and Daniel. If I did something for Daniel like reading him a special story or something, he would give me a present of two chocolates beautifully wrapped up.'

At Christmas the family would head for Dorset, to the village of Litton Cheney. Cecil, the son of a rector, returned to a rectory, this one owned by long-time friends, the painter and engraver Reynolds Stone and his photographer wife Janet. Cecil and Jill were introduced to the Stones by the art historian Kenneth Clark and started spending regular holidays with them in 1962. Christmases in particular became a time for the Day-Lewises and the Stones, who had four children of their own, to get together.

The Stones' home was a remarkable refuge for creative souls like Cecil Day-Lewis. Between 1953 and 1979 it acted as a magnet for some of the outstanding artists, writers and thinkers of the time. Benjamin Britten, Iris Murdoch, Kenneth Clark, John Betjeman, Henry Moore and Joyce Grenfell were among regular visitors. The elegant peace of the house, set at the end of a leafy lane, adjoining a beautiful church, was an escape from the noisy vulgarities of city life. The Old Rectory was a paradise for children too. Daniel spent endless hours boating on the two huge ponds that were hidden away in the Stones' wilderness of a garden and riding their donkey, named Elizabeth Fry after Janet Stone's famous Quaker grandmother.

In 1962 and 1963 the Day-Lewises took over a mini-wing of the Old Rectory on the second floor. Complete with its own bathroom, and even a piano, it was a home from home at Christmas. 'Daniel was a very quiet, gentle child. He was not the sort of child that thundered around being a nuisance. He was a bit detached,' recalled Janet Stone. 'But he was very happy going in the boat or on the back of the donkey with his father.'

Christmases at Litton Cheney were splendidly civilized affairs. On Christmas Eve Cecil would read his poem 'The Christmas Tree' and from Beatrix Potter's *Tailor of Gloucester*. 'Reynolds, my husband, always loved Beatrix Potter. Cecil read because he was such a great reader,' Janet Stone remembered. 'Then the children went to bed with great excitement and we crept into their rooms with stockings.' On Christmas morning everyone made the short trip from the Old Rectory to the church and then the stockings Janet Stone made up for each of her guests were opened around the tree.

The house was also filled with music. Cecil would sing or play the recorder with Jill accompanying him on the piano. Daniel would also break into song, the hostess of those Christmases past recalls. 'He had a lovely voice, he had perfect pitch, he could pick up a tune instantly.' She remembered him singing the Beatles' songs he had learned back at Greenwich. In a family filled with multi-talented individuals, however, Daniel had to compete for the floor. 'There was never a shortage of performers when they were with us, Jill and Cecil both loved the limelight.'

The winter of 1962–3 was one of the severest of the century. The occupants of the Old Rectory found themselves snowed in. 'We got stuck in the snow which we all longed for because it meant we didn't have to do anything we didn't want to do and nobody could get to us,' Janet Stone recalled.

Some of Daniel's most emotive childhood memories were formed in that snow-drifted landscape. Years later he recalled the magic of discovering his childish prayers for snow answered that year. He remembered, too, his father's traditional Christmas reading of 'The Christmas Tree', with its imagery of starless, west-country nights and hard, hoary frosts. The distant recollections of the times he spent there still made his blood run with a 'tincture' of child-like excitement and world-weary sadness, he said.

For all the wonder of Thomas Hardy's Wessex, however,

the Day-Lewises' annual visit to Ireland was the undoubted highlight of each year. The Irish adventures started in 1964, when Daniel was an impressionable seven-year-old, readying himself for the transfer from the mixed Invicta to the all-boys Sherington school. Each August the family would drive through Wales and the West Country to catch either the Fishguard to Rosslare or Holyhead to Dun Laoghaire ferry. From the Irish ports they drove across country, through Cecil's birthplace of County Laois if possible, and head for the rugged coastline of Connemara and County Mayo. For two summers they stayed at the Errisaesk Guest House, in Connemara. Every other summer they spent at Old Head, a wind-ravaged spot overlooking Clew Bay and Clare Island.

Freed from the constraining routine of life at Croom's Hill, Daniel and Tamasin ran riot. Their memories of time spent there were amongst the most magical of their childhood. Ireland, their father's ancestral home, whose 'whispering roots' drew him back late in his life, took up permanent occupancy of a corner of both their hearts.

The highlight of most summers was the annual horse race at the silver strand of Carrowniskey, ten miles or so from Old Head, overlooking the islands of Inishturk and Caher. Daniel was entranced by the sight of local farmers and fishermen placing poles at either end of the beach, while the tinkers set up illegal betting booths. Carrowniskey was the sight of his earliest admitted romance. It was only an imaginary one, however, the first impressionable stirrings of a young boy's heart. 'I fell in love with a girl on a chestnut horse, her black hair flying,' he reminisced once.

Tamasin rode in the horse race. Jill recalled years later how she was terrified that her daughter would be thrown and killed. Tamasin had told her mother that the horse was trained. As she lined up with the others at the start, a voice in the crowd muttered, 'Terrible pony, she'll rear up at the starting pistol.' The horse did no such thing, however, and Tamasin skilfully guided it around the course to finish the race. Her father was so inspired by the sight of his daughter, her red windcheater billowing, her dark hair trailing behind her, that he wrote a poem about it, immortalizing the image as one that time might be able to bury but could not 'unmake'.

Together the family explored the gnarled, battered coastline, catching boats from Cleggan to the island of Inishbofin, visiting Ballintubber Abbey, walking at Croagh Patrick, Holy Mountain, and joining in the fun at the annual pony beauty contest in the fishing town of Clifden. Each summer the children became more and more reluctant to come home. 'They were always full of stories, always slightly sad to be back,' remembered Jenny Dormer.

Ireland's enchantments were indeed irresistible. Cecil would recount how one moment he would be fussed over as the famous Anglo-Irish poet, the next introduced as a Professor of Poultry at Oxford! Old Head was an inspiration for him. He walked, rested and wrote there, soaking up the atmosphere – and the humour – of the land he increasingly regarded as home despite a life and career spent at the heart of Establishment England. He too returned to London invigorated and inspired by his summers there.

By 1964, however, for all the immortal thoughts inspired by Ireland, Cecil's health began to fade. Christmas that year was spent at Greenwich. During the holiday Cecil was rushed to Greenwich's Miller General Hospital after waking up with blood all over his pillow. He had suffered a serious haemorrhage and was kept in hospital for the first fortnight of the New Year. His health was never fully to return.

Over the following years, the pressures of nursing her husband and managing a large house made Jill, already an acutely sensitive individual prone to explosions over matters Cecil would barely raise an eyebrow at, even more volatile. If Cecil's core was the 'blade of ice' he believed all artists needed to create, Jill's centre was a river of molten lava. Vesuvian-scale eruptions became more and more common, although she kept her anger bottled up as much as she could. Years later she confessed that sometimes, particularly when she decided to keep the full extent of her husband's illness a secret, she would drive the car away from Greenwich. Then she would let all the emotions flow. 'It affected me terribly. I used to go and park my car in a back street near Deptford and just scream because of the strain of keeping up the act,' she said.

She understandably felt that she was being cheated of precious time with the man she loved. Sean Day-Lewis's wife Anna was a shoulder to cry on occasionally. 'Jill would talk to my wife about her anger at Cecil's age and infirmity, she did not want him to be so old and so ill,' Sean recalled. 'The house did become a difficult place to be then, one could see that.'

Tamasin, already wise beyond her years, became intensely aware of her mother's temperament. 'One was alert to every nuance in my mother's moods,' she said many years later.

The atmosphere in the house became increasingly tense. Tamasin and Daniel became even more distanced from their father, and, inevitably, the strain began to show. 'I found it quite oppressive. There were an enormous amount of rows, we were always on tenterhooks,' recalled Jenny Dormer. 'I thought then it was very bad for them.'

In this climate, the youngest member of the household became more and more emotional. Jenny and Tamasin had the ability to wind Daniel up into tantrums. 'He was very dramatic with his outbursts. Jill never acknowledged that he was having temper tantrums,' Jenny remembered. 'Usually Tamasin would start it off by saying something like "Mamma's little pet", or something like that. Food was another way of getting at him; saying "You can't have that" would get him going. I used to join in, which was not very nice. When we called him "Mamma's boy" he used to say, "I fucking hate her, stupid cow." And we would say, "If your mother could hear you now!" Very cruel to a little boy and he would rise more and more and grow redder and redder in the face.'

As his health failed him, so too did Cecil's famously equable temper. Tamasin once recalled how a thunderous outburst from her father had had a devastating effect on the kitchen table. The force of his hand as he hit the table left a crack in its surface.

'Towards the end of his life, no doubt because of his illness, he lost his temper much more,' his son Sean remembered.

As the once ebullient atmosphere was darkened by Cecil's

failing health, so Daniel's acts of rebellion became more outrageous. Years later he was to claim they were attention-seeking. At the time they seemed more like an attempt at breaking away from the strictures imposed on him. 'He used to be so good and so nice, and then as soon as they left he became riotous. He was breaking out, breaking away,' said Jenny.

Daniel began to enter his father's holy of holies, the study. 'He would go down to his father's study and pinch a couple of cigarettes, or some of his chocolates, he used to eat violet cream chocolates,' recalled the oldest member of the mischievous trio.

Goaded on by his sister and Jenny, he began to perform for them. 'As soon as they left he would run downstairs and pinch his father's cigarettes. I used to say, "You are not to do that" but he would swear at me and say, "What are you going to fucking do about it? You can't do anything."

'Sometimes Tamasin and I would say, "Go on then, smoke two together," and he would. They were untipped cigarettes because Cecil used a cigarette holder. I used to say, "They will think it is me" and he would say, "Well, you'll just have to buy some and put them in then, won't you?"'

Not content with emulating one of his father's bad habits – after his first illness, doctors constantly advised Cecil to give up smoking – Daniel took up another vice as well. He and Tamasin had been free to drink a glass of wine with their Sunday lunch since early in their childhood. 'Both of them used to savour it because they liked it,' their nanny recalled. As he became more rebellious Daniel disastrously progressed to the hard stuff stored in his father's inner sanctum. 'He was drunk once or twice. I was cooking them something in the kitchen while their parents were out when it happened,' remembered Jenny. 'Once he was really sick, we were scrubbing it up and Tamasin was wondering whether you could distinguish between alcohol sickness and fever sickness!'

When Jenny Dormer left Croom's Hill, to be replaced later by a Spanish au pair, it was clear that Daniel's mutinous behaviour was on the increase: 'He was breaking loose.' Others on Croom's Hill also saw his acts of insurgence grow.

In his manhood Daniel would come to regret that he had

never had a brother. In his boyhood he turned to neighbours like Frankie Gair and Tom Broadbent for an escape from the powerful female influences of Croom's Hill. Tom, three years Daniel's junior, also bore witness to the devilish streak in the boy at number 6.

'He used to come round, put bread on the lawn, and then hide at the end of the garden. He had an air-gun, we would wait for the pigeons to come down and then we would shoot them. We used to hit them, we killed a few. We did it when my parents were out. He was the better shot, I can't even remember him giving me a shot.'

Tom also learned, to his cost, how Daniel had picked up the sharp practices of the marketeers who ran their stalls in nearby Deptford. As he grew older he was allowed to go fishing on the Thames. 'I had this really nice set of fishing flies which were my Grandad's. They were really nice, my grandfather had tied them himself. I swapped them with Daniel for a bar of chocolate!'

Daniel had acquired street-fighting skills too. 'We also used to play fighting games. He used to beat me up quite a lot, not viciously, but he was quite into fighting,' Tom recalled.

Cecil often said that he believed in giving his children some freedom. He called this principle a 'loose leash'. Privately he began to despair at his children's rebellions, however.

He and his oldest son Sean would regularly lunch together near his Chatto & Windus office in the West End. 'Cecil thought of Daniel and Tamasin as being rather revolutionary but that was compared to us being brought up in Devon and saying "Yes, sir, no, sir,"' recalled Sean.

At Sherington School, Daniel's behaviour attracted only mild rebukes. 'He was very, very articulate and hard-working but he was also not that obedient in the sense that he would, if given the chance, avoid working. The intelligent child always finds his way through the problems set by a teacher,' recalled Ian Saunders, who arrived to teach at the school in 1967 and is now the deputy headmaster. He once warned Daniel that he was devoting too much time to playing football and hanging around with a small gang of friends he had made there. 'I told

Daniel that if he did not stop acting the fool he would never get a decent job. Out of the mouths of teachers come such inanities. It's the sort of thing you say to so many people, only once in a million is there any comeback.' (It was to be twice in a million for Ian Saunders. Another, younger pupil at Sherington, Julian Holland, was told, 'He would not come to anything' unless he stopped 'messing around with the piano'. The music world now knows Julian as Jools Holland.)

At home in Croom's Hill Cecil was increasingly distracted. As his health declined steadily, his once solid frame slowly fading away, so too did the amount of energy he had for work. He was finding writing his Nicholas Blake novels difficult – he once joked that he had asked Agatha Christie for help with a few plots – and was relying more and more on his salary from Chatto & Windus rather than his poetry for income. To the many ailments he suffered from, he added claustrophobia. At a party held in his honour at the publishers Collins in 1968, Cecil was so terrified of being trapped in the room where the celebration was being held that he spent the entire evening in the adjoining corridor.

The financial burden became more and more difficult to bear. Luckily Tamasin saved her parents a significant drain on their resources by winning a scholarship to Bedales, the progressive co-educational school in Petersfield, Hampshire. She was the only girl to win a scholarship. Her mother announced the news with a piercing scream as she opened the post one morning. With Jill there were anguished screams and joyful screams. Tamasin knew instantly which category this one fell into and what it meant.

As Cecil slowly recovered his strength, however, his profile received an unexpected boost. He was about to become more famous than at any time in his writing career. On 14 December 1967 he received a letter from the then Prime Minister, Harold Wilson. The Labour Party leader wanted to know whether Cecil would be willing to put his name forward for the job of Poet Laureate. Cecil wrote back to say he would be and within a couple of weeks received another letter with the Downing Street hallmark on the envelope. To his amazement he had been chosen to succeed John Masefield, who had died the previous May, as 'Poet Laureate in ordinary to Her Majesty'.

The announcement was not to be made until the New Year, however. Cecil told the family but they all had to be sworn to secrecy. Tamasin found this particularly difficult. Among her classmates at Bedales was the daughter of one of the other leading poets favoured to receive the Laureateship, Robert Graves. 'I wanted to jump on my desk and shout, "My Pappa has won it,"' she once recalled.

When the announcement was made, however, early in the New Year, Tamasin and Daniel had ample opportunity to share in the celebrations. The newspapers had a field day with Wilson's appointment of Cecil Day-Lewis, former Communist and re-invented Irishman, as the Queen of England's official poet. 'Cecil Day-Lewis (He Once Sold *The Daily Worker*) to be Poet Laureate', read the *Daily Mail* headline.

Cecil enjoyed the limelight. 'You know I am the first Anglo-Irishman to be Poet Laureate. There's a feather in the cap for the old country,' he told a posse of press who descended on Croom's Hill, over tea and Jill's chocolate cake in his study on the day of the announcement. He praised his predecessor, Masefield, 'such lovely manners', said he would try to write about events that touched the public 'like the Aberfan disaster and Francis Chichester's voyage around the world', and modestly resisted comparisons with former holders of his new role, Wordsworth and Tennyson. 'Out of my class,' he said with a gentle smile.

Jill, however, was convinced that friends and neighbours would see it as a sell-out. 'We are waiting for the sneers,' she said pessimistically.

The financial reward was minimal. The Poet Laureate carried with it a salary of just £97, a £70 annual wage and £27 in lieu of the wine or 'butt of sack' that had historically accompanied the honour. But suddenly Cecil was the subject of much interest nationally and locally. The ten-year-old Daniel, Tamasin, Jill and Cecil became celebrities for a month or so as virtually every newspaper photographed them at home at Croom's Hill or walking around Greenwich's historic landmarks.

'There were terrific parties,' Ann Broadbent remembered. 'The thing that gave him greatest pleasure was a letter from an old lady in Ireland who wrote to say that she always wondered what became of the rector's little boy!'

The postbag at Croom's Hill was swollen by Cecil's celebrity. A new, enlarged letter-box had to be fitted to cope with his correspondence. The high profile was less welcome for the Poet Laureate's young son.

Daniel's impeccable manners and cut-glass accent were far from oddities at Sherington. The school was popular at the time with many middle-class parents in the area, including the Labour Minister James Callaghan, who sent his children there. 'It was a very, very good school. It was a boys' school with fairly strict discipline, very strong on games, the upper professional classes could send their boys here rather than to prep school,' recalled Ian Saunders. But the 330 boys there when Daniel was a pupil did reflect the mix of classes in that corner of London. 'We had a very large range of social class and income,' added Saunders.

In later years Daniel claimed that he became the victim of bullying. Despite the odd misshapen vowel and the occasional blasphemy, he was branded a 'poshie'. Unlike the other school scapegoats – West Indian and Asian children – Daniel had an escape open to him, however. His first public act of chameleonism had been to affect the south-London drawl of his tormentors.

'Suddenly one was singled out for being slightly different. In my case it was because I spoke differently. In other people's cases it was because they were the wrong colour,' he recalled years later. 'For me it was easy, I just adapted. My sister would ask me, "Why do you talk like that when you're with your mates?" To her, there was hypocrisy involved. To me, it was absolutely unconscious. It was raw survival.'

High-profile appearances in the newspapers, however, once more turned the spotlight on the 'posh bastard' in the school's midst. Having a father who now took tea with the Queen at Buckingham Palace was 'beyond the pale'. His old teacher has little doubt he was bullied: 'I expect he was, that was the playground pecking order.'

Daniel found himself protected by a gang. Their allegiance was to Millwall Football Club, then home to the most notoriously violent fans in England, among them an elite force called the F Troop. There were also sympathies for the fascist National Front. The gang was on the periphery of the skinhead culture.

By the age of eleven Daniel had shot up in size. He was acquiring his father's stature. 'He had an old face, a mature body for an eleven-year-old. He was grown,' recalled Ian Saunders. He began to spend more time with his rough-and-ready working-class pals. He became fascinated with their world of 'fighting and fishing', as he later put it. Despite his size, Daniel claimed he was of little use in the scrapes he and his suede-headed friends got into. 'I wasn't much good to them, but I had a couple of protectors, and if I got a belt, they made sure someone else got three.'

When his thuggish-looking friends were brought home to elegant, Georgian Greenwich and the home of the new Poet Laureate, however, Cecil realized it was time to act. The 'loose leash' had to be tightened, his son's freedoms reduced. Discipline and order had to return once more.

CHAPTER THREE

ESCAPE TO EDEN

'What does education often do? It makes a straight-cut ditch of a free meandering brook.'

THOREAU, *Journal*, 1850

T HE NIGHT was restless, tearful, terrifying. Yards away, legend went, the slain spirits of the ancient Battle of Solefields still weighed heavily on the darkness. The tangled woods echoed to the sounds of 500-year-old souls, the ambushed victims of Dick the Butcher, Smith the Weaver and their rebel leader Jack Cade.

Cloaked in the suffocating darkness of his new dormitory home, however, Daniel Day-Lewis was haunted more by fear of the living than dread of the long dead. Inside the boarding house he listened to whispered talk of fagging and bullying, of endless prep and compulsory prayers. As the other young voices fell silent, the noises in his eleven-year-old imagination were deafening. Awful things lay ahead.

The following morning at Croom's Hill Jill Balcon picked up the telephone to hear a plaintive, pleading voice. 'Mamma, this place is awful,' her son was sobbing. 'I was so frightened I spent the night sleeping in my trunk.'

Daniel did not take long to decide Sevenoaks School was not for him. That one dreadful night, spent in a fold-up bed, surrounded by five other homesick boys at the school's first-year boarding house, was enough to convince him escape was his only option. His phone call was his first attempt at winning his freedom. His story was a vivid invention, his tears the most theatrical he had yet shed. Back at Greenwich, however, they failed to have the desired effect. It would take him two years to shake free from the shackles of the school he was later to refer to as 'a sort of prison camp'.

In the summer of 1968, while his Sherington school-mates sat the 11-plus or the Junior Leaving Examination to go to comprehensive schools in Greenwich, Daniel had sat, and passed comfortably, the Sevenoaks entrance exam. He and the friends he had made at Sherington would soon be heading in different directions.

In September Cecil and Jill drove him to his new home-from-home, Lambardes, a faceless modern block built specifically for the school's youngest boys. They helped their son unpack his trunk of belongings, wished him well and then left him in the care of Brian and Elizabeth Townend.

The Townends, a salt-of-the-earth couple with a seen-it-all wisdom when it came to the care of their boys, were only months away from celebrating the twentieth anniversary of their arrival at the school. For most of those two decades they had been known as 'Fuzz' and 'Ma Fuzz'. Brian Townend was the proud owner of a magnificent, piratical beard.

They remember Daniel's earliest days there clearly. 'After his first night he produced this story that he had been so afraid to sleep in the dorm that he had to sleep in his trunk,' recalled 'Fuzz' Townend. 'So he told his mother. He couldn't have, of course, the trunk was locked up in a cupboard. It was rubbish but that's what he told her. It was always clear to me that Daniel didn't really want to be at Sevenoaks.'

Daniel's new school was a mere twenty miles or so from Greenwich. Door to door, his father's car – by now upgraded to a Mercedes, despite Cecil's shortage of money – could manage the drive through the suburban blandness of London's south-eastern fringe and out into the sweeping countryside of Kent, the so-called 'Garden of England', in less than an hour. In almost every way Daniel could imagine, however, Sevenoaks was a world away from the school he had left with predominantly happy memories. 'The place was alien and unattractive in every single one of its millions of details,' he said years later, his gift for exaggeration now polished to hyperbolic Irish perfection.

If Invicta's and Sherington's pupils had reflected the multicultural melting-pot that was south London in the 1960s, then

Sevenoaks was a monument to the immovable stability of the English middle classes. When Daniel started there the compulsory wearing of straw boaters – 'biffs' in school slang – had only recently been dropped, 'coloured' boys were still a novelty, and the admission of girls remained a distant dream for the most revolutionary progressives.

From the moment he found himself standing under the shadow of School House, the austere, stone-clad, eighteenth-century building at the hub of the sprawling school campus, Daniel sensed that for all his credentials he belonged more to urban London than to rural Kent. A trammelled order was once again being laid out before him. He no longer wanted to play life by the rules.

For most of his peers, however, Sevenoaks was a school to be proud of, an alma mater with a unique place in history. A school has stood on the outskirts of the Kentish market town for 500 years. The mist surrounding the histories of England's earliest schools is thick enough to allow a small group of them, Sevenoaks included, to compete for the honour of being the country's oldest.

The identity of the school's founder was in no doubt, only the date he opened it was. William Sevenoaks, a merchant, soldier and Mayor of the City of London, whose benign sculpted features still watched over the manicured grounds, established the school in the fifteenth century. Whether he did so in 1418, in a display of generosity after being elected Mayor, or fourteen years later in 1432 as part of his will when he died, seems to be a mystery even the school's official history cannot quite clear up. Either way, Sevenoaks scholars contend, only the secular schools of King's College, Rochester and Cambridge can lay claim to being older.

Sevenoaks also has the distinction of being the only school to be mentioned in Shakespeare. After William Sevenoaks' death the town and the school were overseen by James Fiennes, Lord Saye and Sele. In 1450, when the Hundred Years War with France was at its height and war taxes were bleeding the population dry, he became so unpopular that a rag-tag collection of commoners rebelled against him. Led by Jack

Cade, the upstarts defeated Fiennes's army at the Battle of Solefields. The fighting took place in woods within a few hundred yards of Sevenoaks school.

Before beheading Fiennes Cade accused his prisoner of having committed a series of hideous crimes. One of them was that he had 'most traitorously corrupted the youth of the realm in erecting a Grammar School'. This grisly episode found its way into Shakespeare's *Henry VI, Part II*. Cade and his accomplices, Dick the Butcher and Smith the Weaver, treated their prisoner to the 'health o'th' hatchet', then placed his noble head on a pole.

Impressed as they might have been by such grand links with the literary past, however, Cecil and Jill Day-Lewis were more interested in the school's educational present. They had entrusted Daniel to Sevenoaks for sound practical reasons. During the 1960s the school had won itself a reputation for combining academic excellence and traditional English public school values with a touch of progressive libertarianism. Its pupils were predominantly middle-class, with a sprinkling of 11-plus boys from local Kent County Council schools. Church, cricket and rugby were the school's holy trinity, and Latin was still a compulsory element of the curriculum. Cecil's own education at Sherborne had not been dissimilar. At the same time, under its charismatic headmaster, Leonard Taylor, Sevenoaks had won a reputation for an open-minded approach to schooling.

Cecil was against the idea of Daniel joining Tamasin at the mixed, 'co-ed', Bedales. 'He felt co-ed schools were fine for girls but not for boys,' recalled his son Sean. Cecil and Jill hoped that Sevenoaks' individualistic mix of old world discipline and new age enlightenment would suit their son.

As it turned out, Daniel's time at Sevenoaks coincided with the brief headmastership of a man more interested in the traditional values of the starchier schools. Dr Michael Hinton arrived at the school in 1968 and instantly declared that it should move back to the basics of English life. Morality and religious rectitude were his twin gods. Hinton was worried that the liberal attitudes played into the hands of apathetic boys.

'The result has been a great deal of taking of advantage, of petty theft and petty vandalism . . . of the general evasiveness of which boys are past masters,' the school's official history, written by former master Brian Scragg, records him as having said at the time. 'Our religious and moral education are not as effective as they might be.'

So Daniel once more found his days conforming to a strict regime, his life filled with new rituals and a new lexicon. Breakfast at 8 a.m., school assembly at 9 a.m., classes through the day until 4 p.m. 'Tea and bun' at the end of lessons, supper at 8 p.m., evening 'prep' afterwards, bed and lights out in the dorm at 9 p.m. Uniform rules were strictly applied: grey suits, grey shirts, house ties. 'The attitude was to dress boys like bank clerks and make them behave like adults,' remembered Elizabeth Townend.

As a weekly boarder, Daniel returned home to Greenwich every Friday. But he had to be back at school on Sunday evening in time for supper and one of the school's strictest rituals, 'Sunday At Eight', a church service, a dry, tedious affair.

Like virtually every other child who has been removed from his parents, Daniel was immediately homesick. The sophisticated cosiness of Croom's Hill presented a stark contrast to the coldness of his spartan dormitory. And for a boy who already cherished solitude and privacy, sharing these sleeping quarters with five other boys was traumatic. 'He had been sent as a day boy to an ordinary state school, to suddenly be dropped into a boarding school came as a shock. I was terribly sorry for these children brought along, these dear little boys,' said Elizabeth Townend.

Daniel established himself as a loner early on. A fellow first-year in 1968 remembers him as a fish out of water. 'I was a scholarship day boy, but I spent most of my time with boarders. We all had friends, but he seemed a loner.'

Daniel's sense of displacement was intensified by the fact that, academically, he had much catching up to do. For all its liberal leanings, Sevenoaks was not so radical that it had dropped the classics from its curriculum. Latin and French, subjects unheard of at Invicta or Sherington, were suddenly on Daniel's timetable. He was given extra tuition in both subjects but when he found his studies tough going, a sense of failure quickly set in. 'I was totally inadequate to deal with that particular way of life. I was academically incapable of keeping up. I'd never done Latin or French and I was having all this extra tuition. I had such an overwhelming sense of failure – even at that age.'

His plight was not uncommon. Most of the boys who arrived at Sevenoaks from outside the public school system were novices at Latin. 'I found it tough not coming from a prep school and I found myself dropping a long way behind too,' remembered his former schoolmate. 'In things like Latin which I had not started until I got there, it was an academic school undoubtedly. Masters liked to believe they were progressive on the arts side but it was strongly academic.'

Daniel was suffering outside the classroom as well. A passionate footballer, he found himself having to play rugby instead. Cricket, however, was less of a culture shock. Like his father, he displayed a natural talent for the school's summer game, though not to the extent of outshining Sevenoaks' star player. Paul Downton went on to provide Sevenoaks with the sort of honour which, in Daniel's eyes anyway, the school prized most: an England cricket cap. 'It was a school for academic achievers and athletes, and if you weren't one or the other, you were useless.'

Daniel's curious combination of middle-class manners and south London street-wisdom also marked him out as different. He suffered from taunting and bullying, the sort of treatment traditionalists might deem 'character-building' but which others might call 'character-demolishing'. Older boys played puerile pranks on their juniors. 'Not far from Lambardes was a place called Park Grange. On the way from Lambardes to woodwork there was a ditch called the Hedgehogs. Older boys always used to try to push new boys into it. It was filled with mud. Boys would get into trouble if they turned up caked in mud,' recalled his contemporary. 'There was a bit of fagging still, I remember having to clean older boys' shoes.'

In years to come, Daniel would claim that his time at Sevenoaks induced a perpetual feeling of nausea. However, the school records show that it could not all have been unremitting gloom. If Latin and French were a struggle, the English language presented no such problems. The literary atmosphere of Croom's Hill had clearly had an osmotic effect. Daniel became briefly a star of the school at writing and reading poetry and prose. He won one of the junior writing prizes and, in July 1970, read two of his father's poems at a literary evening. Neither of his parents was present: Cecil was absent through illness, Jill because tickets for the evening had sold out before she applied. She did show up for another public reading, however, this time to hear Daniel read from his own scribblings. Afterwards Cecil said his son's writing was 'rather good'. 'He wrote one about a fox being hunted which shows great empathy,' he told the *Daily Express*. 'I don't think he feels any compulsion to write poetry just because I do. It is entirely off his own bat.' Daniel told the *Daily Mail*, who also wrote of his success, that he had no plans to follow his Poet Laureate father. 'I don't think I want to be a writer,' he said.

One of his English masters remembers him as a talented public speaker. 'He came to me once to borrow a copy of *The Hot Gates* by William Golding. He was reading aloud from an essay called "Billy The Kid" at the junior spoken word festival on an open day,' recalled Hugh Pullen, still a master at Sevenoaks. 'He read aloud rather well. And unlike many pupils he actually returned the book.'

Daniel also began to demonstrate a gift for woodwork. One of his first efforts was a table tennis table. 'All my life's ambition went into this table,' he recalled later. It was taken home to Croom's Hill and installed in a cellar, the scene set for sporting confrontations to come.

Most significantly of all, however, the absolute escapism of acting was fully revealing itself. Daniel had made his first public appearance at Invicta School's Nativity Play, playing one of the Three Wise Men. He recalled once that his first-ever spoken line was 'I bring you frankincense'. There had been brief glimpses of theatrics even earlier than that, for example when he ran around the kitchen at Croom's Hill with a string shopping bag over his head. It was 1961 and he was impersonating Yuri Gagarin, the first man in space. Later, as he entered the dressing-up phase all children seem to pass through, he decked himself out as a guardsman, re-enacting Trooping the Colour. 'I had a rather splendid guardsman's uniform in my dressing up box. My first performance was the Fainting Guardsman,' he was to remember.

At Litton Cheney Daniel also loved dipping into the Stones' fancy-dress box. Janet Stone still has pictures of the Oscar-winner as a small boy dressed up as a Roman centurion in Greenwich and as a policeman at Litton Cheney. He and Tamasin even staged their own childish version of *The Dumb Waiter* for their grandfather, Sir Michael Balcon.

Sevenoaks, however, gave Daniel his first taste of grease-paint. He was cast in a production of *Cry, The Beloved Country*. As a junior member of the school, his role was minuscule. He played a negro spear-carrier, whose only lines, he recounted once, were 'Yes, umfundisi, no, umfundisi'.

If the part was insignificant, the possibilities it opened up in the adolescent Daniel's mind could not have been more vital. At the end of the performance his make-up was never quite removed. He would go to sleep in his dormitory at night, his real self mysteriously and elusively hidden behind a mudpacked mask. 'What I loved about it most was the escape into another world,' he said when reminiscing about it. 'I loved the fact that I could never get all the make-up off, that it made my sheets filthy at night, that I had a licence to sully the sheets.'

Ultimately, however, Daniel and Sevenoaks were not made for each other. After his first, dramatic telephone attempt at escape, he realized that his parents were determined he should stay in the Kent countryside. His removal would have to be the school authority's decision instead.

Shoplifting was rife at the time. Gangs of boys would roam the town, filling their pockets with whatever they could lay their dextrous young hands on. Here was a fraternity Daniel could see a purpose in joining. With the hard-liner Hinton in the headmaster's office, stiff penalties were being doled out. Expulsion would release him, his logic went.

'There was quite an outbreak of shoplifting at the time, it was when shops were starting help yourself shopping. It was an open invitation,' recalled Elizabeth Townend. 'There was a toy shop that was having a closing-down sale and that was when it all blew up. They obviously all dared each other.'

Some of those who were caught were suspended. Daniel, on the other hand, could not get arrested! 'I made endless feeble protests, but they refused to expel me,' he remembered once.

His unhappiness deepened. Compounding his home-sickness, his sense of being a 'non-person', and his academic insecurity, there was another factor which made Sevenoaks, in Daniel's turbulent adolescent mind at least, seem a gaol from which he had to be released.

Boarding school was a bewildering experience in so many senses. Sex was yet another area of confusion. Forbidden and frowned upon it might have been, but homosexuality was as intrinsic a part of life at Sevenoaks as it was at many other traditional English public schools: it had been a fact of life at Sherborne, when Cecil was a boy there half a century earlier.

'What do you expect in a boys' school? If you are going to have boys together like that it is asking for trouble,' recalled Elizabeth Townend. 'It was frowned upon, but how did you catch them at it?'

Daniel told his half-brother Sean that he had aroused the unwanted attentions of some of the school's predatory older boys. 'It was Dan himself who told me. He was an object of desire for the older boys, he was a very pretty boy,' recalled Sean, himself the product of a public school education, at All Hallows School in Rousdon, Devon. 'In my generation at boarding school it was definitely thought as "queer" if you were interested in girls. You crossed over after you left school. Daniel really wasn't very interested in the things that boys got up to at boarding school at that sort of age. It was terribly off-putting for him. He resisted their blandishments because he wasn't into that.'

More than a decade after the experience, Daniel was twice

to draw on his memories of his fellows' adolescent experiments. 'At school boys were always jumping into bed with each other,' he recalled then. 'You got the feeling they were only practising until girls came along.'

His restlessness was compounded by the images of an English Garden of Eden being painted by his sister. Tamasin, who was blissfully happy at Bedales, wrote regularly. Bedales was then at the height of its vogue. Many boys at Sevenoaks listened jealously to dispatches from friends and relatives. All seemed to be revelling in the free-wheeling philosophy of the school. 'Bedales was very fashionable at the time. We all looked on it as a place of great freedom, from a creative point of view it seemed to take things to the absolute limits, it had a lot of attractive points to it,' remembered Daniel's former fellow pupil.

Unlike the rest of the school, however, Daniel was no longer content with second-hand accounts of this co-ed idyll. One morning in his second summer term the Townends walked into the dormitory at Lambardes to discover Daniel's bed was empty. Two other beds at the school were also unoccupied. Daniel, a boy called Pat Herring and another pupil had fled.

'Daniel ran away, which was a sensation, taking two boys with him, Pat Herring and another boy. God knows where they got the money,' remembered Elizabeth Townend. Parents and police were alerted and a search was launched.

The fugitives materialized at Bedales. They had taken the train from Sevenoaks to Hampshire. Eventually Sevenoaks was told that the missing trio was at the school's progressive rival. The headmaster and Daniel's housemaster, 'Fuzz' Townend, drove cross-country to Petersfield to bring the miscreants back to Kent. Before that, however, Daniel had spoken to his parents, explaining his unhappiness at Sevenoaks. According to an account his mother gave many years later, his primary concern was sex. 'He was sobbing, saying how unhappy he was at his single-sex school and then he said: "What's more, I'm sex starved." We found that part so funny,' she told the *Daily Mail*.

His father dealt with the problem in the stoic manner he seemed able to adopt at such times of crisis. Sean Day-Lewis, in his biography of his father, remembered how 'Cecil, at his best in such crises, did not become over-excited. Instead he patiently and quietly attempted to discover what was wrong and what was needed to put things right.' Daniel told his father that he wanted to transfer to Bedales.

Tamasin's school was then one of the most expensive in England. Cecil's finances were somewhat stretched, as they had been periodically throughout his life. The solution, according to Sean, came in the form of an increased scholarship allowance for Tamasin if Daniel enrolled at Bedales too. By having to pay out less for his daughter, Cecil was able to put his son through the school as well. Daniel was accepted and given a place at the beginning of the autumn term 1970.

He arrived at his modish new school a film star, having been hired for his first screen acting role for three reasons: first, he could play football, second, he looked like a south London hooligan, and third, he owned a pair of jeans! Director John Schlesinger had been in Greenwich filming a sequence for his movie *Sunday, Bloody Sunday,* starring three of the bright lights of the British screen: Peter Finch, Glenda Jackson and Murray Head. This tale of a suitably seventies *ménage à trois* – Head's character, a beautiful young sculptor, was simultaneously having affairs with Finch and Jackson – featured some grittily realistic London backdrops. In Greenwich Schlesinger wanted to re-create a park football match. The director arrived to scout around for young talent.

He asked Wendy Mead, owner of the local greengrocer on Royal Hill, whether she knew of a group of likely lads. The posse of schoolboys she rounded up included Daniel Day-Lewis and his friend and neighbour Tom Broadbent. Schlesinger had been at school with Tom's mother Ann and instantly recognized him as a relative of hers. 'You're a Younghusband,' he told him, remembering his mother's maiden name.

Schlesinger also needed a trio of particularly mischievous-looking lads to play another scene in which they were to walk casually down a street, scratching cars with broken glass. Both

Daniel and Tom had the look of potential trouble-makers. Schlesinger took one glance at them and ended the shortest casting session either would ever undergo with the words: 'Yeah, you'll do. Have you got any jeans?' Both boys did, and so two film careers were born, one to move on to greater things, the other to end at the close of a memorable day. 'The best bit was playing football, there were a couple of guys who said they were Tottenham reserve players,' recalled Tom Broadbent.

Schlesinger's eye saw something in the dirty-faced angel that was the fourteen-year-old Daniel Day-Lewis. When the movie was released, the football scene featured the briefest of close-ups of him blowing a chewing-gum bubble. And when it came to enacting the car-vandalism scene, it was Daniel who was told to take the lead. The boys were to walk down the road and 'scratch' three parked cars.

'We were each given a broken milk bottle that had its edges rubbed off so that it could not scratch too deep. Behind the milk bottles we had a piece of chalk. We were only meant to rub the chalk on to the first two cars, and then we were supposed to scratch the last car. We had one dress rehearsal, with the stars walking one way, us walking the other,' remembered Tom.

The enterprise was profitable for all concerned. Tom and Daniel pocketed £5 each for their day's work. *Sunday, Bloody Sunday* went on to become a critical and box office success. Schlesinger, Jackson, Finch and writer Penelope Gilliatt all won Oscar nominations for their contributions.

That August Daniel set off for Old Head in Ireland, hugely relieved to have been freed by his father from his Sevenoaks 'prison cell'. Yet, grateful as he and Tamasin were for such acts of fatherly support, brother and sister were beginning to step up their rebellion against their parents' strictures. Back in Greenwich Tamasin was drinking in local pubs and going out with older men, much to the annoyance of Jill in particular. On one occasion Tamasin, ensconced at the home of a friend of Cecil's, suffered the embarrassment of having her mother ring up after midnight demanding that the man drive her daughter home immediately.

Already emerging as a formidably independent spirit at Bedales, and now grown into a strikingly attractive young woman, Tamasin deeply resented being treated like a child. 'Our childhood was quite puritanical,' she admitted many years later. 'We were still seen to be children in adolescence, which was a huge contrast to life at Bedales – where we were treated as burgeoning adults and encouraged to make our own choices.'

That summer, at Old Head, as Daniel excitedly readied himself for his move to Bedales, Tamasin's frustrations brought her into direct confrontation with her father. In Sean Day-Lewis's biography of Cecil, she recalled how she had started dating a Dublin boy that summer. By then seventeen, she was so smitten by the boy that she was disappearing with him every night. When her father discovered what was going on he summoned her to his sitting room.

'I don't want my daughter to be a whore or tart,' he exploded when Tamasin told him truthfully what she was doing. She had an inkling of her father's secrets and hit back accusing him of 'double standards'. Cecil once confided that he thought his only daughter 'a tremendous tough'.

Daniel's public act of rebellion in running away from Sevenoaks bonded brother and sister even closer. Like most siblings, they still had their disagreements. But now that her brother's angelic image had been irretrievably shattered, an affectionate closeness was developing. It has grown ever since. 'I thought she was terrific, but she didn't like me,' Daniel said once. 'Maybe it was because I smiled at everybody and got away with murder. But as soon as I got into trouble she saw that I was OK.'

From the moment he arrived at Bedales that September, Daniel felt as enthusiastic about the school as his sister. He came to call it 'bliss'. The contrast with Sevenoaks was instantly obvious; the school's alumni summed it up. Sevenoaks' favourite sons were England cricketers; Bedales boasted the offspring of actors and authors. Lord Olivier was among the high-profile parents.

Uniforms did not exist. Instead of dull grey compulsory

jackets and ties, pupils wandered around in come-as-you-please clothes and colours. At the start of the 1970s Bedales boys and girls dressed for Woodstock rather than the Square Mile of the City of London. Hippyish tie-dyed shirts, jeans and Jesus sneakers were *de rigueur*. Teachers were called by Christian names, or even nicknames. The headmaster, a dashing, dynamic sports lover called Tim Slack, was known to everyone as 'Tigger'.

The laissez-faire lifestyle was reflected in the school magazine, the *Bedales Chronicle*. A flick through its pages during Daniel's days there was as likely to throw up an anarchic comic strip called 'The Irresistible Rise of Superpunk' as a wordy comparison of Hopkins and Eliot as poets of the religious experience. When Daniel arrived its columns were used to debate whether Bedalian students should be allowed to smoke or not.

If Sevenoaks was like a prison camp to Daniel, Bedales was a holiday camp in comparison. Another new world was opening up to Daniel. At last it was one he could be part of. Founded at the end of the nineteenth century as an alternative to the rigidity of the public school system, Bedales provided Daniel with the freedom he needed after years of suppression. It was a place to shed the chains of his childhood. He relished it.

In the autumn of that year, 1970, Cecil had come to Bedales to speak. Despite his weakening health, he accepted an invitation from headmaster Slack. Robert Graves, passed over by Harold Wilson in favour of Cecil for the Poet Laureateship, was also invited to deliver a speech at around the same time.

In the hip vernacular of Bedales, the Poet Laureate's lecture was a 'jaw'. 'Jaws' were held in the school's Lupton Hall on Sunday evenings, around seven. They were serious affairs. 'You had to wear a suit and tie, or if you were a girl, your best frock,' remembered a contemporary of Daniel's, Carlo Gebler, son of the writer Edna O'Brien.

Speakers ranged from rabbis to imams, writers to film producers. The twenty-minute talks were designed to open Bedalians' young minds to the infinite possibilities that lay ahead of them. Cecil's speech certainly did that. Decades later the words he used that evening seem like a map of his son's future.

For all the enjoyment the Poet Laureateship had brought him, Cecil had never shaken off the view that artists, like children in his Victorian-valued past, should be seen and not heard. 'Otherwise you tend to get people talking about the "funny, nice man who talks about architecture" and they may forget about the poetry,' he used to say. In his 'jaw' he once more argued his case. 'The artist's calling demands that he be disinterested: should have no axe to grind: should rid himself as far as possible of the notion of his art as a way of self-advancement,' he said, his presence filling the hall, his voice an intoxicating blend of soft Irish and grave Anglo-Saxon.

'I find it difficult to imagine that any artist who is not a mere doodler with words or paints or notes can be a materialist. The sources of his art are so deep – though it must use space and time, the art springs from a region where time and space are unimportant. The poet knows that spirit is a wind which "bloweth where it listeth",' he added.

Three human qualities made a true artist, the ageing eminence concluded: 'Patience, joy and disinterestedness.' And he ended his speech by addressing those words to his own child. 'Remember, my son, those words – patience, joy, disinterestedness.'

Somewhere the seeds of his message were settling in Daniel's still restless mind. They would not bloom for years, but his words took immovable root. By 1971 both he and Tamasin were offering their father fleeting glimpses of their potential. It had been one of Cecil's friends, the American poet Robert Frost, who said: 'You don't have to deserve your mother's love, you have to deserve your father's, he's more particular.' All Cecil's children lived under the shadow of their father's achievements. There was no sense of Stephen Spender's criticism, of superiority, far from it. 'He was a terrific encourager. But like most offspring of famous men I could never quite lose the need to try to impress him,' according to his oldest son Sean.

At seventeen, Tamasin had felt for years that the only way

she would become close to her father would be through achievement. 'I had to win his respect through my work,' she told Sean years later. Daniel, too, admitted to being intimidated more by his father's aura of importance than any understanding of his reputation. He was too young to appreciate that. 'I was probably in awe of him. I had great respect for him, not because I knew anything about him but because he commanded respect.'

Tamasin in particular was responsible for placing a celebrated feather in the Day-Lewis family cap. In 1971 King's College, Cambridge decided to open its historic doors to women. Tamasin, a shining academic star at Bedales, became the first girl to win a scholarship there. Her headline-winning breakthrough won her the respect she craved. But then she decided not to go up to university immediately and took a year off. Her good looks had already brought her to the attention of some of London's leading fashion photographers. She spent her year enjoying the glamorous life of the catwalk model, working for the designer Jeff Banks at the Paris shows and for the Fabiani collection in Rome.

In his adolescent mind, at least, Daniel still had some way to go. Back at Bedales he took the first steps by emulating one of his father's first achievements. He began to establish himself as an actor capable of tackling more demanding roles than mere blacked-up spear-carriers or bubble-blowing extras.

Bedales' drama productions were overseen by the formidable Rachel Fields, one of the longest-serving teachers. Her dark, Transylvanian demeanour and cutting tongue had earned her the nickname 'Drac'. When excited, Fields would beat her chest violently. It was an intimidating package. 'She was feared,' remembered Carlo Gebler. 'She was sarcastic and very accurate, which was an unfair combination when you are twelve and she is fifty-two.'

For all her ferocity, she had a shining reputation for developing young talent. As Daniel started out at Bedales, the school magazine was reporting the soaring success of one of Rachel Fields's most recent prodigies, Simon Cadell. Impressed by Daniel's enthusiasm, she cast him in his first school production towards the end of 1971. In Shakespeare's *A Winter's Tale*, staged at Lupton Hall, Daniel was to play the same role his father had taken on almost half a century earlier at Sherborne – Florizel.

Cecil and Jill both travelled to Bedales to see their son's introduction to serious theatre. Dressed in a white ruffled shirt and classical Shakespearean tights, he looked dashingly romantic. And even though the school review of the play made no mention of his debut afterwards, singling out only a dancer called Susie Carpenter-Jacobs for her excellence, his parents were bursting with pride. Years later, Jill claimed she saw a natural talent instantly. 'What impressed me was not so much the way he spoke his lines, but the intensity with which he listened to the others,' she said. 'That's how you can tell a real actor.'

Cecil was equally excited by his son's performance. Back in Greenwich he had nothing but praise for Daniel's interpretation of the role he knew so well. 'Excellent, excellent,' he told friends and family. Perhaps, after all, the speck of adolescent clay was shaping himself.

CHAPTER FOUR

THE GREAT SCYTHE

'There are two themes for poetry. One is death, the other love, and the bridge between the two is transience: everything passes away.'
CECIL DAY-LEWIS, *Observer*, October 1968

OUTSIDE ANOTHER elusive English summer was in its first, faltering flush. Only weeks earlier Cecil Day-Lewis had watched skeletal elm trees battered by a 'racking' April storm. Now, through his bedroom window, under chalky blue skies, those elms were still and in leaf.

Inside the poet's room, however, for all the ethereal shafts of sunlight and vases of bright garden blooms, the faces were wintry white. They faded in and out of focus, spoke in voices hushed and respectful, their features resigned to the inevitable. Man too must abide by the seasons. Cecil Day-Lewis knew that better than most.

In another corner of the house Jill Balcon's voice could no longer mask the growing panic within her. There was still no sign of her son Daniel. She offered another private prayer that he would not be too late.

The scene was The Lemmons, the country home of Jill's closest friend Elizabeth Jane Howard and her husband Kingsley Amis. It was Sunday, 21 May 1972.

All day Jill had been ringing Bedales in an effort to get through to Daniel. Staff there were told to pass on the message, he was to catch the first available train to Hertfordshire. His father was gravely ill.

Only seven weeks earlier Daniel had travelled from Greenwich with his parents and Tamasin to the Amis home. It had been decided that his mother and his increasingly weak father should spend some time there while Jill was working at Elstree

Studios, in north-west London. The studios were a gruelling ninety minutes or more by car from south-east London. The Lemmons, on the other hand, was a mere quarter of an hour away in the picture-postcard village of Hadley Common.

Cecil, now a pale, cadaverous shadow of his former robust self, was incapable of fending for himself. The strain of nursing her husband had taken its toll on Jill, who was near exhaustion, but she hated the idea of leaving him alone for any longer than absolutely necessary. When her friend offered to put them up she accepted instantly. The arrangement was even more appealing because Elizabeth had a nurse called Tessa in the house looking after her own ailing mother. So, on 6 April, Cecil walked slowly out of the front door of Croom's Hill, climbed into the family Mercedes and, with Jill at the wheel, watched the masts of the *Cutty Sark,* the Canaletto skyline of Wren's riverfront, and finally, the steel-grey waters of the timeless Thames fade from view. He was never to see his beloved Greenwich again.

The Amises had a self-contained bedroom and bathroom on the ground floor of their house. Cecil was delighted by the move; the change of scenery lifted the eternally rootless writer considerably. After regaining his strength from the upheaval, he even penned a short poem in honour of his new hosts, which he called 'At Lemmons'. It was a typical blend of Cecil at his most sentimental and his most resigned. He thanked his hosts for 'sweetening' the atmosphere in his sick room, but accepted his failing grip on mortality. When he read the poem Kingsley Amis broke down and wept.

Despite his failing health Cecil brought a breath of fresh air to the house. He rode around the gardens in Elizabeth's mother's electric wheel-chair, sat in the courtyard listening to pieces of his favourite music – Mozart, Schubert, Bach and Chopin – and encouraged his friends to read to him in bed. His good nature was infectious. Often Kingsley Amis would drop by for an evening drink, but only on condition that he did not make Cecil laugh too much in case he had a heart attack.

Cecil was also cheered by a visit from his son Nick. His

second son from his first marriage had become an elusive figure within the Day-Lewis family. After graduating from Oxford he had moved to South Africa and later Australia. 'He kept getting engaged at Oxford and got engaged to a South African woman and went straight there after he graduated. He eventually escaped from that marriage and got married to someone else, ending up in Melbourne,' explained his brother Sean. Nick's visit to The Lemmons was the first time father and son had seen each other in ten years.

The new, extended, Amis–Day-Lewis family had celebrated three birthdays at the house: Kingsley Amis's fiftieth on 16 April, Cecil's sixty-eighth on 27 April and Daniel's fifteenth two days later. For Daniel's his mother made one of her grandest birthday cakes. He was also given a second cake to take back to his school-friends at Bedales.

The atmosphere at The Lemmons was, if anything, even more fiercely intellectual than at Croom's Hill. Daniel remembered later being in awe of the 'ferociously high-powered' exchanges he heard between Kingsley and his son Martin. It made him feel, he said once, 'like a cockroach in the corner'. As the Amises' guest's health faded, it would also have made Daniel aware of how few opportunities he had been given to establish such a rapport with his own father. All he had provided was trouble, he would later think to himself.

Less than a fortnight after his youngest son's birthday, however, it was clear to all that Cecil was losing his battle against his illness. Jill's close friend Ursula Vaughan Williams, Daniel's godmother, rushed to be at her side and along with Elizabeth Jane Howard they remained with the Poet Laureate as he slipped in and out of consciousness throughout the weekend. By Sunday evening Tamasin had arrived and Sean had been contacted and was on his way. The worry was Daniel and whether he would arrive at his father's bedside in time.

Cecil's struggle had been a long, tenacious one. For months, however, he had been almost totally immobilized. As Daniel had stood on the stage at Bedales, back in December, proudly soaking up his father's applause at the end of his performance as Florizel, he had been oblivious of the superhuman effort behind his appearance at the school that night. The night before Cecil had lost his footing and fallen down the stairs at Croom's Hill. He was 'black and blue with bruises'. Only his will-power had carried him through his son's finest hour.

Cecil had long before sensed that his time was close at hand, even though Jill and the children had decided to protect him from the truth. He had gone into hospital in March 1971, shortly after returning from a trip to Rome where he laid a wreath commemorating the 150th anniversary of the death of the poet John Keats. With the laurel-leaved wreath in his hand, he had told the assembly at the city's Protestant Cemetery: 'Keats came here to Rome in a last desperate attempt to throw off the disease that was killing him. His name will be on the heart of every man and woman who loves Romantic poetry.'

Back in England, a few weeks later, doctors told Jill that her poet husband had also developed an illness from which there was no hope of recovery. They had discovered pancreatic cancer. It was only a matter of months.

Aware that time was running out, Jill had taken Cecil on a series of short holidays. Mostly they had travelled alone, leaving Tamasin and Daniel to their studies. That summer, however, the family had taken one last trip to Ireland together. Cecil had once more been returned to his ancestral homeland and the wind-whipped coastline where his roots seemed to whisper most eloquently to him.

Throughout that year he had continued to make the occasional public appearance as Poet Laureate. In the winter he had even spoken at the House of Lords where he delivered Lord Byron's maiden speech as part of a celebration of another great poet's life. The effort drained him so severely that he collapsed of exhaustion the following day at home in Greenwich.

Christmas had been spent at Croom's Hill, where, with his customary generosity, he treated friends and neighbours to champagne. His neighbours in Greenwich were not told of his condition but they sensed the terrible truth. Jill's close friend Ann Broadbent remembers visiting the house during those final months.

'It was never mentioned that Cecil had cancer or was dying. And in fact not long before they moved to Lemmons, Jill rang up and said, "Come over to dinner, it'll be only you, wear your oldest clothes,"' she recalled.

'So I thought I would wear my very oldest clothes which turned out to be a very old Victorian dress which I had to corset myself prodigiously to get into at all. What I had forgotten is that Victorian ladies never ate when they were corseted. They ate before.

'Halfway through dinner I realized I was going to faint, so I got up and made for the door. I fell like a log over Cecil's lap. It couldn't have been a better thing because by that time everybody was worrying about him. The evening took off like a light.'

Nothing could lift the gloom at The Lemmons on the evening of 21 May, however. Cecil, his strength ebbing and flowing, would occasionally ask someone to read to him. After Elizabeth Jane Howard read extracts from *Pride and Prejudice*, he thanked her with a whispered 'marvellous stuff'.

Later Tamasin went into her father's room to say goodnight. 'Goodbye,' he murmured in return. Moments later he suffered a spasm of pain and had to be given a pain-killing injection that would knock him out. As he faded from consciousness Jill arrived in the room, relieved at having just made contact with Daniel. Sean Day-Lewis recounts in his biography of his father how Elizabeth Jane Howard told Cecil, 'It's Jill.' He whispered, 'I know,' and dropped into a deep sleep.

After catching the first train that Monday morning, Daniel arrived at The Lemmons at 10 a.m. His half-brother Sean had arrived shortly before and was at Cecil's side. Daniel was rushed straight into his father's bedroom. There he saw Cecil surrounded by a circle of women in dressing-gowns. He was ushered to his father's bedside and given his right hand to hold. One minute later Cecil Day-Lewis slipped quietly away. It was as if he had clung to life until his son had arrived at his side. No words were exchanged, but somehow he must have sensed that Daniel was there. He could leave now.

That May Monday morning, at the age of fifteen, Daniel

Day-Lewis said goodbye to the father he had held in awe, the inspirational figure to whom he had yet to prove his own worth. There would come a time when he would regret his father's passing every day. He would grow to wish he had proven himself a better son, provided his father with fewer problems, achieved more before his passing. He would come to mourn the missed opportunities to listen and learn. He would come to miss the wisdom and the words.

Yet at first Daniel felt strangely numb. He was chillingly unmoved by the events of that morning. Like Cecil witnessing his own mother's departure from this life, there was 'no pain, no perturbation, no sense of parting'. Years later Daniel would describe those deathbed moments as 'that bizarre, alienated, emotionless first encounter with the great scythe, which left me reeling from my own indifference'. At another time, too, he would talk of the theory of eternal return, how 'human beings are constantly making decisions blindly, making the same mistakes from generation to generation, which then affect the rest of their lives'.

Cecil's childhood loss explained much about his strengths as an artist and his weaknesses as a man. That morning his own passing sowed the same divergent seeds deep within his son.

During those first hours after his father's death, Daniel spent much of his time with Tamasin, the sister he had become increasingly close to. The shared sense of loss, however minimal it was in Daniel's case at the time, brought them even nearer. Sean Day-Lewis remembered seeing Daniel and Tamasin comforting each other. 'As soon as my father's last breath was drawn everybody left the room. Daniel and Tamasin went to chat together in the garden. It was obvious to me that was not to be interrupted, they wanted to be together and that image has lingered,' he said.

The death of the Poet Laureate was announced publicly that Monday. Kingsley Amis added a brief statement: 'Cecil died peacefully after a long and exhausting illness which was largely free from pain. To the end he continued to show those qualities of humour, cheerfulness and good nature that all

72

those who knew him would recognize as characteristic. He never complained.'

The following day's obituaries were kind. 'C. Day-Lewis – the gentle revolutionary', the *Daily Mail* headline read. 'He was, as a man, much liked. As a poet, he left his mark on the history of his time, which is more than can be said for many who made more noise,' Anthony Hern wrote.

During the next few days it was decided to bury Cecil in Dorset, his favourite English county, in the same graveyard as his favourite English writer, Thomas Hardy. 'Because it was decided not to tell my father that his last illness was fatal he never felt moved to express a preference about where he should be buried,' Sean told newspapermen after the private funeral, conducted by the local vicar and Cecil's friend, the Reverend Austen Williams from St Martin-in-the-Fields. 'He never put down firm roots either in his native Ireland or in England. But I am sure he would have approved of Stinsford. He often visited the church as a Hardy pilgrim.'

At the funeral guitarist Julian Bream played a piece by one of Cecil's best-loved composers, Bach. At the end Jill crowned the grave with a chaplet of laurels from the Amises' garden.

On the Sunday after the funeral, Kingsley Amis paid tribute to the man who had died with such dignity at his home. In an article in the *Observer* he described the 'habitual cheerfulness' of the house guest to whom he grew so close during those final weeks. 'We were always on the best of terms. It was difficult to be on any other terms with Cecil,' he wrote. 'He gave us all in the household and the many friends who came to see him an unforgettable object lesson in how to die.'

Later that year, in October, a memorial service was held at St Martin-in-the-Fields. It had been Cecil's hope that, if there were a memorial, his favourite piece of music, Fauré's *Requiem*, would be played. Representatives of the Queen and the Prime Minister were present, as were Britain's leading literary figures, Cecil's successor John Betjeman, Auden, Spender, the Amises, H. E. Bates, Lord Clark and Laurie Lee among them, filling the church to hear the BBC Concert Orchestra and Chorus majestically fulfil the poet's wish.

In the aftermath, Daniel's emotions remained jumbled, the inevitable, delayed shock yet to rumble into tangible form. He went back to Bedales where the subject was never raised. 'Nobody mentioned his death at school. Not one person,' he recalled once. 'I was brutal about my father's death. I thought, he's not alive any more, life goes on – and I didn't think about it for a couple of years. I didn't begin to feel sorry, not for years.'

And so, instead, he went back to pouring his energies into his main interests: woodwork, sport and his growing passion for acting.

Encouraged by his first taste of cinematic stardom with John Schlesinger and the bitter-sweet triumph of Florizel, Daniel became one of the leading lights of Rachel Fields's drama activities. Carlo Gebler, two years his senior, directed and shared the stage with the young Daniel. 'I remember I directed a production of a Thornton Wilder play, *Our Town*. He was in that. I also remember him in Shaw's *Man and Superman*, which I was in as well. I remember him as this long-haired boy, perfectly polite, quite cordial and friendly. There were those who loved the idea of performing and being a performer, but he was not one of those.'

School productions were nervous affairs, Gebler remembered. Pupils were too concerned about incurring the wrath of Rachel Fields or sneaking into the tunnel-like corridor that ran under the Lupton Hall stage for a sly cigarette between scenes to observe the performances of others. 'I remember Daniel being perfectly fine, but there really were more important things to worry about,' he recalled.

One of Daniel's most eye-catching roles came in a production of Pirandello's *Six Characters in Search of an Author*. He played the part of the Son in the well-received piece, which co-starred some of his closest friends, including Lesley Verner as the Leading Lady and Seamus Dalton as the Leading Man. Daniel's performance won him his first eulogistic review. School theatre critic Tim Williams praised Daniel's portrayal of 'indifference hiding vulnerability'. Accidentally, the *Bedales Chronicle* could have been describing the inner turmoil within Daniel himself.

As his true emotions were suppressed, he revealed to his school-friends a melancholic side to his nature. He became, and remains, prone to brooding introspection. A darkness settled in behind the eyes of the boy with the still angelic smile.

Months after burying his father, in the summer 1972 edition of the *Bedales Chronicle*, Daniel offered a telling glimpse of the emotions seemingly bottled up deep within him. He contributed an untitled essay to the magazine. It remains the only piece of fiction published in his famous name.

Daniel's story was that of a young boy witnessing the massacre of his parents. The killings were carried out by the Black and Tans, the infamous British soldiers who fought a bloody guerrilla campaign against the Irish as London applied martial law at the end of the Anglo-Irish War of 1919–21. The story combined the brutal, four-letter-word-filled language Daniel had picked up in Greenwich with some strident teenage politics. Perhaps the latter had been picked up from his father. Irish politics, like English politics, was a matter for the dinner table rather than the public platform. Cecil did not generally get involved, but as an increasingly frequent traveller to Ireland he had been drawn to the ancient troubles as a source of material. His collection of Irish poems, *The Whispering Roots*, written in the 1950s, is laced with such work. 'Kilmainham Jail, Easter Sunday, 1966', written on the fiftieth anniversary of the Easter Uprising, and the shooting of the men who signed the Proclamation of the Irish Republic, is among the most powerful.

The teenage Daniel was clearly inspired by the same subject. Instead of lyrical poetry, however, he expressed his feelings in blood-lusty prose. He named his hero Finian, the Christian name of his nephew, Sean and Anna's son. Finian hates the English and dreams of running away to join the IRA. His convictions are deepened after witnessing his family butchered before his eyes.

The story is filled with vivid language. At one point the leader of the British troops screams: 'Open up, you Irish pigs, and take a deep breath because it's the last one you'll be taking in the world.' Later, after describing the massacre, Daniel's dialogue includes the line: 'Did you see that snotty-nosed brat writhe and squeal when I shuved the bayonet up its ass?'

There were other signs of latent rage within him. When he arrived at Bedales Daniel had been determined that he would not again suffer the bullying and the sense of isolation that made his time at Sevenoaks so hellish. He had already established himself as one of the school's elite pupils, 'select' in the Bedalian language, and was venting some of his anger on other, vulnerable pupils.

There are shades of Cecil Day-Lewis and his 'razorlike contempt' in Daniel's descriptions of how he used his wicked tongue as a weapon. 'I had a sharp tongue and I took pleasure in using it,' he admitted to *The Times* in 1989. 'I knew how to get to people.' School-friends remembered how dark and menacing this side of Daniel could be. 'There were black days when you never went near him,' one remembered. Daniel himself once summed up the boy of those darkest Bedalian days in two simple words: 'morose and spotty'.

His family were clearly worried that Daniel would drift in an even more directionless state without a father-figure to guide him. Cecil may have been remote, but he had been a tower of strength during times of crisis. Daniel was also entering a phase of his life when he would need fathering more than ever before. 'It is always terrible to lose one's father, but Cecil died at a very bad age for Daniel. It was very traumatic for him,' recalled his Croom's Hill neighbour Margot Gair.

Daniel's grandfather, Sir Michael Balcon, became a more influential figure. 'He was tremendously easy for me to talk to. I think probably as a younger man, during my mother's childhood, things had been different – he had been rather strict, a difficult man to get close to,' he recalled years afterwards. Teachers at Bedales, including the headmaster Tim Slack, also gave the teenage Daniel as much paternal guidance as they could.

Sean Day-Lewis remembers once talking to Elizabeth Jane Howard. She believed that Sean, himself a father of two children, Finian and Keelin, could help significantly. '"He needs someone to father him, why don't you have a go?" she said to me once.'

Daniel's mother had a sea of troubles of her own to contend with. Cecil's will was published in September, three months after he was buried. He left £52,571 after death duties. He bequeathed his property to Jill, and half of all his copyrights to his first wife Mary.

While the will was sorted out, Cecil's assets had been frozen. This had left Jill, whose acting work provided her with barely enough to cover the costs of maintaining Croom's Hill, in difficulties. Eight months after Cecil's funeral she had not settled the £25 fee she owed *The Times* for announcing the burial. She had suffered the indignity of receiving a fiercely worded final demand and then having other newspapers print the story. 'They must have known they would get paid eventually,' she said. 'I am terribly upset.'

Adding insult to public injury, she then encountered problems getting the widow's pension she was entitled to. The forms were due in within three months of her husband's death. She had not submitted them until the last moment and received a stiff reply mentioning the lateness of her application. Her reaction was, once again, emotive. Explaining her predicament to the London *Evening Standard*, she raged: 'The next thing I know I receive a curt letter demanding to know why the form was received eight days after the statutory period had elapsed. So I wrote back saying, "Because I am still recovering from nursing a cancer patient and you have just caused me even more distress." People think that because I was married to the Poet Laureate and was left a nice house I'm sitting pretty.'

The sensitive actress, who had been widowed at the age of forty-eight, was also deeply upset by newspaper talk about Cecil's successor as Poet Laureate. Bookmakers were taking bets on the appointment; even Cecil's friend W. H. Auden had been mentioned. He dismissed the rumours as 'tosh'.

Jill described that as 'turning the knife'. 'It makes me so ill. Of course a new one has to be appointed but to place bets on it – it's all so inhuman. I don't want sympathy. Just a little humanity,' she told the *Standard* in late September.

As if these difficulties were not enough, Jill was already becoming frustrated at her inability to interest anyone in buying Croom's Hill. Every creaking floorboard, every corner of the house reminded her of her loss. But, at an asking price of £70,000, there were no takers.

Back at Bedales Daniel turned more and more to theatre as an escape from the cruel realities of life. His education had filled him with a sense of acting's infinite possibilities. Shakespeare, Chekhov, Pirandello, Shaw, even Sam Shepard ... 'Drac' Fields fuelled her pupils' imaginations with an eclectic mix of the modern and the classical, the light and the dark. Daniel was beginning to hear a calling of kinds. In the summer of 1973 he enrolled with the National Youth Theatre.

Founded in 1956 by Michael Croft, the NYT's 'theatre for all' principles drew dozens of youngsters from diverse backgrounds together every year. Through the school holidays, over a period of three years, it built a beginners' guide to the nuts and bolts of the theatrical profession. More adventurous than even progressive Bedales, its curriculum ran from Shakespeare, Sheridan and Lorca to Miller, Wesker and Friel. Graduates of this bold young breeding ground had included Timothy Dalton, Ben Kingsley, Derek Jacobi, Helen Mirren and Michael York.

Daniel arrived to discover five productions planned for that summer: two Shakespearean, *Richard II* and *Romeo and Juliet*, and three more modern pieces, *Geordies' March*, *The Petticoat Rebellion* and *The Children's Crusade*. But his first experience of the communal chaos of larger-scale theatre left him somehow cold. He returned to Bedales at the beginning of the autumn term in 1973 resigned to spending the following summer anywhere else but among a group of aspirant actors. The doubts crept in.

Years later he described the experience as 'seedy and distasteful'. He remembered that for the following months, although he continued to act at Bedales, his long-term ambitions focused more and more on the tranquillity of the woodwork shop, and the tactile relationship between mastercraftsmen and their materials.

78

Until then he had 'a perception of the theatre that had been unshakable from the age of twelve,' as he once put it. 'Suddenly weighing the two things, the theatre seemed to be an occupation to be deeply mistrusted, as opposed to the honest, tranquil world of craftsmanship.'

With his mother's attention concentrated on rebuilding her own life and tying up the loose ends following his father's death, a once more confused Daniel was entering his most wayward phase at Bedales. The school's frontier philosophy carried with it a natural danger. Why should its eager youngsters restrict the spirit of experimentation to the classroom? Drug-taking has remained a problem at Bedales to the present day. 'I was aware of it, there were a few people at school who did it,' remembered Carlo Gebler. That Daniel, rudderless and still rebelling at the constraining forces he had been subjected to in the past, was attracted should come as no great surprise.

The precise details of what happened to Daniel in 1973 remain shrouded in something of a mist. Within the Day-Lewis family his brief confinement to a hospital was barely talked about. 'This whole thing about the overdose has grown over the years. At the time when I did hear about it, some months after it happened, it was not a big deal,' said Sean Day-Lewis.

Only Daniel's own, rather opaque account of the events remains. According to the story he has volunteered frequently over the years, he accidentally took an overdose of migraine tablets. He had been prescribed them, had started to find taking them fun, and had gradually increased the dosage to an almost lethal level. He had no idea of the drugs' hallucinatory powers and was taken ill. When he was diagnosed by doctors their prognosis was that he must be under the influence of serious drugs. He emerged from his trip to discover that he was being treated as a heroin addict.

'It happened because I was messing about with drugs,' he has said. 'It was a complete accident.' At various other times he has described the experience as the most frightening – and, in some ways, the most inspiring – of his life. Daniel remembers waking in a room, being watched over by women in masks. 'They told me I had destroyed my system and would never leave. They locked me in isolation with a nurse while I hallucinated,' he told the *Daily Mail* in 1989. 'To get out I had to behave with a degree of sanity which was madness in itself.' Several times since then, perhaps with a hint of exaggeration, he has described that performance as the greatest of his life.

Whatever the reality of Daniel's near-fatal overdose, the after-effects of this latest in a series of incarcerations in his short life were spectacular. During his final years at Bedales he was galvanized into action. By the time he came to leave he had lived through 'the happiest days of my life'.

By 1974 he was one of the stars of the school. He did not return to the National Youth Theatre for a second summer, but instead, again with Rachel Fields's expert guidance, took on a challenging range of roles. He played Vershinin in Chekhov's *Three Sisters* and produced a junior school adaptation of J. P. Donleavy's *Fairytales of New York*.

His most highly praised piece of acting came in another Shakespearean role, however. The *Chronicle* raved about his innovative fool Feste in a 1975 production of *Twelfth Night*. 'Rather than playing Feste as the middle-aged cynic Shakespeare could have had in mind,' the review read, Daniel played him as 'an extremely elusive and enigmatic youth'.

An enigmatic other-worldliness was also becoming apparent in the eighteen-year-old actor. The review described him as 'a man who fitted where he chose, always an alien but never obscured in the background'.

Daniel was in the foreground in almost every area of the school by now. He was installed as star of stage, soccer pitch and cycle track.

Headmaster Slack was a passionate cyclist. The great event in the cycling calendar was the 'Le Mans' race around the school and surrounding countryside. Daniel hurled himself into the sport, flying around the Hampshire lanes on his racing bike in preparation for the contest. A lifelong love of two-wheeled speed was born.

A burning will to win blazed through in everything he did. Sean Day-Lewis remembered taking him on at table tennis in the basement at Croom's Hill. 'I can remember he was very competitive. They had the ping-pong table in the basement. I played him and just about beat him. I was terribly keen to win too and I remember his mother saying how disappointed he was because he liked to win,' he recalled.

Daniel's football had apparently always relied more on his competitive streak and his enthusiasm than on outright native skill. Friends remember him as being quick, very direct, but one-footed. 'His own game on the wing was very fast and gangly, the most right-footed player I've ever seen,' one contemporary, Richard Tomlinson, commented years later.

His exploits on the football pitch drew a devoted female following. By the summer of 1974 he was known universally to his fan club as 'Dan Day-Pinup'! DDP was the star attraction in a team strong on good looks, if short on modesty. The *Chronicle*'s summary of the 1973–4 season tempered the news that the team had suffered 'a number of mundane draws and crushing defeats' with the observation that 'although this season's team were not always an unqualified success as footballers, this was offset by the fact that they were undoubtably [sic] the dishiest bunch o' fellas ever to grace the Bedales football scene'.

The following season Daniel was elevated to the captaincy of the first team, after the departure of Ian Dow. The *Chronicle* reported that the new skipper 'combines Ian's impeccable conduct on the field with an uncompromising personal philosophy centred around the concept of winning football matches'.

As they started another campaign, the team's appeal for support again played on the sex appeal of Dan Day-Pinup and his foot soldiers. It read: 'Witty, articulate, intelligent, curvy, vivacious and above all extremely entertaining to look at. Why don't you come and watch us more often?'

The young women of Bedales hardly needed an invitation to stand on the touchlines. Daniel was the main object of desire among the girls. Unlike at Sevenoaks, the overtures were not unwelcomed.

Bedales, despite its libertarianism, did not condone sex. *In flagrante* violations brought expulsion. But, just as bed-hopping homosexuality was an illicit fact of life at Sevenoaks, full-blooded expressions of heterosexuality were part of the secret landscape of the Eden that was Bedales.

Sex was a risky, nocturnal affair. Boys and girls slept in separate buildings and the grounds were patrolled by vigilant teachers at night. The thin beams of their torches crawled along the school walls like Stalag searchlights – but to little avail. Bedalian boys and girls were expert at slipping in and out undetected for late night liaisons at secret locations around the school grounds.

One seventies' Bedalian, the journalist Mary Ann Sieghart, recalled in *The Times* how 'pupils who wanted to sleep with each other tended to head for the great outdoors'. The favourite venue when she was there was a sandy quarry nearby. Members of the theatre group also had access to a secluded hut. 'The pressure to have a boyfriend at that time was incredibly strong. If you could not attract a boyfriend you were deemed a social reject by the boys. And once you were a reject, no boy would want to go out with you anyway,' she wrote.

Two particular teachers led the school's moral police force, Sieghart recalled. One would patrol the grounds of the school at night with a torch and dog. His female counterpart slept in a room near the only ground-floor window of the girl's house that was not barred. 'She was always said to leave booby traps such as broomsticks on the wooden stairs leading down to the window.'

For the girls of Bedales in the mid-70s, Daniel Day-Lewis was the school's ultimate catch. 'Every girl was hopelessly in love with him,' remembered one. 'He became something of a legend, the grooviest boy ever at Bedales.'

Tamasin's presence at Bedales and his female-dominated childhood had spared Daniel the sort of terrors other adolescent boys faced when it came to forming friendships with the opposite sex. He was also free of the sexual confusion that was a legacy of many Bedalian boys' early years at single-sex boarding schools. Judging from the phone call he made to his mother after escaping Sevenoaks, he already had the hyperactive mind of an avowed heterosexual adolescent!

One of Daniel's closest girlfriends was Jennifer Hall, like

him the child of famous parents. She had been sent to Bedales by her father, the theatre director Peter Hall, after the break-up of his marriage to her mother, the actress Leslie Caron. Caron had devastated Jennifer's father by running off to Los Angeles with Hollywood's most notorious young roué, Warren Beatty.

The school was as healing an experience for Jennifer as it was for the son of the late Poet Laureate. She was sent there with her brother Christopher. 'This proved to be a fabulous decision for us, providing a stable environment until the age of eighteen,' she recalled later. 'Whatever else was happening, we knew we would always be back at school in term-time.'

Unlike in Greenwich, where Daniel had been teased for being the son of a famous father, eminent backgrounds counted for nothing at Bedales. This helped ease the pressure of living under the shadow of famous parents. 'You didn't think about it,' recalled Carlo Gebler. 'Your parents were not celebrities, they were the people who wiped your bottom.'

Daniel and Jennifer's friendship failed to develop into anything more profound. Soon after leaving Bedales, Jennifer married an apple farmer. The marriage did not last.

'Jill always said he would break her heart,' recalled Sean. The two, however, have remained friends ever since.

The one girl who did claim a lasting place in Daniel's affections was a tall, willowy beauty in the same year as him. Sarah Campbell would remain a part of his life for more than a decade. In years to come, friends would call the pair the great loves of each other's lives. Gentle, thoughtful and possessed of the same eye-catching, angular looks as Daniel, Sarah and the Bedales 'pin-up' were a striking couple.

By the summer of 1975, however, Daniel's time in the Garden of Eden was coming to its close. With the prospect of entering the real world drawing ever nearer, he began to think about his future. Academically he had done well enough to get two A-levels. University seems not to have been on the cards, however. His choices narrowed down to two very differing options – woodcraft or stagecraft.

Daniel was an exceptionally talented woodwork student. Under Bedales master David Butcher, he had built on the raw talent he had demonstrated at Sevenoaks. His finest work had been a grand, round dining table fashioned from pine and walnut. He had made caned chairs to accompany it and had installed it back at Croom's Hill. He also made a Welsh dresser, which he gave to the school.

As he weighed up his future he decided to apply for jobs in both professions. He set his sights high. David Butcher had spoken of the apprenticeship courses being run by John Makepeace, then emerging as the most celebrated cabinet-maker in England. Daniel decided to apply to him.

On the drama front Rachel Fields and his mother had always spoken highly of the Bristol Old Vic Theatre School. Jill Balcon had fond memories of her time working at the Old Vic company in the West Country and had maintained friends down there. Daniel opted for Bristol rather than RADA or one of London's other famous schools.

He began work on his applications, the rest he would leave to fate. If one, or both, rejected him he would have his answer. 'It would be a sign from the gods, it was not meant to be . . .'

CHAPTER FIVE

FANNING THE FLAMES

'Acting is a masochistic form of exhibitionism. It is not
quite the occupation of an adult.'
LAURENCE OLIVIER, Time, 1978

T HERE HAD already been an early-morning tour of the
troops. Amidst the deafening chaos of whirring lathe-
wheels, screaming chainsaws and crushing hammers,
there had been order. The discipline of a workshop. As vital as
the discipline of an army. John Makepeace's routine is as regi-
mented today as it was then.

As he eased into his chair and sifted through the morning
mail, the cabinet-maker's eye was drawn to one letter more than
any other. Embossed, unexpected and intriguing, it was headed
'Buckingham Palace'. Daydreams of ennoblements, contracts or
even invitations to take tea with the Queen quickly faded, however, when he skimmed forward to the scrawled signature at the
foot of the second page. The surname was, of course, familiar.
The Christian name was not. He would never forget either.

The letter the cabinet-maker received from the nineteen-
year-old Daniel Day-Lewis in the summer of 1976 was the most
remarkable job application ever to descend on his desk. Clearly
well researched, polite and well presented, it would have won
its writer an interview regardless. The royal insignia, however,
sealed it.

'It was the most extraordinary experience,' he remembered.
'And it all started with this letter from Buckingham Palace.'
Daniel introduced himself as a former pupil of Bedales,
interested in an apprenticeship. 'It ran for two, very well-
composed sides. At the foot was a P.S. which said, "You might
wonder why I am writing to you on this paper, I have a friend
who lives there!"'

Makepeace's reputation was already established. He was then based at Farnborough, near Banbury in Warwickshire where his main business was converting farm buildings into houses and workshops. His success had already enabled him, however, to start planning a move to a much grander setting, Parnham Hall, a majestic stately home near Beaminster, Dorset. There his reputation would spread around the world.

Five-year apprenticeships under Makepeace's watchful eye were much sought after. Only a handful of trainees was accepted each year. The teacher scrutinized every one of his potential pupils' applications with a master-craftsman's eye for detail.

Daniel's letter did the job that was required of it. John Makepeace was intrigued to meet its resourceful writer and invited him to Warwickshire for an interview. By the time Daniel arrived, the cabinet-maker's curiosity was barely controllable. In the time that passed between the invitation and the interview, he had received a series of testimonials recommending he accept Daniel Day-Lewis.

One was from Norman Brick, the head of Kodak in the UK, and an acquaintance of Makepeace. Another was from Lilian Browse, the author and art expert, an old neighbour of Sir Michael Balcon in West Sussex, whom the cabinet-maker also knew. The third, and perhaps most impressive, was from Peter Hall. The director, then in the process of establishing the National Theatre on London's South Bank, had first got to know John Makepeace when he visited his workshop to make a documentary about his work. Daniel, no doubt with the help of his Bedalian friend Jennifer Hall, persuaded him to put in a good word too.

'These were not lightweight testimonials by any means. It was so interesting to me that someone had taken all those steps and had researched people who were important to me in my life. There was no way I could ignore an application like that,' he remembered. 'It also meant that the interview was quite loaded before I had met the poor chap.'

Daniel arrived for his interview and spent an hour with John Makepeace. As master weighed up novice, however, he quickly sensed that the eager would-be apprentice was torn between joining his profession and following another career. 'I remember him as being quite self-possessed. Even then he was open about the fact that theatre was a possibility and he mentioned it at the interview,' he recalled.

When he asked Daniel about how much woodwork he had carried out since leaving Bedales, doubts began to creep in. 'He had no evidence of his work or his application in terms of having done very much. He was six months out of school when I met him and my challenge to him was "What have you done since school if this is so important to you?". He said that he did not have a workshop or any tools and it was impossible for him to do anything at home. That sent loud alarm bells ringing in my spine.'

Makepeace did not want to discourage Daniel, but at the same time he needed to be convinced of his dedication. 'My response was "Go away and we will meet again, when you have something to show me." I was looking for evidence that this was really what he wanted to do. I am fairly tough on these things.'

He never saw Daniel again. Nor did he ever discover who his friend at Buckingham Palace was. Instead he accepted, a few years later, a true member of that household, David Linley, son of Princess Margaret and the photographer Lord Snowdon, and an ex-Bedalian too.

John Makepeace's decision deprived his profession of a potentially brilliant craftsman. Cabinet-making's loss was to be acting's gain.

Daniel left Makepeace determined to prove himself good enough to join his business. With his mother's blessing, however, he had also applied to his one and only theatre school, the Bristol Old Vic. Its principal was the late Nat Brenner, one of the most respected teachers in English theatre. He too was clearly impressed by Daniel's letter. He was invited for an interview and was offered a place immediately.

Daniel's decision was a difficult one. The craftsman's life held a magnetic hold over his young imagination. 'The life of a cabinet-maker seemed infinitely more pure,' he remembered years afterwards. He saw a serenity in men like Makepeace and David Butcher, the Bedales woodwork master, that he too yearned for. 'They seemed to have found the secret as far as I was concerned,' he recalled once. 'They were peaceful, beautiful men and I suspected that as long as I worked in the theatre I would not find the secret.'

He has also admitted that the idea of having to succeed as a creative artist terrified him. He was not sure that a life spent exploring the stormiest outposts of his own mind was an attractive prospect. 'I probably felt my mind wasn't a place I would feel comfortable.'

His mother's mind was occupied with more practical considerations. She wanted her son to have a stable, successful career. She knew the perils and pitfalls of her profession. She was equally torn. Her friend and neighbour Ann Broadbent recalled that Jill, her own career still blighted by the 'I'll never work again' insecurity that is the reality of life for all but a chosen few actors, was reluctant to commend her son to the same fate.

'Certainly Jill didn't know what to advise. 90 per cent of actors are resting 90 per cent of the time,' she remembered. 'She just didn't know which way would be the better because she knew that he was good as a carpenter.'

Jill left her son with few illusions about the actor's lot. 'As far as my mother's concerned, she'd have been only too happy if I'd chosen another profession,' he told the American magazine *Film Comment* years later. 'Very few people who work in the theatre or the business actually wish it upon their children.'

Eventually Daniel made his decision. Ablaze to do something with his until now listless, unfulfilled life, he wrote to Bristol and Brenner accepting a place.

It was a welcome piece of good news at Croom's Hill. On two occasions the year had threatened to bring more tragedy to the family.

On 16 February Tamasin had been travelling down from Liverpool to London on an overnight train. She was by now studying for her finals at Cambridge, and, tired from endlessly burning the midnight oil, was grabbing a few precious hours of sleep. Her peace was shattered by an enormous explosion of sound. She woke to find herself bleeding profusely. She had been showered by broken glass. Her face had been torn to red, raw ribbons, there were beads of glass in her eyes.

The express had been travelling at 80 mph when a goods train heading in the opposite direction passed by. Somehow a door had swung open on the goods train, smashing its way into the side of the London-bound train. As passengers and guards frantically administered first aid to Tamasin and five other victims of the freak accident, the train pulled into the nearest town, Bletchley, in Buckinghamshire.

There surgeons operated on the six casualties. Others were treated for shock. Luckily Tamasin's injuries were mostly superficial. The doctors told her that her eyes had miraculously escaped laceration and that the wounds would heal. Her modelling days, however, were over.

Worse was to follow. Later that year Jill, who had been feeling unwell for some time, underwent a series of tests by her doctors. She was told that she had breast cancer and that the only option was a mastectomy.

The effect on the family was devastating. The disease had already claimed the life of their father, and Daniel and Tamasin were numbed by the cruelty of it all.

Years later Jill and Tamasin admitted that they never spoke about the cancer. The operation was a success and Jill made a complete recovery. 'People told me that she was terribly distraught by this because her father had died of cancer, but she didn't say so directly to me and she hasn't referred to it since,' Jill confided in an interview with the *Daily Mail* eighteen years later. 'I tuned it out to some extent,' Tamasin said at the same time.

The difficulties at home made Daniel's move to Bristol all the more liberating. It was as if one chapter in his troubled life, a period darkened by death, illness and insecurity, was drawing to a close. Having chosen a profession and a direction in which to take his life, he was determined to make the best of it.

Set in a Dickensian, dock area of old Bristol, a sea-port city built on the profits of slave-trading in the nineteenth century, the red-brick Old Vic Theatre has for decades been one of the most august in England. Its nearby school has been a breeding ground for talent. Miranda Richardson, Gary Oldman and Greta Scacchi were among the raw talents polished there in the 1970s.

Daniel's teachers included Rudi Shelley. He had arrived at the school three weeks after it opened in November 1946. Before that he had taught in Cardiff, where one of his brightest students was an intense, burning, blue-eyed young man from the steelworks town of Port Talbot, Anthony Hopkins.

Shelley had worked with Jill Balcon when she was establishing herself. His first impressions of the accomplished actress's son were mixed. 'I knew his mother when she was at the Bristol Old Vic Company. Jill was practically a beginner then. I became very attached to Danny, but there has always been a certain loner side of him,' he recalled.

Under Shelley, Brenner and the other tutors, students went through an intense training programme. There were ballet classes, improvisation sessions. They learned to bare their souls, strip themselves of the layers of inhibition life had already padded each of them with.

Daniel realized then that he had been suppressing his feelings for years. From the day he returned to school after his father's death, numbed and cold at his loss, he had maintained an air of untouchability. Now he was being forced to uncork his emotions. He also had to learn to integrate his naturally self-sufficient personality within a group. It was traumatic, but it was also a relief.

'I'd always felt isolated, protective of myself, of all my fears,' he told writer Fionnuala McHugh in The Times in 1989. 'I knew that I'd never let anyone see me care. It was all "Don't mess with me." I'd spent years, years carefully retaining what I'd considered to be my dignity.

'And when I went to theatre school, the deal was that unless you could learn to make a complete idiot of yourself in front of other people very quickly, there was no point in being there.'

Shelley saw Daniel suffer through that process. 'He found it dreadfully difficult, denuding himself psychologically. But then everybody does,' he said. 'People who say they do not are either hyper-exhibitionists or I don't believe them.'

As he adjusted to the process of baring his soul publicly, Daniel's overwhelming feeling, however, was joy. At last he had found a direction in his life. He was working towards a goal and he relished it. 'It was a tremendous relief to be working hard at something for the first time in my life. I thought going into the theatre would encourage the fire to rage.'

During his first two years he threw himself into his studies. The days were long, 10 a.m. until 11 p.m., and intense. In the first year Daniel and his fellow students worked on individual scenes from plays rather than complete works. Chekhov's *The Cherry Orchard* and Shakespeare's *Romeo and Juliet* were among the classics deconstructed in the classrooms. 'One wasn't allowed near a stage for the first year or so. We were like overstrained greyhounds straining in the slip,' he remembered once.

In the second year students were divided into groups of eight. The teams would devise improvisational plays of their own. Even on the football pitch Daniel had remained an individual. For the first time the lone wolf learned to be a team player. 'With the theatre you have no option but to trust the other actors around you. So for me it was a good time, especially as I had never liked groups; it was a kind of battle I had to fight within myself to get into working with them.'

For all the fraternal spirit within the theatre school, however, Daniel could never quite rid himself of his isolationist instincts. Bristol's pub and club scene was buoyant at the time. Clubs like The Granary, a jazz pub around the corner from the Old Vic, and The Dugout, smoke-filled and subterranean, were a magnet. Theatre students burned the candle at both ends there. But, despite the openness he was displaying in the theatre workshops, Daniel kept his distance. Some skins would never be shed. 'It is quite common for people to give up their whole social life to the theatre and I quite respect that. I remember when I first went to Bristol it was quite a big deal, there was a club everyone went to.'

91

The adrenalin surge that was keeping his peers going until the small hours of the morning did not materialize in Daniel. 'I was expecting this thing, this is the stage, this is the lifestyle.' Instead he went home to the flat he had rented in Clifton, a twenty-minute walk from the theatre, read, slept, lived life according to his own rules.

Again a legend grew around his enigmatic behaviour. 'People developed, in their minds, on my behalf, a very mysterious life I must be leading, but I just needed to be on my own. I think it bothered people initially, they saw it as a sort of aloofness, which it wasn't at all.'

Daniel's single-mindedness was unmistakable when an old childhood friend bumped into him in the street. Tom Broadbent had gone to Bristol University to start a social sciences degree. As he walked out of the front door of his digs near the campus one day, he saw his former neighbour and pigeon-shooting partner walking down his street.

'It was right outside my house, I lived opposite Manor Hall. We both recognized each other straight away,' recalled Tom. The two young men got talking, but Daniel was clearly preoccupied. 'I remember that first time he had to go back and learn his lines, he seemed very intent on it,' Tom said.

The two saw each other occasionally, but it was obvious that Daniel was absorbed to distraction. 'He seemed very happy in Bristol, really into it. I used to tell him how hard I thought it must be learning lines, and he would say, "It's not that hard if you try",' according to Tom.

Daniel's living conditions were a far cry from the grandeur of the Croom's Hill home where Tom had last seen him. He visited his flat on a few occasions. His life there seemed solitary and introspective. 'It was quite a pokey little upstairs flat. People were not ringing on his bell.'

At Bristol, under Brenner and Shelley's guidance, Daniel absorbed the techniques of the so-called Method, and the teachings of Stanislavski. Years later Daniel admitted he found it an almost terrifying approach to his craft.

'Stanislavski was at the root of the training I had at the Bristol Old Vic, although they used only parts of it. I trusted myself entirely to that place and that approach, thinking, if I'm going to spend three years there I should do it unquestioningly.

'About three years after I left I picked up a copy of Stanislavski which I'd resisted doing while I was there, thinking that they'd chosen the parts of that approach they want to use. It scared the life out of me.'

In one sense, however, Daniel had already committed himself to a form of Method acting for life. 'One of the things I immediately discarded was the notion we were taught that all actors were only actors so long as they were working. In the back of my mind I reserved the right to be out of work rather than do something I didn't believe in,' he told the Irish writer Deirdre Purcell years later.

His greatest sadness during those first three wildly exciting years as a full-time actor was the loss of his grandfather. Sir Michael Balcon died on 17 October 1977, at the age of eighty-one. His obituary in *The Times* the following day predicted that his films would stand as his epitaph. 'The history of the British film industry would have been sadly impoverished without them.'

After Cecil's death Michael Balcon had become a far more available source of wisdom for Daniel. There had always been a distance between Cecil and the film producer, partly because of their very different backgrounds, partly because of the manner in which the married poet had won the heart of his only daughter.

'They had an accommodation but they never saw much of each other. My father always rather hoped that he would use one of his detective novels for a film,' said Daniel's half-brother Sean. 'But Balcon was very hot on people not using their family ties. My wife used to write film reviews at Northcliffe Newspapers and she had to ring him up. He was furious, he told her she was using her name to get things.'

During the five years following his father's death, Daniel had grown to respect his grandfather in a way he had not been able to as a boy. The way Balcon, whose family had been Yiddish-speaking, re-invented himself as an Englishman fascinated him. 'He never dwelled on his past,' Daniel recalled later. 'He was so determined to be English that I never heard any Yiddish or Hebrew until I left home.'

As grandfather and grandson had got to know each other better, both had benefited. 'I felt very intimidated by him when I was a kid,' Daniel remembered. 'But after a while I got to know him as a bright, generous man who had an appetite for many things and understood young people. He became more and more open-minded as he grew older and I grew to love him more and more.'

Daniel distinguished himself at Bristol. At the end of his third year at the theatre school he was one of only three students accepted by the Bristol Old Vic Company. There he fell under the influence of the company's much respected artistic director, Richard Cottrell. 'He was, for me, the first person that really inspired me in the professional theatre,' as he put it later.

Under Cottrell Daniel performed in *A Midsummer Night's Dream*, *Edward II* and *Troilus and Cressida*. His most prominent roles, however, came in Nigel Williams's *Class Enemy* and Mike Stott's *Funny Peculiar*.

The former was a savage piece, performed at the New Vic Theatre in 1980, and set in a brutal London comprehensive school. Written off by their teachers, a group of six lower-class schoolboys systematically destroy their classroom, their fury and frustration spiralling violently. Daniel, readopting the patois of his native south London, hurled himself into the role of a boy called Iron. His passionate performance, for the first time, caused him physical damage.

Tom Broadbent and his mother were among the crowd who watched him in *Class Enemy*. Ann Broadbent remembered visiting Daniel in his dressing room afterwards. 'They were breaking up wooden desks, and they really were hurting each other. Afterwards I sat in the dressing room pulling out splinters from Dan's hand with a needle.'

She also saw him in *Funny Peculiar*, in which he played a simpleton called Stanley. He wandered the stage delivering inane one-liners like 'Where I go for training there's a lad sold his head!'

Again Daniel was impressive. 'I went with my brother who was not at all used to the theatre. Dan was playing this half-wit. In the interval my brother Tony said, "Poor Dan, he's quite all right normally,"' Ann recalled. She knew then that the little boy she first saw running around shouting 'Helicopter' was set to take flight in his chosen career. 'When I saw him that first time I realized he was a very good actor.'

Class Enemy in particular represented a significant moment for Daniel. If he still had lingering doubts about the validity of what he was doing, whether acting was in any way worthwhile, they disappeared with that play.

As the 1980s dawned Britain was convulsed by class conflict. Margaret Thatcher's Conservatives were tightening the newly won reins of power, unemployment was soaring, demonstrations and rioting were rife within the inner cities. The disaffected anger which had first roared into life with the punk music movement moved from the recording studios to the streets. *Class Enemy* was the ultimate expression of that working-class rage. *Gotcha* by Barry Keefe was presenting the same message elsewhere. In theatres around England a new breed of angry young man was emerging. Young British actors like Tim Roth, Gary Oldman and Phil Daniels were doing what their American heroes, from James Dean and Marlon Brando to Robert De Niro, had been doing for years. Daniel described it years later as 'poetry created out of the life of someone who can't express himself'.

During his time at Bristol Daniel had learned to express himself more eloquently than at any other time in his life. Years later he remembered the exhibitionistic joy of being a junior member of his profession. He loved to shock and surprise his colleagues.

'What was always rather wonderful was when you were The Kid in the company and no one gave a toss and you were fed a scrap and you took it and you chewed it and you spat it out and everyone was amazed at this kid who'd been just shuffling around and making tea for people,' he explained once.

Another of the bright talents at Bristol then was a self-effacing Lancastrian with 'a face like a stone archway'. Daniel understudied for Pete Postlethwaite in *Edward II* and had been directed by him in *Funny Peculiar*. The older actor watched the rising star of the company at work in the rehearsal rooms and on stage.

'We all saw this extraordinary pyrotechnic work going on and we thought, "Oh, no, not another one of these! Can't we lose him somewhere?"' he recalled years later as that actor appeared on the cover of *Time* magazine.

But there was to be no losing him now. He had found a voice and a vocation. The fire was ready to rage.

The discoveries of March 1980 were, if anything, even more sensational than those Daniel was making within the walls of the Old Vic. Almost eight years after Cecil Day-Lewis died, the first biography of his life and work was published. Sean, his eldest son, now a senior, much respected figure at the *Daily Telegraph,* had spent years poring over the sporadic collection of papers and correspondence his father had left behind. His book, *C. Day-Lewis: An English Literary Life,* painted an affectionate and honest portrait of his father. Too honest, however, for the liking of some. Daniel's past served up its secrets.

During the course of his research Sean, who as a nineteen-year-old had seen his father leave him, his mother and brother, to begin a new life with his second wife, Jill Balcon, unearthed much. He found his father to be a quiet philanderer, a man who, by his own admission, was 'a good starter of affairs who found it hard to sustain a marriage'. The love quadrangle between his mother, who had died in February 1975, Rosamond Lehmann and Jill was made public for the first time. So too were Cecil's various flings, including one in which he made love in a tree!

Most revealing of all, however, was Sean's discovery that he, his brother Nick and his half-sister and -brother Tamasin and Daniel were not Cecil's only children. One of his affairs had produced another son.

Daniel was at the Old Vic when news of the book's revelations began to reach the family. By now Tamasin too was living in the west of England. Since leaving Cambridge she had become a successful TV producer. Beginning as a researcher for Anglia TV in Norwich, she had moved on to the BBC and was now installed in Bristol at the Corporation's studios on Whiteladies Road, within a few minutes of Daniel's Clifton home, as an assistant producer. At the BBC she had met and fallen in love with a rising management star, John Shearer. She and Shearer had moved into a mill house in the sleepy Somerset village of Splatt in 1979.

While Daniel and Tamasin maintained a stoic silence, their mother vented her anger. By now Jill had sold Croom's Hill and moved to Petersfield, home of Bedales, where she had found new happiness with another distinguished man of letters. Antony Brett-James was a soldier turned military historian. He served in Burma with the Royal Signals before becoming Head of War Studies at the Royal Military Academy, Sandhurst and one of the world's leading experts on Napoleon. He retired from his post in 1980, at the age of sixty. He had met Jill during a spell working at Chatto & Windus, where he had been a reader and publicity manager. Their romance had started while she was still in Greenwich.

Although Jill and Brett-James never married, Daniel in particular came to consider the eminent writer as a fatherly figure, referring to him in interviews as his stepfather. His dependability was never more appreciated than when the biography of Jill's late husband was published.

Sean Day-Lewis recalled that it was Brett-James who contacted him to complain that Jill had not received a copy of the book. He telephoned the journalist at his home in Hammersmith, west London. 'When this book did not get to her as soon before publication as she thought it ought to, she got him to ring up and complain.' Jill, who had built a warm relationship with Sean over the years, made no effort to speak to him. 'Jill didn't ever write to me or speak to me about it, not even a thank you note for sending it to her. She just wrote to the publisher saying this will cause terrible pain to all Cecil's children.' She has not spoken to Sean since. Tamasin spoke to him many months later. 'She said she found it a bit relentless, all the indiscretions. Some of it they did not know at the time.'

Sean once heard at second hand that Daniel was distressed by the book and wrote to him. Daniel wrote an angry letter back. His anger was centred on the fact that this had to be the subject of the first communication between them in a long time. 'Since then he has referred to it as "the ill-fated book",' Sean said.

Years later, however, Daniel admitted that the book had helped him form a more realistic image of a father-figure who was beginning to occupy his thoughts more and more. 'I was just glad to find out things that brought him to life again,' he told *Vogue* magazine in 1985. 'He was in danger of becoming a symbol. If you choose to judge yourself by someone else's actions, you have to make sure you understand what those actions were.'

Reaction elsewhere was less emotional. Many of the reviews praised the son's balance in paying tribute to his father and his poetry and exposing his other life simultaneously. 'Much as it may have pained him, as he had to live it all again and then relive it in print ... he holds a delicate balance between a deep filial affection for his subject and an honest appraisal of the brazen infidelities,' Cecil Wilson wrote in the *Daily Mail*.

Sean discovered the existence of Cecil's fifth child when he visited a farmer's wife called Edna Elizabeth Currall, known to everyone as 'Billie', in Musbury, the village where he grew up. She had met the poet in the local pub, the Red Lion. There was an instant attraction and the couple, both married, conducted what Cecil in his diaries called a 'wild, preposterous and devouring affair'. The result of the affair, which Cecil used in fictional form in one of his Nicholas Blake detective novels, was a son, born in September 1940. The son, christened William, and Billie's husband John were unaware of the identity of the real father. Cecil did know, however. Sean told how, soon after the birth, his father bought Billie a pram for their child. It was the last thing he ever bought the boy, according to Sean.

Daniel has never talked about how learning he had another

half-brother affected him. After learning of his famous pedigree in 1980 the farmer's son remained in the West Country, no doubt curious and perhaps proud of the progress of his blood relative over the following years. As far as Sean Day-Lewis, who kept in contact with the Curralls, is aware, Daniel never spoke to or met his half-brother. Now he never will. William Currall died in 1993, in Cheshire, aged fifty-three. His mother had passed away a year earlier.

CHAPTER SIX

THOSE TWO IMPOSTERS

'I wish I could be like Shaw who once read a bad review
of one of his plays, called the critic and said: "I have
your review in front of me and soon it will be behind
me."'

BARBRA STREISAND, *Playboy*, 1977

T O THEIR friends they were the perfect fit. They shared
the same head-turning looks, the same sensitive, cul-
tured nature. They had grown from school sweethearts
into adult soul-mates. For Sarah Campbell it could have been
that way 'for keeps'. For Daniel Day-Lewis, however, separation would always be just a casting agent's phone call away.

Since Bedales Daniel and Sarah had shared a lasting love. It
had survived Daniel's time in Bristol and Sarah's years at university. In 1980, as Daniel returned to London after leaving the
Old Vic, they shared the first of two homes they would make
together.

The two-bedroomed flat in West End Lane, West Hampstead, was owned by an old schoolmate of Sarah's, Clare Montefiore, like her friend the daughter of an Oxford University
don. The couple lived there off and on for more than two years.
During that time Daniel would give his flatmates a glimpse of
the greatness ahead of him and the sadness in store for the one
relationship in his life friends and even family believed would
end in marriage.

His one-year contract with the Bristol Old Vic Company
over, Daniel had returned to London expectantly. The hard
realities of his profession, until now unfamiliar to him, suddenly fell into confidence-flattening focus.

'I had far too easy a time of it, which made things terribly
difficult when I arrived in London, thinking it was all going to

be like that,' he recalled years later. 'That's when the power decided that it was time I was brought to heel.'

While many of his fellow Old Vic students had spent a year competing with each other for every available role, Daniel had remained cosseted in Bristol. 'Some of my mates had been out of work from the moment they left school. For me there was a kind of delayed shock of having to face up to that,' he explained. 'I had my first bout of unemployment for about five months. It was desperate.' He spent those months in West Hampstead, living rent-free at Sarah's friend's flat.

Daniel's local dole office was at Neasden, north London. He signed on and started collecting a paltry £14 a week. True to the promise he had made to himself at Bristol, however, he spent months refusing work which did not interest him.

Years later he would come to claim that he spent much of the time 'wrecked'. It was only when he saw himself in the mirror on the morning after a particularly punishing night before that he realized what he was doing to himself, he said. 'I looked like a demon. I got out my running shoes and started pounding the track.'

As far as his flatmates in West Hampstead were concerned, however, Daniel was at his most disciplined when out of work. Only when he was in work did he get 'wrecked'. He stuck to his principles with an iron will. 'He was absolutely straight when he was not working. When he was unemployed he never drank at all, if he got work he would go on a bender,' recalled Simon Dunstan, Clare Montefiore's ex-boyfriend, who shared the flat with Daniel and Sarah for almost a year.

The ferocity of his determination made Daniel an awkward customer to live with. 'When he was working he was absolutely brilliant, when he wasn't he would be very gloomy indeed and he wouldn't treat himself well at all, he would not allow himself to whoop it up. He could be quite dark. He could be desperately serious, sensitive with a bit of a temper. He would sometimes say things that were quite rude. He could be difficult to be around.'

Ironically, the first offer of work after his return to London came in a phone call from the West Country city he had left with such happy memories. A panic-stricken member of Bristol's Little Theatre explained that the actor who was due to play the lead in a production of John Osborne's *Look Back in Anger* had walked out on the first day of rehearsals. Daniel later recalled the voice telling him: 'I don't know anything about you, but these people I'm working with say that maybe you should come and do this play.' There would be better prepared, more ego-friendly phone calls. At the time, however, the caller's lack of etiquette could be forgiven.

Daniel leapt at the chance, immediately packed his bags and left West Hampstead. Grabbing a copy of Osborne's play and jumping on board a train back to Bristol, he began the most demanding assignment he had yet faced. There were just three weeks left before the opening night. 'I had seen the play a couple of times but didn't know the part intimately well,' he recalled later. 'I did know that the character Jimmy Porter was a kind of modern-day Hamlet.'

The three weeks flew by. 'It was the fastest study I had ever done,' he recalled. Theatre critics care little for excuses, however. As Daniel stepped into the role of Jimmy Porter, the part that had lent a voice and a name to the Angry Young Men of the British theatre twenty years earlier, he also walked into the first bad reviews of his career. The harshest lessons of his chosen trade were coming thick and fast.

He admitted afterwards that he was shocked at the experience. The *Bristol Evening Post* brutalized his performance, accusing him of inexperience, a lack of emotional depth and portraying Porter as a spoilt, middle-class brat rather than the ranting, working-class force Osborne had intended him to be.

'The one in the *Evening Post* was my initiation, it was like being blooded,' he told another city newspaper, the *Western Daily Press*, weeks later, the wounds barely healed. 'It sounds arrogant to say it, but it came as a shock to receive bad reviews. It was the first time I had seen my name linked with so many unattractive adjectives. It upset me, it really did.'

He took his punishment in trouper tradition. He went out on stage the next night, resolute that he would improve and learn from his experience. *Look Back in Anger* eventually became a near sell-out and a financial success for the Little Theatre. There were even good reviews to be pasted on to the wall alongside the *Post*'s assassination. Daniel admitted that he felt 'very emotional' when he read the first positive criticism of his performance. Kipling donated acting its most apposite epigram: 'If you can meet with triumph and disaster and treat those two imposters just the same . . .' During his fiery baptism Daniel faced his two imposters. He emerged unscathed.

The proceeds from *Look Back in Anger*'s success were syphoned back into financing a new play. Christopher Bond's adaptation of Bram Stoker's *Dracula* was to be one of the most ambitious productions staged at the Little Theatre. Daniel was asked to stay on and once more take the lead.

Bond's stock was high at the time. He had produced a particularly gruesome version of the story of Sweeney Todd, 'The Demon Barber of Fleet Street'. *Dracula* would tap into the same vein. Anticipation was high, but in the run-up to the opening night, at the end of February 1981, Bond decided to indulge in a little theatrical hype. National and local newspapers, always interested in the Old Vic's more spectacular productions, were suddenly told that there would be no advance photographs of the new *Dracula*. They would all have to wait until the opening night to glimpse the Gothic monster the innovative producer had created.

Daniel stoked up interest with the odd enigmatic interview. 'There will be ghastly pallor, and blood and fangs,' he teased the *Western Daily Press* reporter with a half-smile. The only clue to what was in store was the fact that the young actor was wearing a bobble-hat beneath which there clearly lurked a secret.

The creature that emerged on stage at the Little Theatre that opening night was a terrifying throwback to the classic Nosferatu of the silent age, with Max Schreck as the vampire. With his hair dyed blond and savagely shorn, his promised fangs in place, Daniel evoked the spirit of that monochrome masterpiece. His Count Dracula was hailed as a sinister triumph. There was no blood-letting in the columns of the *Evening Post*. Dracula stalked the stage every night for a month.

Daniel's second spell in Bristol proved a high-profile show-case. After one Saturday night performance he was driven from Bristol to Liverpool where he had landed a small part in a BBC TV play, *Artemis Two*, by David Rudkin. He had been spotted at the Old Vic and was hired for a day's work.

His television debut had come even before that, however. His darkly handsome features first graced the small screen in an episode of the BBC's hit 'private-ear' series, *Shoestring*. The show, about a Bristol-based radio phone-in host with a flair for detective work, had in 1979 turned its star, Trevor Eve, into a national idol. Daniel showed up in one episode as a disc jockey. Years later he joked that he carried on receiving money for the cameo long afterwards. 'I still get an occasional 35p from the BBC because it has been sold to some island in the South Pacific,' he said. 'It's nice to have an income.'

He returned to London, Sarah and the West Hampstead flat, the memory of his first brief flirtation with joblessness behind him. 1981 was to be one of the busiest years of his life.

Sarah had taken his sudden disappearance to Bristol in her stride. She understood the importance of his work and his need occasionally to spread his butterfly wings, the couple's friends recall. 'The impression was that he needed to have space, you could not pressure him, you could not put him up against a wall,' recalled Simon Dunstan. 'That is why his relationship with Sarah lasted so long, because she was so wonderfully gentle, she would allow him to be Dan. He had the space and he respected her for that. It can't have been easy for her.'

Life in the flat conformed to the chaotic rules of every other twentysomething household in London at the time. 'There was a lot of playing house, we were all quite young, so we stayed in a lot, had lots of parties,' said Simon Dunstan.

Daniel's dress sense at the time was anarchic, his flatmate recalled. The boy who could not leave his nursery without a tie and who had been packaged in stockbroker greyness at Sevenoaks was still rebelling. Japanese army boots, leggings, bandannas, leather and ripped jeans were his trademarks. 'There was an element of style to it all. I remember when he was Dracula he wore a dog-tooth checked suit. With his short, dyed blond hair he looked striking.'

He imitated Keith Richards, the ultimate rock and roll survivor, Simon Dunstan remembers. 'He would tie a bandanna around his knee and pretend to be Keith. He could make himself look great, he had a great flair for design.'

On the streets of post-punk, 1981 Britain, Daniel's exotic new uniforms turned heads. In the casting offices of the English film and theatre profession, however, they drew mystified blanks. As his management company, Leading Artists in St James's, London, began to put his name forward for movie roles, Daniel was asked to clean up his act.

'My agent had had various complaints about my appearance because I was notoriously scruffy and often unshaven. I went to one interview, for a director whose name I shan't mention, but I won't ever work for him, that's for sure. He let it be known to my agent that I should go back looking more presentable the next day – which I found humiliating.'

His experience with Sir Richard Attenborough, however, proved conclusively that old cinematic saw 'nobody knows anything' – even when it came to dress sense. Daniel had been asked to see the veteran British film-maker's casting director as Attenborough put together his most ambitious movie to date, the life and times of the Indian leader Mahatma Gandhi. Daniel assumed that he was being considered for a pukka part as a member of Her Majesty's military on the sub-continent. Accordingly he dug up one of the few suits he possessed – second-hand, of course – and somehow conjured up a bow-tie. He went along to the casting agent's central London offices and presented himself for inspection with a ramrod-straight back and the well-pressed precision of a guardsman. The agent took one look and said: 'Can you come back next week and try not to look like a poet's son.'

As it turned out, Attenborough was looking for a dark-haired Englishman to play a racist South African bully boy. For the next seven days Daniel returned to his razorless previous life, roughed up his street clothes and returned to see Attenborough himself in his best biker-from-hell outfit. It was an interview he would never forget. 'He said, "How tall are you?" And I said, "Six foot one and a half." He said, "You're a good boy" – and that was the end of the interview,' he recalled later.

Two weeks after finishing Dracula, Daniel, his blond punk hair dyed back to its natural raven colour, headed off to India to join a stellar cast, led by Ben Kingsley who had been chosen to play Gandhi. It was his first movie role since John Schlesinger cast him as a tearaway in *Sunday, Bloody Sunday*. For the moment he was not worried about being typecast as a hooligan.

Daniel played a menacing young thug called Colin. His opening line in a major movie was memorable in its own way. It was: 'Get off the pavement, you bloody coon.' His scene was set in Pietermaritzburg, Southern Africa, in 1893, when Gandhi was crusading for civil rights there. At the time 'coloureds' were not allowed to walk on the pavements. Gandhi challenged this, boldly walking along a pavement and towards Daniel and two other youths, played by Ray Burdis and Daniel Peacock. Attenborough's concern over Daniel's height was made clear in the scene. The racist ruffian towers over the tiny figure of the pacifist Gandhi. Kingsley, as Gandhi, got the final line in the scene. As the loathsome Colin was about to flex his white supremacist muscles, he was distracted by the voice of his mother demanding to know why he hadn't gone to work and what he is up to. After sheepishly explaining that 'we were just trying to clean up the neighbourhood', the saintly leader smiles at the deflated Daniel and says, 'I think you will find there is room for us all.'

The scene also featured a young British actor who had already made a major impact. Ian Charleson played a vicar called Charlie Andrews, who remained Gandhi's closest non-Indian friend throughout his life. Charleson had already made his mark with his portrayal of the runner Eric Liddell in the Oscar-winning 1981 movie, *Chariots of Fire*. Charleson and Daniel became friends during filming in India, which conveniently doubled for South Africa. Fate would conspire to link them together again later in their careers.

Even though his role in *Gandhi* was minimal, the experience of being involved in a movie of such scale was precious to Daniel. Everything about the production was epic. Attenborough had cherished the idea of making the life of Gandhi for eighteen years. As he tirelessly hawked his idea around Hollywood the standard response was: 'A movie about a little brown man with bandy legs and a tea towel round his middle? Where's the love interest? Do us a favour, Dickie!'

But he did not let such studio put-downs deflect him. Finally, in 1980, he raised the finance – a massive chunk coming from the Indian Government itself – and he was in business. In November, he and a massive, ninety-strong crew had begun filming in Porbandar, Bombay, Poona, Putna and Udaipur. By the time they reached Delhi to film Gandhi's funeral all of India wanted to be involved in the project. A crowd estimated at 350,000 – most of them onlookers-cum-extras working for nothing – filled the centre of the city to watch the funeral cortège file past.

More revealing for Daniel, however, was the small-scale miracle that was Ben Kingsley's performance. Attenborough's aim was explained in the opening dedication. 'No man's life can be encompassed in one telling . . . what can be done is to be faithful in spirit to the record and to find one's way to the heart of the man.' Kingsley had found his way to the heart of the Mahatma with astonishing effect. He exuded a serenity, almost a saintliness on set. Even when he was not before the cameras there was a discipline and a peace to him that commanded reverence and respect. So stunning was his re-creation of the Mahatma that elderly Indians started calling him by Gandhi's nickname, Babu. 'No, no, you mustn't do that. I'm only an actor,' he would say, slipping out of his spell momentarily.

As a wide-eyed novice, Daniel could not have wished for a more inspirational lesson in concentrated professionalism. Kingsley deservedly walked away with virtually every major film award, including the Best Actor Oscar for 1982.

Back in England in the summer of 1981, Daniel took his first step towards becoming a recognizable television face. Ronnie Wilson, a leading director at the BBC, had been impressed by Daniel's Dracula in Bristol. He cast him in *Frost in May*, a four-part dramatization of a quartet of autobiographical novels written by Antonia White. He was given the part of Archie, the first husband of the heroine of the series, played by Janet Maw. His was not the only young face in this production being given a first substantial television role. The part of Nanda in the opening episode was played, to much acclaim, by a sugar-sweet thirteen-year-old called Patsy Kensit.

Filming went on through the long, hot summer of 1981, a summer memorable for more rioting and the wedding of Prince Charles and Lady Diana Spencer. 'I remember us having champagne on the set the day of the Royal Wedding,' recalled Janet Maw, who became a close friend of her on-screen husband. She too discovered a young man happiest when at work. 'One of the things that was so refreshing about him was that he was obviously a very fine actor, but there was no great ego or any preening or any macho thing in the way, he was just Daniel. He just wanted to get on and do the best job he could. There was no moody front, no image being presented, everyone liked him. He was very self-effacing, not in a pathetic way but in a very up-front kind of way. He was incredibly striking, he had those very striking features, but he was also incredibly easy to talk to and great fun.'

Daniel and Janet, along with writer Alan Seymour, director Ronnie Wilson, producer Ann Head, and actors Elizabeth Shepherd and John Carson became a tight-knit group of friends. 'We had dinner several times at Alan Seymour's house, quiet gatherings,' Janet recalled.

Daniel and Janet also started playing tennis at courts in Brook Green, west London, near Sean Day-Lewis's home. 'He was very good, which surprised me because he was so tall and slim, I didn't expect him to be so strong.'

In the autumn Daniel was cast in another television production, *How Many Miles to Babylon?* He spent most of September and October back on Irish soil, on location around the town of Rathdrum, County Wicklow. *How Many Miles to Babylon?*, produced by the BBC's Innes Lloyd and adapted from Dubliner Jennifer Johnston's novel, told the story of two young men – one privileged, one poor – in turn-of-the-century Ireland.

Daniel played Alexander Moore, the well-heeled son of an Anglo-Irish landowner, heir to an estate with its own stables and horse stock. His friendship with the estate's expert horseman Jerry Crowe, played by Christopher Fairbanks, carried the two young men all the way to the trenches of the Second World War.

Daniel and Christopher became close friends. Before heading off to Ireland, they had immersed themselves in their parts by drinking in the Irish enclaves of north London. 'It was Method drinking,' recalled Simon Dunstan. 'They went to Biddy Mulligan's, a hairy Irish pub in Kilburn. They used to drink lots and talk in an Irish accent. Daniel was good at it anyway. They would have got beaten up if the people there thought they were taking the piss, so it was a good test, I suppose.'

Both Daniel's debut TV series were transmitted early in 1982 and won him his first national recognition. Brilliantined and moustached in *How Many Miles to Babylon?*, he drew comparisons with Jeremy Irons, another quintessentially English actor, then on his way to worldwide acclaim for his part in *Brideshead Revisited*. 'I knew people would say we looked alike. Personally I can't see it,' Daniel told the *Daily Mirror*. 'If it results in my getting another part as good as this one I'll be pleased. But I don't really want to be compared with another actor,' he added politely.

Reviews for both performances were glowing. *Daily Mail* critic Mary Kenny's praise would have pleased Cecil Day-Lewis. She singled out Daniel for his authentic Irish accent in *How Many Miles to Babylon?* when it was transmitted in February. Three months later Daniel's Archie was hailed as 'outstanding' by Julian Barnes in the *Observer*. Patricia Craig in the *Times Literary Supplement* went further. She thought the character one of the few advantages the dramatization had over the Archie of the original novel. 'Daniel Day-Lewis makes something cogent and coherent of it,' she wrote. Sean Day-Lewis, as the *Daily Telegraph*'s TV critic, warmly welcomed the series, lauding Janet Maw and Patsy Kensit for their contributions. As for Archie, he reined in his critical instincts, 'declared a brotherly interest' and said nothing more. Privately, however, he was highly impressed.

Daniel later admitted to mixed feelings about the way of working life in British television. The perennial financial strait-jacket within which programme-makers were forced to work was too limiting, he felt. 'The system doesn't let one work the way one wants to work. Even in Britain where the BBC and Channel Four give more time and resources to TV than maybe any other country in the world,' he told the American magazine *Film Comment* a few years later. 'But it's still too rushed, too cost-conscious.'

Despite the encouraging reviews for his first two major roles on television, however, Daniel spent the first two-thirds of 1982 once more languishing among the ranks of the 'resting'. His second taste of joblessness was, if anything, worse than the first. 'It was very rough. I felt that I was gathering some momentum and suddenly, whoosh, it happens. If one needs humility, it's not difficult to find humility, and I felt very humble.'

Once more depression set in. The blackness Bedales had seen was a feature of life at West Hampstead. 'He saw himself as a tragic person, a tragic hero in a sense,' recalled Simon Dunstan. Memories of his father had by now become a haunting influence. 'There was a sense of sadness, more sadness than there might have been otherwise. His father was God to some extent.'

As Daniel endured his spell of unemployment, however, there was an unmistakable sense that such humbling experiences would soon end for ever. It was almost as if it was his destiny to reach the heights of his profession, Simon Dunstan recalled. 'He had the very highest ambitions. He wanted to be Gielgud. He took himself and his work very seriously. And with Daniel it was all or nothing.'

Sarah was the perfect foil for him, according to Simon. She was working on a doctorate. She too passed through phases of introspection. 'She was an excellent cook, a brilliant designer, she was very well read and incredibly gentle,' said Simon.

Daniel and Sarah made a distinctive-looking couple, he

with his ever-changing hairstyle, she with her long blonde hair and delicate beauty. They were noticed wherever they went together. 'They were both incredibly angular, they looked great together. They used to do these wonderful body sculptures where they would link arms and she would pull Dan on to her shoulders. He would lie on her back, they looked great,' their flatmate recalled.

For all his anxiety to succeed, Daniel sometimes found it difficult to play the public game required of rising young actors. He would dread going to showbiz parties that his agents would arrange for him. 'He came back from one where he had been with Sarah and he had not said a word the whole evening. People came up to him and he just froze,' said Simon Dunstan. 'Personal exposure was difficult for him, he was a very private person. He has very strong emotions but he has this iron reserve as well, so the two are in tremendous conflict all the time which makes it scary.'

One of Daniel's escapes was cycling. The love of biking instilled in him by Tim Slack at Bedales remains with him to this day. 'He had this bike that his mum bought him which he converted down to one gear. He cycled very hard, when he does something it is total,' his flatmate remembered.

As well as cycling and running, he once more started playing football. He joined up with a group of other out-of-work actors and began turning out for a so-called showbusiness XI. Today an appearance by the one-footed winger would draw vast crowds wherever he chose to turn out. On those wet, windy Sunday mornings on the cramped pitches of Hackney Marshes in north London, however, there were no such acts of worship. It was only years later, when actors from Britain's television soap opera *EastEnders* joined the team, that crowds began to appear.

By the autumn of 1982, however, Daniel was back on the right track. He was cast in one of the West End's most critically acclaimed productions, *Another Country*. Producer Julian Mitchell's play, set in an upper-crust English public school, was loosely based on the young life of the spy Guy Burgess. It explored the suffocating effects the sadism, militarism and homosexuality of public school life had on the young men of England. In Burgess's case those forces drove him eventually to betray his country and become an agent for Communist Russia.

Seven years earlier, Julian Mitchell had helped Daniel's mother return to the West End stage for the first time since her husband's death. She starred in his version of *A Family* by Ivy Compton-Burnett, which opened at the Apollo in 1975. Now it was her son he sought out after the departure of *Another Country*'s original leading man, Rupert Everett. The tall, lean Everett had been in the part of Guy Bennett for six months since the play opened in March 1982. He was already being lined up to reprise the role in a movie version to be directed by Marek Kanievska.

Mitchell had originally considered Daniel for the supporting role of Judd in the spring. The physical similarities between him and Everett had counted against him, however. 'They looked at these two long drinks and said perhaps not,' he recalled later. The rejection was doubly disappointing because the play was to open at Greenwich Theatre, the refurbished old music hall that stood across the road from 6 Croom's Hill. Now, however, Daniel was being asked to take over from Everett. 'I was terrified, I had never worked in a big London theatre before,' he confessed.

The play's themes resonated loudly in Daniel. His act of over-the-wall rebellion against the constricting order and underground homosexuality which he had encountered at Sevenoaks did not produce a fall-out to compare with Burgess's treason. But he still understood the oppression at the play's heart.

Having reviewed the play once, the West End critics gave Daniel's new-look Bennett a miss. Word of his performance was soon circulating among agents all over London, however. His performance also won him the devotion of a group of flamboyant young fops who would turn up for every one of his appearances. The unwanted attentions of Sevenoaks returned.

Simon Dunstan and a girlfriend, Penelope Dening, turned up to meet Daniel for dinner after the show one night to discover him besieged by the fans. They were clearly infatuated with the dashingly handsome new Bennett. He dealt with them with politeness and tact. 'They were this clique of white-gloved young men in fifties' clothing and spats. They wore weird make-up and their hair was greased back. They were like something out of a Noël Coward play,' recalled Penelope Dening. 'Their leader called himself "Bedford",' added Simon Dunstan.

Daniel chatted briefly to his fan club in his dressing room at the Queen's Theatre. 'He was very gracious, but he kept a distance,' Penelope remembered. Over dinner at Manzi's restaurant Daniel called the group his 'backstage Johnnys'. 'He said they came every night to see the show. I wondered whether he was gay, but Simon said, "Oh, no."'

Daniel played Bennett for eight and a half months, through the winter of 1981 and into the spring of the following year. It was a gruelling experience that left him 'dribbling'. As he took his curtain call on his last night, however, he knew he would have little time to recover. The next morning he was booked on a flight to Tahiti and his first substantial film role, in a lavish new version of *The Mutiny on the Bounty*.

His farewell to *Another Country* was a spectacular too. He recalled later how he got so drunk with the friends he had made that he was lucky to catch his plane. 'I remember the last night I got hopelessly intoxicated – to such a degree that someone had to pack for me the next day.'

The true story of how, in 1789, the crew of a British Navy ship overthrew its tyrannical captain, William Bligh, to colonize a desert island paradise in the Pitcairn Islands, was well-tilled cinematic soil. *The Mutiny on the Bounty* had been filmed twice before, each time with award-strewn success.

Director Frank Lloyd's 1935 version won a Best Picture Academy Award. Its leads, Charles Laughton as Bligh and Clark Gable as the leader of the mutineers, Fletcher Christian, were both nominated for Oscars.

Almost three decades later, in 1962, Hollywood put the *Bounty* to water again, this time casting Trevor Howard as the dictatorial Captain and Marlon Brando as Christian. Directed by Lewis Milestone, the film was a mixed success. Brando's extraordinarily strangulated English accent raised eyebrows among critics, and even his box-office appeal failed to deliver a financial hit. Somehow, however, the second treatment of *Mutiny on the Bounty* picked up a nomination for Best Picture in its year.

In 1984 a Welshman and an Australian were to take on the central roles, Anthony Hopkins as Bligh and Mel Gibson as his upstart officer. Faced with a familiar film voyage, scriptwriter Robert Bolt took a different tack and told the story through the court martial Bligh was given for his incompetence in losing Her Majesty one of her ships. Laurence Olivier played Bligh's chief inquisitor, Admiral Hood. Daniel had won the role of John Fryer, Bligh's second-in-command.

The movie had been years in the planning. Originally intended as a project for Sir David Lean, it had been taken over by producer Dino De Laurentiis after the great English director told its original backers, Warners, that he wanted to make two movies at a cost of $37 million each. His reputation still tarnished by the disappointment of *Ryan's Daughter* in 1970, Lean was refused the money.

At $24 million this was a slimmed-down yet still grand-scale version of Lean's *Bounty*. Both its leads were at crucial stages in their careers, the Australian emerging as one of the most bankable international stars after the success of two *Mad Max* movies and *The Year of Living Dangerously*, and the Welshman embarking on a new ascent in a rollercoaster career.

The uncredited star of the movie, however, was the $4-million replica of the original *Bounty* that had been built specially for the film. Outwardly every hand-crafted inch of the magnificent 133-foot-long vessel, every length of its 10,000 square feet of Scottish flax rigging, faithfully re-created the 230-ton coal-carrier that had been given its first assignment, a journey to the Society Islands, on 23 December 1787. Beneath the authentic, Stockholm-tarred surface, however, the ship was a steel-hulled, diesel-engined cruiser that reflected the best sea-faring science could offer at the time.

Daniel travelled out to the South Seas, along with a largely British cast that also included Liam Neeson, Bernard Hill, John

114

Sessions, and Phil Davis. The shoot was to last sixteen weeks. Filming took place in New Zealand and on the island of Moorea, near Tahiti, where the original motley crew of the *Bounty* had found the fruits of paradise so irresistible. Daniel and his colleagues found Moorea equally enticing. They based themselves at the Kiora Hotel on Moorea.

Daniel's character, Fryer, could have averted the most famous mutiny in British naval history. Appointed by the Admiralty to supervise the *Bounty*'s expedition to bring Tahitian bread-fruit back to feed the slaves of Jamaica, he had objected to Bligh's ambitious plans to circumnavigate the globe via Cape Horn. His troubles began when Bligh went ahead and sailed into desperate storms.

After voicing his disagreement Fryer was replaced as second-in-command by Fletcher Christian. He remained faithful to Bligh, however, and with his captain and seventeen others was cast adrift in a 23-foot boat, to spend forty days at sea before finding land on the island of Coupang, Timor.

Daniel played Fryer with an air of square-jawed, stiff-upper-lipped superiority. His face forever wreathed in scowls and sullen grimaces, he made a fitting second-string villain of the piece.

There were grimaces galore off camera too. The modern *Bounty* also proved itself a far from happy ship. The production was plagued with problems, the main one being that Hopkins and director Roger Donaldson did not hit it off. The pugnacious son of Port Talbot took offence at threats from Donaldson that he would 'come down hard on him' if he gave him any trouble.

When Hopkins, who had become particularly close to Daniel, Bernard Hill and Phil Davis, 'a nice bunch', considered the inexperienced director was being unfair on them and other members of the cast, he exploded. At one point, in front of the entire crew, he unleashed a Bligh-like verbal assault, calling Donaldson 'a fucking idiot'. Hopkins later told his biographer Quentin Falk that he found Donaldson 'a rude, arrogant man'.

If relations between the star and the director did not augur badly enough, there was also a series of strange happenings that made some wonder whether the movie was in some way jinxed. First, the engines of the *Bounty* inexplicably stopped at precisely 5 a.m. on 28 April. The ship's skipper, J. 'Mack' McGuire, could offer no explanation whatsoever. A member of the production crew pointed out that Captain Bligh was woken from his sleep by a flintlock-wielding Fletcher Christian at 5 a.m. on 28 April, 194 years earlier.

Then Neeson's mother telephoned the remote island to describe to her son how she had had a terrible dream where she had been chased by a man 'with a crooked finger and a black arm'. Back in Ulster, the strapping actor's mother had no idea that her son was playing a character called Churchill – with a deformed finger and an arm that had been charred black by burns!

The film was clearly fated in some way. Hopkins recalled later that Tahiti had a 'spell-like' effect on people. 'You begin to go stir-crazy because there's nowhere to go.' Daniel found the experience equally unsettling. He later described it as 'four months of sitting around waiting for the sun to shine'. 'Everybody found their primitive instincts,' he told *Elle* magazine a few years later. 'We kind of punched each other a lot, did our fertility dances. It was a desperately sad place to be.'

Hopkins later credited Daniel with providing him with one of the more positive legacies of their time in Tahiti. During their long days waiting for the sunshine, the old hand and the newcomer talked endlessly about their craft. Daniel had suggested that Hopkins, unhappy in Hollywood, might consider going back to the stage after a long break. Bligh took his young officer's idea on board. His return to the National Theatre in *Pravda* soon afterwards marked the beginning of a revival in his fortunes that was to take him to uncharted heights.

When *The Bounty* was released in 1984, however, it divided the critics wildly. While some praised, others fired bruising broadsides. 'A long voyage to nowhere,' one called it. 'One question arises as you settle down to watch *The Bounty* and it remains unanswered 133 minutes later,' wrote David Castell in the *Sunday Telegraph*. 'Why?'

The most damning criticism of Daniel's contribution to the film came from the acid-queen of the American critics, the *New*

Yorker's formidable Pauline Kael. She disliked the movie, calling it 'misshapen'. And she disliked Daniel Day-Lewis even
more. She wrote: 'as the skinny-faced John Fryer ... Daniel
Day-Lewis sticks out; he seemed like a bad actor'. Careers have
been killed by such withering words. Kael, however, would
come to form a different view of the 'bad actor'.

Daniel returned from his South Seas sojourn to join the
Royal Shakespeare Company. He had been hired for the RSC's
'small-scale' tour, an annual attempt to spread the Shakespearean word to the farthest-flung corners of the provinces.
The contrast between the soft-scented winds of Tahiti and the
multi-million-dollar extravagances of *The Bounty*, and a rain-
lashed English winter and obscure school halls and leisure
centres in Margate, Walsall and Barrow-in-Furness could not
have been greater.

The tour ran from October through to the end of January
1984, with performances in twenty-two towns normally
starved of top-class theatre. The two productions were *A Midsummer Night's Dream*, in which Daniel had the part of Flute,
and *Romeo and Juliet*, in which he had the role of the eponymous hero. His fellow-travellers included emerging talents like
Philip Jackson. The tour was led by the veteran actress Sheila
Hancock.

Daniel's Romeo won almost universal praise. Playing
opposite Amanda Root as Juliet, he looked dashing in shim-
mering leather. The *Walsall Observer* described his Romeo as 'a
fidgety, staccato romantic with a growling voice and a youthful
discovery of love'. The *Barrow News* praised 'a swashbuckling,
moody and romantic Romeo', while its local rival the *Westmorland Gazette* was impressed by Daniel's athleticism. 'Romeo was
a lusty, dedicated lover capable of swarming up ropes and
killing his opponents, yet vulnerable enough to love Juliet,' its
critic wrote.

The final performances before Christmas 1983 were held at
a school in Tiverton, Devon. Daniel's performance there attracted his half-brother Sean and his wife Anna, in the West
Country for the festive season. Sean thought the play flawed.
'He was a wonderfully good-looking Romeo, and that was part

of the problem. He was if anything better looking than Juliet, which didn't help the play.'

The Tiverton performance also attracted critics from the national newspapers in London. *The Times* praised him. 'Daniel Day-Lewis had the looks of Giuliano de Medici and the ardour and wit he brought to a different lover's role in *Another Country*,' Anthony Masters wrote. The *Observer*'s new critic, Michael Ratcliffe, was less impressed, however. He thought Juliet far outshone her Romeo. 'Amanda Root is the best all-round Juliet I have seen: young, irrepressible, humorous, reckless and wise . . . she is the find of the tour,' he wrote before adding, 'Daniel Day-Lewis lacks heart and metal in the voice.'

Others who saw him in the role disagreed. His co-star from *Frost in May*, Janet Maw, recalled: 'I liked his Romeo very much, he had this ability to express feelings without becoming a wimp. Even then he had that particular distinguished air about him, and I am not talking about class, there was just something special about him.'

Daniel inadvertently made his greatest impression of the long tour in Barrow. In *A Midsummer Night's Dream* he was playing the part of Flute, one of the acting troupe readying to play at the Duke of Athens's wedding. In the play within the play he appeared in a billowing white lace dress as the tragic lover Thisbe. As he delivered some of the play's funniest lines, he was apparently overcome with a violent attack of the giggles. This quickly spread to the audience and soon the entire theatre was doubled up. It was 'perhaps the high spot of the evening', the *Westmorland Gazette* reported.

For Daniel, however, it was a rare high spot. As his mother had discovered years earlier, the grind of provincial touring was a far from glamorous experience. The nightmarish sights and sounds of life on the road, that years earlier had been recounted for fun by Jill, became a drab reality. Among Daniel's most vivid memories of life as a travelling Shakespearan player, he would recall, were 'the ghastly smell of cabbage in dosshouse corridors and fag ash in the basins'.

He developed a particular dislike for the regalia of classical theatre, tunics and tights so revealing it felt 'like having a

Right: The laughing policeman. A youthful Daniel at Litton Cheney. (*Janet Stone*)

Below: Brother and sister. Daniel, the embryonic actor, in his plastic Ben Hur best, and Tamasin, the embryonic film-producer, happy to stay on the sidelines, at home in Greenwich. (*Janet Stone*)

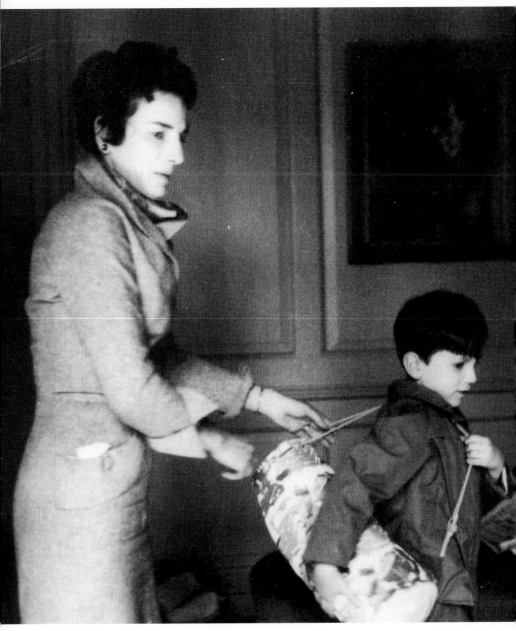

Rush hour at Croom's Hill. Jill Balcon prepares her son for school. (*Janet Stone*)

Right: Number 6, Croom's Hill, Greenwich. (*Janet Stone*)

Below: On Pappa's knee. Daniel and Cecil Day-Lewis in the study at Litton Cheney. (*Janet Stone*)

Left: Daniel and a bonfire Guy Fawkes share a ride on the Stone family's donkey, Elizabeth Fry, as Cecil looks on at Litton Cheney. (*Janet Stone*)

Below: "A man who fitted where he chose, always an alien but never obscured in the background. . ." 'Dan Day Pin-up', as Feste in *Twelfth Night*, Bedales, 1975. (*Bedales School*)

Right: 'A complete wanker'. With Amanda Root in *Romeo and Juliet*. (*Donald Cooper*)

Below: Dracula at the Half Moon. (*Donald Cooper*)

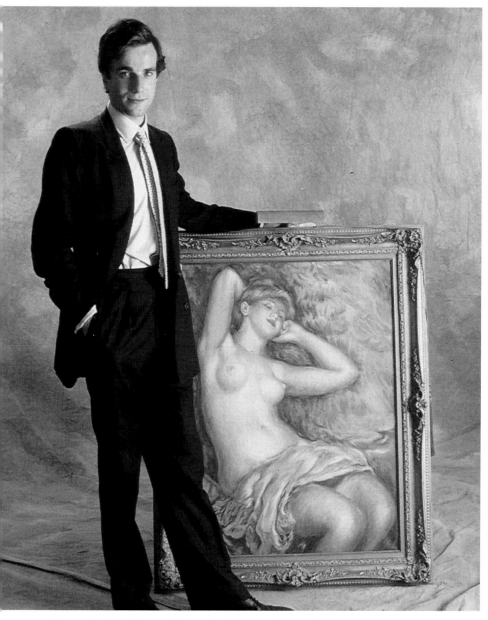

Above: As Henderson Dores in *Stars and Bars*. (Nancy Moran/Katz)

Facing page: As the poet Mayakovsky in *Futurists* at the National Theatre, London, April 1986. (*Donald Cooper*)

Above: Darkness descends? In London during interviews for *The Unbearable Lightness of Being*, August 1988. (*Rex*)

Below: A horny cripple from Crumlin. As Christy Brown in *My Left Foot*, with Brenda Fricker as his mother. (*Alpha*)

halogen lamp inside one's crotch'. Matinee audiences, often swelled by busloads of pubescent schoolgirls, were the bane of his daily life. 'You'd walk on stage and wait ten minutes for audiences to stop howling with laughter.'

At the end of the tour Daniel had been due to move on to the RSC and Shakespeare's home, Stratford-on-Avon. Before the end of the run he voiced his unhappiness and arranged to talk to the RSC's management back at its Barbican headquarters in London. He walked into the meeting to discover a panel of directors ready to discuss his future. 'I was so bowled over by the pretentiousness of that one gesture that I knew instantly my brief and rather soiled love affair with the RSC was finished for good,' he recalled later.

The stern-faced panel apparently had assumed that Daniel's unhappiness was a cover story. It seemed that they believed he had won a film role and wanted to betray the theatre for its vulgar relation. 'Suddenly it was as if I'd become the principal of a kindergarten. I said, "I have the pleasure to inform you that I have no other work – neither film nor television nor theatre. But I would rather be out of work than be unhappy with the Royal Shakespeare Company."' The clubbishness of English theatre has irritated him ever since. The idea that film is somehow 'a Faustian sell-out' has aggravated him even more.

Daniel later wrote his time as a roving Romeo down to experience. 'It was assumed that the classics were a good line of work for me because I enjoyed speaking verse and had the right nose for it,' he mused. As for poor Romeo, he dismissed Shakespeare's great romantic hero as 'a complete wanker'.

Shakespeare would, however, return to haunt him again.

CHAPTER SEVEN

COMING OUT IN THE WASH

'It is not that the Englishman can't feel – it is that he is afraid to feel.'

E. M. FORSTER, *Abinger Harvest*

REGAL IT was not. It was the language of late night Saturday Deptford and the Millwall terraces, 'class enemy' Cockney, threatening, bullying, and once more irresistible. The last time Daniel Day-Lewis had wanted something badly enough to compose such an unforgettable letter he had written it on Buckingham Palace headed notepaper. Stephen Frears neglected to admire the type of script the young actor used when he wrote to him in 1984. He was too shocked by the language to notice.

'Don't be fooled by my polite education,' Daniel had written. 'I've got some very unpleasant friends.' The letter went on to explain that those nasty friends would inflict serious damage on the British director if the leading role in his in-the-pipeline project with the writer Hanif Kureishi did not come its correspondent's way.

Daniel had been sent a copy of Kureishi's script, titled *My Beautiful Laundrette*, by his agent Julian Belfrage. It was the story of a yuppie Pakistani, launching a washeteria business against the backdrop of growing racism in urban Britain. The two leading roles were Omar, the Asian embodiment of eighties entrepreneurship, and Johnny, a squat-dwelling old school-friend and one of the Pakistani community's chief persecutors. It was on the face of it an unlikely story to bring to the cinema screen. As Daniel read on it became even more unlikely. It turned out that Johnny's racism was little more than

120

an expression of his boredom. By the end of Kureishi's screen-play he had – in a neat reversal of the old colonial order – become Omar's lover and laundrette dogsbody, proving as useful with his fists as he was with a squeezy-mop.

Daniel saw the script at the end of 1984. He knew instantly that Johnny was his passport out of the typecast cul-de-sac he felt he had been heading down.

After his falling out with the RSC he had been busy with theatre and television work. For five months he worked on a five-part BBC drama series, *My Brother Jonathan*, based on Francis Brett Young's novel. Daniel played the eponymous Jonathan, a righteous doctor tending to the needy in a deprived, working-class English town. The series traced his relationship with his family and particularly his brother, Harold, played by Benedict Taylor. It was the kind of role Daniel's dark good looks and impeccable pedigree qualified him for perfectly. Jonathan, the son of a poet and an eternally dramatic, ex-actress mother, was perhaps closer-to-home than any character he had yet played.

It had been the major difference between his and Jonathan's childhood that had fascinated him most, however. 'I was really pleased when I realized my relationship with Harold is such an important element of the series,' he told the BBC's *Radio Times* magazine. 'I've always longed for a brother. It's something I've thought about all my life. In acting you find occasions when a part enables you to play out certain games. And here I was presented with an opportunity to do what I've always wanted – suddenly I was given a brother to play with. It was great!'

Daniel researched his part ferociously. He had moved from West Hampstead to South Kensington where Sarah had bought a top-floor flat in Queen's Gate. 'It was a very beautiful flat,' recalled their ex-flatmate Simon Dunstan, a frequent dinner guest. 'It wasn't very big, it was at the top of a mansion block, it had a roof garden. It was beautifully decorated. There were paintings of Dan's on the wall, I remember.'

Being in Kensington meant some of London's best libraries were now on Daniel's doorstep. He spent hours poring over surgical textbooks. The series' medical adviser, a Dr Hobbs, even allowed him and director Tony Garner to stand in on a major operation. 'The surgeon was secretly disappointed we showed no signs of passing out,' Daniel said later.

For all the enthusiasm he showed during filming, however, he admitted afterwards that the part was simply too wholesome. 'I am only capable of playing one nice person every two years. The rest of the time I have to spend getting rid of the nasty side, so as to be able to operate as a human being,' he confessed later. '*My Brother Jonathan* exhausted all my powers of compassion and philanthropy.'

By the end of 1984 a familiar role had provided an antidote to the good doctor. Christopher Bond's production of *Dracula* had travelled the 120 miles or so from the West Country to the Half Moon Theatre in the East End of London. The bleached suede-head Nosferatu of Bristol days was back to haunt audiences. The albino hair and mortician's slab make-up made him look 'as if all the blood had been drained out of him'. Again his inventiveness was being rewarded with good reviews.

Welcome as his return to working with Bond was, however, Daniel feared his screen roles were limiting him. Once he had read Kureishi's script for *My Beautiful Laundrette* he knew he had found the part that would break the mannered, middle-class mould. It struck the same chord as *Class Enemy* and *Gotcha* years earlier. It was anti-Thatcherism with a twist. It had a rare and powerful relevance. Daniel knew he had to do it. So did virtually every other actor who had cast eyes on the script.

Frears, a roaring bundle of nervous energy from Leicester, had launched his film career with *Gumshoe* starring Albert Finney in 1971. He had then waited thirteen years for his second feature, the gangster movie *The Hit* starring John Hurt and Terence Stamp, spending most of the intervening years making some of the best television films of his time. He knew of Daniel's work in *Frost in May* and *Another Country* and already had him down as a possible candidate for the part of Johnny. But he was on a list which included two of the most energetic members of Britain's new wave, Tim Roth and Gary Oldman.

Frears had already interviewed Daniel for a gay role in another movie he had been planning for years, the biopic of Joe Orton, *Prick Up Your Ears*. When he eventually got to make the film, however, he gave Gary Oldman the part of the outrageous playwright. He claimed he was not convinced by Daniel's accent. When he had walked into the room affecting a warped-vowelled south London drawl, Frears said he asked Daniel, 'Why are you talking in a working-class accent? You're the Poet Laureate's son!' Daniel later denied Frears's account and said that he had exaggerated the story.

Whatever the truth was, Frears saw something in the poet's son and during the weeks leading up to final casting on *My Beautiful Laundrette* asked to see him twice. The first time Daniel wore what he later called his 'day-to-day-rockabilly' look. Once again his scruffy uniform was perfect for conveying the menace his potential employers were looking for.

By the time of his second visit he was stalking the stage as his peroxide vampire at the *Half Moon*. His reprise interview with Frears went well enough. As he left, however, Daniel was riddled with fears. He conceded in later years that his distinguished name might have helped him early in his career. 'You're judged by how many people know your name. Day-Lewis is not a name that's ever been associated with my profession, but it may be that someone once let me audition because it rang a bell,' he said.

As he pursued the part of Johnny, however, he was worried that his pedigree might count against him. He began to convince himself that Roth and Oldman, both less privileged products of London's inner city, were more natural choices. Was Frears going to hold his famous upbringing against him once more?

It was then that he decided to put poisonous pen to paper. Daniel later admitted that he had threatened to break Frears's legs, 'both of them', if he passed him over for the part.

'The letter was fairly vile, but I only wrote it to him because I knew he would understand it. He is not easily intimidated and it wasn't intended to intimidate him, it was just making a point and he took the point!'

Frears described the letter as 'disgusting'. 'I guess he wanted to prove he wasn't posh, that he could be nasty. I thought, well, if he wants it that badly. Actors are like that, you know. A good part – it's like sex to them. They can smell it.' Soon, however, the menace of the letter, whether mock or real, would be forgotten. Frears had made an inspired casting choice and Daniel was about to tackle his first substantial film role.

Daniel and Johnny were not such polar opposites as they might have first appeared. Until he began acting, Daniel too had been aimless in life, he too had channelled that lack of direction into destructive behaviour, albeit self-destructive in his own case. He also had the ghosts of his Greenwich past to draw on. As a young boy watching Millwall and its notoriously thuggish supporters, Daniel would long since have had his first, putrid whiff of football terrace fascism.

He looked for physical props. One came from the grave of his last theatrical part. The character of Count Dracula had once more been laid to rest, but Daniel decided against dyeing his hair back to its natural black. He started to grow the colour back in naturally. As a result he looked as though he had a punkified shaving brush on his head. The effect was striking. He arrived on set ready to shock.

His apprenticeship on *The Bounty* and *Gandhi* proved providential. Both Ben Kingsley and Anthony Hopkins had been masterly at shutting out the extraneous din of the film set and concentrating on delivering their performances.

'When you know the camera may be on for thirty seconds, you have to know precisely where you are coming from, to be able to arrive at the necessary place at the moment the camera is switched on,' Daniel once explained. 'A lesson I learned quite early on is that, much as one loves to talk to the people that are around, and there are always interesting people on film sets, it's very important jealously to preserve the time between takes.'

The twin pressures of the budget and workings with Frears made it all the more important for Daniel to be ready for every shot he appeared in. Channel Four had commissioned Frears to make the movie on a shoestring budget of £600,000. If there was a director at work in Britain capable of turning the movie around in that time it was Frears, who had a very low boredom threshold and a hatred of slowness. 'Slowness is infuriating, especially when you're trying for some kind of spontaneity,' he declared.

Filming began on 25 February 1985. The shoot was to be condensed into six intense weeks. Locations were set in south London, amidst the urban greyness of Stockwell and Vauxhall, on the banks of the Thames. The laundrette, on Wilcox Road, Vauxhall, was in fact a shoe shop. Art director Hugo Luczyc-Wyhowski spent £10,000 converting the store into a high-tech washeteria.

Daniel succeeded in maintaining the self-containment he needed throughout the shoot. 'He kept himself to himself. He was very pleasant, but he was focused on his role,' remembered one of his fellow-actors, Derrick Branche.

When it came to the homosexual love scenes, however, Daniel found himself breaking with his new no-small-talk rule. Hanif Kureishi, who had worked out five drafts of the script with Frears before filming started, admitted that he did not set out specifically to write a drama about two gay young men. 'It just started. It came from the characters. I didn't think, "I'm going to write a gay film now!"' he explained.

The role of Omar had been won by a little known Asian actor, Gordon Warnecke. This was his movie debut. Omar and Johnny's was a forbidden love. Their moments of affection together came after work or after dark, in darkened alleyways or locked offices. One of the scenes was filmed in a parked car in a particularly run-down area of Vauxhall. After finishing the film Daniel recalled how some malevolent-looking local Jamaicans watched fascinated. 'It felt very tense, there was a bit of whistling.'

Both men admitted they were nervous about their most intimate scenes together. After each of their passionate embraces, they broke that tension by reaffirming their heterosexuality. 'We swilled a lot of Listerene then talked earnestly about our girlfriends,' Daniel remembered.

For all the flipness, however, both actors realized that a

convincing portrayal of Omar and Johnny's love for each other was crucial to the film. 'Gordon Warnecke and I approached it as a love affair, like any other love affair. It wasn't sensationalized,' Daniel recalled later. 'Those two boys who wouldn't stop kissing seemed natural and that has nothing to do with my sexual inclinations. In the end it's no different from doing *Romeo and Juliet* with someone you don't know.'

Frears tried to lighten that tension with humour. 'Stephen was remarkably tactful,' Daniel said, tongue firmly in cheek, in an interview with the magazine *Photoplay* at the time of the film's release. 'Before each scene, rather than drawing us aside and having a few quiet words with us, he shouted at the top of his voice, "Who's on top?"'

Daniel praised Frears for opening his eyes to much that was new. 'It was virtually my first film, and it was frustrating for him to work with someone who obviously wasn't stupid but who couldn't understand why he was filming it from this or that angle,' he remembered. 'I couldn't stand disappointing him and I wanted to understand all the time.'

His eagerness to understand the demands of cinema even took him into Frears's cutting room for three weeks after filming was complete. It was there that the complexities of the film-making process finally began to fall into place for Daniel. 'That was the moment when I thought, "That's why! That's why!"'

Frears had been drawn to the story from the instant it dropped through the letter-box at his Notting Hill home. 'It was a very accurate and ironic analysis of Britain under Thatcher, a really strong piece of radical writing,' he said at the time. 'It is somewhere above market forces and terrible men with cigars, and that, for a director, is very protective.'

Kureishi's intention was to shatter the stereotyped view of Anglo-Indian culture, until then a cliché dressed in turbans and khaki English Army tunics, a constant echo of a distant imperial past, represented in the eighties by films like *Gandhi* and Merchant–Ivory's *Heat and Dust* and TV series like *The Jewel in the Crown* and *The Far Pavilions*. 'Stephen and I wanted to do something about life in England today, as opposed to all that

Raj crap they've been serving up for the last two years. I invented a word for the Raj films, I called them Easterns. With Lord Mountbatten as Gary Cooper, Lady Mountbatten as Marlene Dietrich and Gandhi as Chief Sitting Bull.'

The gulf between the sort of films the radical Hanif Kureishi was burning to make and the productions the Anglo-Indian trio partnership of Ismail Merchant, James Ivory and Ruth Prawer Jhabvala had been serving up for two decades was as broad as the Bay of Bengal. Close as Daniel had become to Kureishi and his ideas, however, when he got an invitation to see director Ivory soon after the end of filming *My Beautiful Laundrette* he accepted immediately.

The trio was preparing to start filming an adaptation of E. M. Forster's 1908 novel, *A Room with a View*. The story of the romantic awakening of a repressed young English girl during an Italian holiday had been adapted for the screen by Prawer Jhabvala. Filming was set for Tuscany and England.

Merchant and Ivory were assembling a cast combining established names with relative newcomers. Maggie Smith as the over-bearing chaperon Charlotte Bartlett, Denholm Elliott as the common-sense Mr Emerson, and Judi Dench as the romantic novelist Miss Lavish, led the 'old wave'. Helena Bonham-Carter, a beautiful young English actress, had been given the plum role of Lucy Honeychurch, the sheltered Edwardian who loses her innocence abroad, an instinctively independent woman with the sort of 'undeveloped heart' that Forster found so fascinating.

The two young male roles, George Emerson, the virile, handsome but 'unsuitable' son of a Socialist newspaperman whom Lucy falls for on holiday, and Cecil Vyse, the appallingly arrogant, priggish egotist to whom the heroine is unhappily engaged, were both uncast. It seemed that either part was Daniel's for the taking.

He pored over the book and the script, comparing the two characters. One would offer him the chance to play his first unashamedly heterosexual romantic character and perhaps dispel any ideas among casting agents that he preferred gay roles. The other would provide him with the chance to make one of Forster's most dislikable characters flesh.

In his office Ivory asked Daniel, still sporting the last remnants of Johnny's shaving-brush coiffure, which of the two he saw himself as. 'I said no one in his right mind would ever admit to seeing himself as Cecil,' Daniel recounted later. 'And I'd rather play him than be him, understand what it is to be that man and thereby avoid the possibility of ever being him.'

As of that moment, the most unattractive role in the film was his. Like Bonham-Carter and Julian Sands, who was given the part of George, Daniel agreed to accept a modest fee of around £20,000 for the role. If the film, being made on a tight £2 million budget, returned a profit, they would share in a percentage of it.

At the time the money mattered little. Cecil represented the sort of challenge and the sort of showcase for his abilities that Daniel had been so eager to find. 'I do find flawed human beings more attractive – damaged goods,' he said once.

By the time he joined the production in June 1985 the crew had spent four and a half troubled weeks in Italy. Italian traffic noise and the wettest year in Europe for half a century had made shooting difficult. They returned relieved to Tonbridge, in Kent, for the last six weeks of filming.

From the moment his character first appeared in the living room of the Honeychurches' Surrey home, it was evident that Daniel had made the right choice of role. Heels clicked together, cheeks pinched, eyes fluttering, Cecil Vyse oozed pretentious arrogance from every pore. In his opening line he announced his engagement in Italian: '*I promessi sposi*, she has accepted me.' From then on Daniel's transformation was a wince-inducing wonder every moment his brilliantined figure appeared on the set. He turned to the tricks of his craft to make Cecil flesh. He wore pince-nez spectacles, carried a walking cane and wore a straw boater. 'English actors love the bits and pieces, the canes and glasses, well, I do anyway,' he said at the time. 'But they must be subsidiary to what is going on at the centre.'

What Merchant, Ivory and the distinguished English cast

thought even more miraculous, however, was how Daniel managed to make one of Forster's least sympathetic characters pitiable. Somehow he loaded the moment when Cecil proved too inept even to kiss his fiancée properly so that one felt sorry for the poor wretch. By magic he pulled off the same trick when Cecil, so wrapped up in himself and his intellect, reads a passage from Miss Lavish's novel without realizing he is describing Lucy's love for George. Most poignantly of all, he transformed the moment when Cecil is told by Lucy that their engagement is off into a time to share in his sorrow. This he achieved with a simple stroke of genius: he took off his shoes. During filming Daniel decided that Cecil should hear Lucy's news with his shoes in his hands. 'Shoes are strange things,' he explained afterwards. 'If you take your shoes off in a situation in which you are vulnerable, you'll feel ten times more vulnerable.'

Soon after finishing the movie Daniel explained what had drawn him so inexorably to Cecil. He told *City Limits* magazine: 'What drew me most towards Cecil is that he inhabits my nightmares. The person who can't open his mouth without saying something that will alienate human beings rather than attracting them.' He also admitted, however, that he did feel sympathy for him. Such suppressed outsiders were to become increasingly irresistible.

The fruits of Daniel's work on *My Beautiful Laundrette* and *A Room with a View* were yet to be released. Word about his accomplished double act was already flying around the industry, however.

Almost immediately after finishing work with Merchant–Ivory Daniel headed north, to Liverpool and Bradford, to star in another high-profile production. He had been cast in the role of Dr Kafka in Richard Eyre's production of Alan Bennett's *The Insurance Man*.

Bennett, the most gifted writer in England, had based his story amidst the claustrophobic Prague landscape of Kafka's classics *The Trial* and *Metamorphosis*. In it a young man named Franz, sacked for having a strange rash on his skin, seeks compensation from Dr Kafka, the insurance man of the title.

Franz Kafka had himself been such an insurance man by day. By night his experiences in the dark, suspicious, bureaucratic world of pre-First World War Prague fed his imagination as a writer.

The production had its troubles. Bradford, grimly doubling for the Czech capital, had almost witnessed a tragedy when a mock hanging scene misfired. A sixty-five-year-old extra, Jack Ferry, had been seconds away from choking when the crew noticed his safety harness had wrapped itself around his neck twenty feet above the ground.

Daniel was becoming a more self-absorbed character on sets. He seemed oblivious to all that was going on around him, Bennett recalled. In the diary he kept during shooting he wrote that 'Dan Day-Lewis, who plays Kafka, has a stooping, stiff-necked walk, which I take to be part of his characterization. It's certainly suited to the role, and it may be derived from the exact physical description of Kafka given by Gustav Janouch. Even so, I'm not sure if the walk is Kafka or Dan, since he's so conscientious he seldom comes out of character between takes and I never see him walking otherwise.'

Daniel revealed, however, that his Kafka was not quite the humourless brooder that history had him marked down as. 'Kafka wasn't the gloomy character everyone thinks he is from his books,' he told Geoff Sutton in the *Daily Mail*. 'I took the plunge and played him as he appeared to his colleagues. Whatever the inner turmoil, they saw him as tireless in his ambition, charming and considerate.'

Shooting on *The Insurance Man* ended in August. By then *My Brother Jonathan* was already winning Daniel more praise. As the series was aired on BBC2, Britain's TV critics switched on to the young man who had set Bedalian hearts beating: 'Dan Day Pin-Up'. Hilary Kingsley of the *Daily Mirror* spotted him first, calling him a 'handsome, frightfully sincere young hero to swoon over' after the first episode had been aired. She had mixed feelings about the 'plus-fours and lace hanky melodrama' but pledged she would tune in for ulterior motives. 'It's over the top but don't snigger. It looks lovely and Dr Jonathan could be just the tonic you need.'

As he emerged from his Kafkaesque cocoon, however, Daniel was on the verge of acclaim that went beyond his appealing bedside manner. With his usual ruthless efficiency, Stephen Frears had finished editing *My Beautiful Laundrette*. Neither he nor Kureishi nor anyone else could have predicted what was about to happen.

Laundrette had been made specifically for television and Channel Four. It had been shot on TV format, 16-mm film. In September 1985, however, it was premiered at the Edinburgh Film Festival. Daniel, along with Kureishi, travelled up to Scotland for the screening. 'Hanif and I went up to the Edinburgh Festival to see the first preview of *My Beautiful Laundrette* with no other intentions than having a good time, getting pissed and seeing some old friends,' he said at the time.

One of the first people the film's young star bumped into was John Schlesinger. The boy he had cast as a car-scratching hooligan in *Sunday, Bloody Sunday*, fourteen years earlier, had become a man. Little else seemed to have changed, however. 'He must have thought I'd gone through a natural progression from one thing to another without very much in between,' Daniel recalled.

My Beautiful Laundrette took the Festival by storm. Within hours of its first screening, critics were raving. 'If this ground-breaking, extraordinarily intriguing and undoubtedly controversial production does not reach at least some of this country's cinemas there isn't a great deal of hope for any effective collaboration between the small screen and the large,' wrote Derek Malcolm, the influential critic of the *Guardian*. 'Frears, Kureishi, Jaffrey and the two boys Gordon Warnecke and Daniel Day-Lewis deserve our congratulations, together with everyone concerned in this audacious, entertaining and possibly trend-setting venture.'

In the *Financial Times*, Nigel Andrews hailed *Laundrette* as 'one of the best Channel Four films in years'. 'The British soul is alive and well in this marvellous allegorical yarn.'

Suddenly Kureishi and Daniel were the toast of the town, and the film's producers Sarah Radclyffe and Tim Bevan were the most sought-after faces in the bars and restaurants of elegant Edinburgh. Offers of international theatrical distribution started pouring in. 'People urged us to allow it to be shown in the cinema, arguing that although initially it would be seen by less people, it would receive wider critical coverage,' Kureishi explained later.

Radclyffe and Bevan struck a deal with Orion for American cinema rights. It was to open in five cities the following spring. In Britain Mainline Pictures bought the rights to premiere the film in fourteen towns and cities.

It was released in cinemas across Britain at the end of November. With the eulogies of Edinburgh still ringing in everyone's ears, newspapers and magazines scrambled to profile the actor already being earmarked as a major new film star.

In the interviews he gave Daniel waxed nostalgic about the parallels between Johnny and his friends on the F-Troop at Millwall. 'We lived in Greenwich, which is hardly the Front Line, but I grew up in Lewisham and Deptford. I was known as the posh bastard. I had to use a lot of camouflage to survive,' he told the London *Evening Standard*. '*My Beautiful Laundrette* was almost like a home-coming.' He also credited a contingent at Sevenoaks for providing him with an early understanding of homosexuality.

The latest set of reviews were, if anything, more sensational than those of Edinburgh. 'Social historians of the future will have to reckon with it. It is provocative, illuminating, funny and tragic,' wrote Alexander Walker of the *Evening Standard*.

Kureishi collected much of the praise. 'The film has a richness of wit and conception one had despaired of seeing in British movies. Kureishi should surely be given a permanent resident screenwritership in UK cinema,' enthused Nigel Andrews, writing about the movie for the second time. 'As played by Daniel Day-Lewis and Gordon Warnecke, no more convincing examples of eighties youth exist on the screen at the moment,' declared Derek Malcolm, doing the same.

Daniel was singled out amongst a cast that was universally celebrated. 'Daniel Day-Lewis is extraordinarily good, apparently "Saaflunnon" born, as the rakishly handsome, fairly inarticulate yet tender-hearted ex-thug,' wrote the *Daily Mail*'s critic Shaun Usher.

'Johnny is a hypnotizing mixture of strengths and weaknesses,' remarked Ann Lloyd in *Films and Filming*. She predicted great things for both Daniel and Gordon Warnecke. They 'clearly have far to go,' she prophesied.

Within months the film was picking up its first major award. In February 1986, Stephen Frears, uncomfortable in a dinner-jacket, strode up the steps at London's Savoy Hotel and collected the *Evening Standard* award for the best British film of 1985.

The success of *My Beautiful Laundrette* had already given him a green light to go ahead with his long-cherished *Prick Up Your Ears*. A major Hollywood career would soon follow. He admitted afterwards that the success of his movie was a complete shock. 'I mean, a story about a gay Pakistani laundrette owner?'

For the movie's new discovery, Daniel Day-Lewis, a world of possibilities was also opening up. *My Beautiful Laundrette* was 'the first film that I ever passionately wanted to do', he said. 'It was the first time that I understood what an enjoyable process filming could be, even though it was agonizing at times.'

The agony and the ecstasy were only just beginning.

CHAPTER EIGHT

'WHO IS THIS DANIEL DAY-LEWIS GUY?'

'There's a divinity that shapes our ends,
Rough-hew them how we will.'
WILLIAM SHAKESPEARE, *Hamlet*

7 MARCH 1986. In New York it was a day like any other. The concrete canyons of Manhattan echoed to the 'wap-wap' wails of sirens and the 'asshole' exchanges of yellow cab drivers. In Times Square posters for the week's big movie, *Down and Out in Beverly Hills*, with Bette Midler and Richard Dreyfuss, were up. So, over on Wall Street, was the Dow Jones, three points on the day, closed at 1699.83.

The city's newspapers were in no doubt that stock in a new, young British actor would soon be heading the same way too. If there was a single day that dictated Daniel Day-Lewis's success, the first Friday in March 1986 was it. Filmic fate decreed that *A Room with a View* and *My Beautiful Laundrette* opened in New York on the same day: Merchant–Ivory's film at the Paris on Fifth Avenue and 58th Street, Frears and Kureishi's at the Embassy on Broadway and 72nd Street.

The critics could barely believe that the creator of the effete Cecil Vyse and the street-wise Johnny was the same person. Daniel had combined the sort of naturalistic English acting America still held in awe, all bits of business and twitches, with the mean, moody malignance of the Method, an American export to the world. The punk and the prig, the strutting peacock of gay pride and the strait-jacketed bundle of repressed sexuality made a city and then a nation double-take as one. 'I was thought to be a reincarnation of Beelzebub, because of the transformation,' Daniel came to say.

The city's, and America's, most influential newspaper, the *New York Times*, welcomed both films enthusiastically. Its respected critic Vincent Canby called *A Room with a View* 'a holiday out of time'. He called *My Beautiful Laundrette* 'a fascinating, eccentric, very personal movie'. He also called it 'the first real sleeper of the year'.

He saved his most generous adjectives for Daniel, however. After praising Helena Bonham-Carter for a 'remarkably complex performance', Canby wrote: 'Spectacular too is a new young actor named Daniel Day-Lewis, who plays the insufferable Cecil Vyse with a style and wit that are all the more remarkable when compared to his very different characterization in *My Beautiful Laundrette*.' He praised his Johnny as 'a man of almost unbelievable patience and reserves of decency – qualities that Mr Lewis realizes in a performance that has both extraordinary technical flash and emotional substance'.

Pauline Kael in the *New Yorker* heaped praise on his Cecil. For the first time she mentioned Daniel's name in the same breath as the greatest of English stage craftsmen. 'Day-Lewis brings it off with the sweet ease of a Gielgud,' she wrote.

New York Magazine's David Denby dusted down racier adjectives, 'rambunctious' and 'juicy' among them. '*My Beautiful Laundrette* is a work of substance,' he added.

Days later an inquisitive America was profiling the new discovery. The *New York Times*, again, led the way. Writer Leslie Bennetts introduced the chameleon to a new continent. 'Although they are both English, Cecil and Johnny could hardly be more different. They don't even look alike,' she wrote. 'Casual moviegoers . . . might never connect the two.' In his first major American interview, Daniel dutifully ran off a résumé of his life and career so far: privileged childhood, troubled teens, the reasons he was drawn to acting. 'It seemed like the only kind of alternative world into which I could escape,' he told Bennetts. And he explained why he had been attracted to the two men who had made him a star. 'So many kids aren't able to find their own morality, and it really interested me that Johnny managed to change his attitudes through guilt,' he explained. 'The thing I liked about

Cecil's character was that he made me laugh. I love being idiotic.'

As all this was unfolding, 3500 miles or so away on the stage of the Cottesloe Theatre on the south bank of the Thames, the chameleon that was 'Mr Lewis' was wearing yet another mask. His head shaven closer than for either of his Draculas, the skinheaded Daniel was finalizing rehearsals for a new production at the National Theatre. Dusty Hughes's highly ambitious *Futurists* was set in post-Revolution, 1921 Russia. There a group of fiery young geniuses fought, sometimes literally, to present their views of the new order being mapped out for their country.

Following *The Insurance Man*, Daniel was once more working with Richard Eyre. Eyre had cast his Kafka as Mayakovsky, the poet, one of the most strident voices of the period. The play's subject and its large cast – twenty real-life artists from the time had been woven into Hughes's piece – presented a challenge for audiences and critics alike.

'It's about history – Russian history after the Revolution – and about a group of poets, writers and painters who became the new mouthpiece of the new state. Eventually all that energy became a problem to the new state,' Daniel told *Midweek* magazine in the week before the play opened. Mayakovsky 'gave himself entirely to the Revolution', Daniel explained. 'He was really a lyrical love poet, but he spent years travelling around in the service of the state, lecturing to crowds of ten thousand. And in the end, as he wrote in a later poem, he crushed the throat of his own song.' Daniel's own father had of course faced the same dilemma. At least Cecil had been able to end his flirtation with Communism when he realized the doggerel damage it was inflicting on his poetry.

As America heralded Daniel, life back on the boards helped him to keep his perspective. 'I couldn't let all the attention get to me,' he said. 'If your feet aren't on the ground in the theatre you're in trouble.'

Not that he was feeling above it all. Unknown to his new American fans, Mr Lewis was capable of taking his chameleonic talents to such extremes that he was barely noticeable in a film. In November 1985, between *The Insurance Man* and

Futurists, he had travelled to France to appear in a low-budget movie being made by first time director Conny Templeman. The Anglo-French *Nanou*, starring the promising young Imogen Stubbs and Jean-Philippe Ecoffey, told the story of an English girl and her impulsive adventures in the rural Lorraine region of France. Daniel played the ex-English boyfriend of the heroine. After the heady hat-trick of prominent roles in *My Beautiful Laundrette*, *A Room with a View* and *The Insurance Man*, however, Daniel once more found himself reduced to a near cameo walk-on. By the time the film came out, a year later, his contribution had been reduced to blink-and-you'll-miss status.

Each day at the National was filled with further reminders of the fickleness of his trade. 'I could look at the unknown actor sitting next to me and think, cynically, in six weeks they'll be saying the same ecstatic things about him they are now saying about me,' he mused. He remembered the acclaim the 'new discovery' Ben Kingsley had won after his astonishing work on *Gandhi*. 'The critics were calling him "this extraordinary new actor"! And Ben Kingsley had been turning in smash performances in the Royal Shakespeare for twenty years.'

Still, there was plenty to tempt his ego. *Futurists'* opening on 17 March drew widespread praise. Charlotte Cornwell, Roger Lloyd-Pack and Jack Shepherd were well received but most critics singled out Daniel's ranting, raving performance as Mayakovsky.

Daniel 'could be the hottest property since Jonathan Pryce', Michael Coveney of the *Financial Times* wrote. 'Daniel Day-Lewis's gaunt, shaven-headed Mayakovsky convinces me, as no reading has ever done, that the hooligan bard was a spellbinding public performer,' declared Irving Wardle of *The Times*. Jack Tinker in the *Daily Mail* praised his 'powerful physical menace', Michael Billington in the *Guardian* thought Daniel's an 'outstanding vignette'.

The success of *Futurists* meant certain sacrifices, however. Mayakovsky's notices meant that Daniel could not attend a gala premiere for *A Room with a View*, held in the West End weeks after *Futurists'* opening night. So while Daniel raged at the Cottesloe it was left to Merchant–Ivory and most of his co-stars to curtsey, smile sweetly and engage in Edwardian-style small-talk with the guest of honour, the Queen Mother.

The critics engulfed *A Room with a View* with their praise. Iain Johnstone in the *Sunday Times* called it 'perilously close to perfection'. Alexander Walker in the *Evening Standard* homed in on the actor he now proclaimed an heir to the great Paul Scofield. Under a headline that read 'Daniel's a perfect snob!' Walker relegated the rest of the cast to supporting roles. 'Movies generally don't make for revelations,' he began. 'You don't often have to look twice at a character the minute he appears, once to register sheer surprise and again to enjoy and admire it.' Daniel's transformation from punk to prig left Walker drooling. 'He walks through life like a supercilious tuning fork, tingling correctly to each tiny cultural shock.' Daniel 'dominated' the film, his acting had 'walked away from the player and taken on a life of its own'.

The morning after the Royal Premiere the man now being simultaneously hailed as the new Gielgud, Scofield and Pryce, made a rare television appearance, on the breakfast station TV-am. The sight that greeted the housewife-dominated audience was as confusing as the conundrum now baffling New York and London. Interspersed with clips of the genteel Cecil were the comments of a world-weary-looking skinhead. Supposedly they were the same person. Even more confusingly, the skinhead was talking in a politely clipped English accent and mourning the fact that he had not been able to meet 'Britain's favourite grandmother'.

In a central London hotel room no more than two miles from TV-am's Camden headquarters, the bearded figure of Philip Kaufman was casting a bleary eye over the morning's TV offerings. The iconoclastic American film director was about to leave London, a fruitless search for the leading man in his latest and most ambitious project almost over. A channel-hopping moment later and his anxieties were disappearing.

'I didn't really know his work. I'd been on my last morning in London during which time I'd seen lots of actors. Still Tomas hadn't walked through the door. Then I flipped on the television set,' he recalled later. 'There was this bald-headed guy.

There was something about his look – a little wildness and sexuality and a sense of humour that told me he might be right.'

His first phone call of the day echoed the conversations across the Atlantic: 'Who is this Daniel Day-Lewis guy?' It turned out that Kaufman had been discouraged from seeing the wolfishly good-looking young Englishman winning such critical acclaim back in his native America. Kaufman was looking for an actor capable of playing Tomas, the lascivious hero of Milan Kundera's novel *The Unbearable Lightness of Being.* Casting agents had told the director Daniel was too young for the leading role of Tomas, in the book a middle-aged neuro-surgeon.

For a director whose reputation had been made by flying in the face of others' advice – Kaufman had defied doubters in Hollywood by translating Tom Wolfe's sprawling space-race epic, *The Right Stuff,* into an Oscar-nominated critical triumph – that news was enough to persuade him to talk to Daniel. 'I think it was in my favour that he caught me at that time of the morning, because I looked about fifty,' the cause of all this consternation recalled later. 'It was eight o'clock in the morning and I was completely knackered. Haggard, wrecked from the night before.'

Daniel read the book and the script, written by Jean-Claude Carrière with the co-operation of Kundera himself. He was not familiar with Kundera's work. Within a few pages he realized why it had been considered unfilmable.

The Unbearable Lightness of Being, hailed as a contemporary classic when it was published in 1984, blends profound philo-sophy with a tragi-comic love story. Set in Czechoslovakia during the 'Prague Spring' of 1968, it tells the story of Tomas, a sexual adventurer whose free-wheeling ways are compromised by his love for a beautiful country girl, Tereza. Tomas is torn between his love for Tereza and his purely sexual relationship with an outrageous artist, Sabina. The two represent the lightness of a life without the burden of commitment and the weight of expectation long-term love brings with it. What to choose, light or weight?

139

Awed with admiration for the writer, but confused as to how his book could be translated into a cogent movie, Daniel travelled to Paris to meet Kaufman, producer Saul Zaentz and Carrière. They spent a day talking about how the unfilmable could be turned into the filmable. 'The whole thing just seemed bizarre. Maybe that in itself made it more appealing to me. As it was with Phil, obstructions often make things more appealing,' Daniel said. At the end of the day's discussions he was persuaded to stay in Paris to meet Milan Kundera himself. Days later he was offered the part. He accepted.

Zaentz and Kaufman were working to a budget of $17 million. Given the difficulty of the material they were working with, however, they were not about to blow their budget on million-dollar stars. Lena Olin, a member of Ingmar Bergman's theatre company in Sweden, had been cast as the mysterious Sabina. The search for Tereza was proving more difficult, however. Kaufman had seen a number of European actresses but few had generated the energy and naïveté of Tereza. With the first day of shooting looming, however, he had hired an actress. 'But I was unsure about my choice,' he admitted.

It was then that another young actress came in to read for a minor supporting role. The doe-eyed French actress Juliette Binoche, then twenty-one, had won critical acclaim for her role in Leos Carax's *The Night Is Young*. Daniel was there for her audition with Kaufman. All three were taken aback at what happened. 'Juliette came in to read for a small part at the very last minute, just before we were to begin shooting, and Daniel was there,' Kaufman explained later. 'There was something about her . . . She and Daniel did one scene together. It was an extraordinary moment. All three of us were very startled.' As she left the room, Kaufman confided later, he and Daniel fell into each other's arms. The search for Tereza was over.

The chemistry between the two actors was irresistible. With only days to go before filming and despite the fact that her English was far from perfect, Binoche was given the film's key role. According to reports the relationship between the two young stars was to evolve into something deeper.

In 1986 Czechoslovakia, like the rest of the Eastern bloc, was still constrained by the crumbling forces of Communism. Freedom was still three years away. The remarkable events of 1968, when new Communist Party leader Alexander Dubcek declared his intention to introduce a more democratic form of Communism, only to be crushed by Soviet tanks within six months, were central to the story. But there was no possibility of Kaufman and his crew filming in Czechoslovakia. After a brief flirtation with Yugoslavia they decided to film in Lyon, France, where areas of the city bore a striking resemblance to the Czech capital.

Daniel, however, travelled alone to Prague. In some ways the chameleonic transformations he had made in the two roles which had elevated him to star status had not been such vast journeys. Cecil and Johnny had represented two aspects of Daniel's diverse experiences during his early schooldays. There were no flesh-and-bone role models for the prosy Edwardian or the pompadoured punk. But on the streets of Deptford and Lewisham and in the elegant drawing rooms of Greenwich, Litton Cheney and the Amises' house, The Lemmons, he had perhaps glimpsed raw material he could draw on. As he came to play Tomas, however, he was staring at a blank canvas. Creating a convincing Czech would present him with his sternest challenge.

In the book Kundera provided few clues about the way Tomas looked, dressed, worked and played. Daniel spent two weeks soaking in as much detail as he could about the way Tomas's countrymen lived. His dedication to understanding the characters he portrayed was now all-consuming. Shortly before the release of *The Unbearable Lightness of Being*, he made one of his earliest attempts to describe it. 'The preparation I do is an absolute confusion and if I went through the details of it, it would just sound like a shopping list and that would make it sound very mundane,' he explained to *Films and Filming* magazine. 'Overriding all that is a kind of central mystery which you're unaccountable for and that's whether any of this stuff is of any use and whether the end-product justifies the groping around you do.' Unsurprisingly he soon stopped attempting to explain his method again.

Part of the 'groping around' process was spent watching genuine brain surgeons operating in Prague. During the early part of his movie Kaufman planned to film Daniel at work in the operating theatre. He needed to look as self-confident in the environment as Tomas, a man who whistled to himself as he sawed open patients' skulls. He returned to the clinical world he had first visited for *My Brother Jonathan*. 'I was able to get a kind of sensory understanding: the smell of an operation, the view of an operation. But you can't, unless you're very stupid, believe that that qualifies you to cut people's heads open,' he said, explaining his research.

Only once did the vivid scenes he witnessed overcome him. 'I did feel really ill on one occasion,' he admitted later. 'I'd been intimidated by the surgeon, a tyrannical Pole, who started throwing instruments around. I could sense his need for me to fall over and it became a battle of wills. I did leave the room, but I came back.'

Back in London he worked on a convincing Czech accent with RADA voice coach Elizabeth Pursey. He also struck lucky when he met a Czech director, Ivan Passer, who had been in the country during the turmoil of 1968. 'I was having lunch with him and I didn't know he was from Prague but I recognized the sound that was coming out of him and asked if I could borrow him for an afternoon,' he told *Films and Filming* later. He carried his taped conversations with Passer throughout the shoot. His final touch was to have a gold dental crown fitted: they were common among Czech men at the time. It was the last detailed change he needed to become Tomas.

As filming began he felt comfortable that he would be able believably to play a brain surgeon. As with *My Beautiful Laundrette*, Daniel was most concerned about the sex scenes he had to play. There was an abundance of them, with both Lena Olin and Juliette Binoche. Most of them demanded that he was naked.

'If I had thought about thousands of people seeing me nude, I wouldn't have been able to walk on the set,' he said, publicizing the film later. 'The nude scenes presented me with enormous difficulties. They were a harrowing experience, I felt so vulnerable.'

After seemingly endless days having the lean contours of his body scrutinized from every conceivable angle by the camera lens of cinematographer Sven Nykvist, he eventually relaxed. 'There's no going back after that. There's no longer any point in hiding my frail body from the world,' he announced when the months of striptease were over.

The Unbearable Lightness was to be the most demanding film Daniel had yet worked on. Even though he was in most scenes in *My Beautiful Laundrette*, the film was shot in six hyper-active weeks. His contribution to *A Room with a View* had taken a similar length of time. Shooting on *The Unbearable Lightness* would go on for eight long months, with its male star working twelve to fifteen hours a day.

The effervescent company of Juliette Binoche helped make the process more bearable for Daniel, however. He admitted that her Tereza had been one of his main reasons for doing the film. He was drawn to the vulnerability and spirit of the character. As rumours of an off-screen relationship began to emerge, however, Daniel adopted the stance he has continued to take ever since. He said nothing either way.

In London, *Today* newspaper reported that the two had fallen in love. Daniel was attributed with the enigmatic quote: 'Obviously, we are very close.' Later in America the style magazine *Interview* attempted to prise the truth out of him. 'If I have avoided the question up till now, is it likely that I'll start speaking about it at this moment? I can't account for what people say. They allege what they want to allege. I haven't contributed to that and I don't intend to. They'll just have to draw their own conclusions,' he told writer Christina de Liagre.

By the end of the eight-month marathon he was emotionally and physically exhausted. *Another Country* had stretched him for a similar length of time, but there at least the load had been lightened by a supporting cast and the occasional day off. *The Unbearable Lightness* revolved around him. He was its star, its focus. There was barely a scene in which his presence was not pivotal.

He had also immersed himself in Tomas to such an extent

that many of his colleagues were unable to separate the player and the part. Kaufman confessed he was baffled. 'It got so I wasn't able to distinguish them in my mind, Daniel was Tomas or Tomas was Daniel,' he said after finishing the film.

Conveniently, perhaps, the confusion also hazed over the reality of relations between Daniel and Juliette Binoche. Clearly the characters of Tomas and Tereza were hopelessly in love. But if Tomas was really Daniel and Tereza was really Juliette?

By the time shooting had come to an end Daniel was torn by other forces. As his immersion in his characters was becoming more complete, so too the process of breaking away was becoming more difficult. He knew he desperately needed rest. 'I needed to go to a rehabilitation unit,' he said. But he also knew that the best way to rid himself of the ghostly presence of Tomas was to lose himself in another role.

Luckily his mind had been made up for him. Six weeks after filming was completed on *The Unbearable Lightness of Being*, he was contractually bound to star in his next movie. He admitted later that he was so drained by *The Unbearable Lightness* that he had considered breaking that contract. The facts that *Stars and Bars* was a comedy and that he was set to make it with his friend the Irish director Pat O'Connor combined to keep him from a potentially suicidal move. It also helped that the character he was playing was one he understood much better than the complex Tomas.

Daniel had been committed to starring in a screen adaptation of English novelist William Boyd's 1984 book *Stars and Bars* for more than a year. He was to play the hero, Henderson Dores, an emotionally strangulated English art dealer working in New York.

Boyd's book had been a best-seller. It told the farcical story of how Dores's pin-stripe straight life unravels after he is sent on a mission to the Deep South to procure an Impressionist masterpiece. The part required the sort of comic touch Alec Guinness and Peter Sellers used to provide the late Sir Michael Balcon. The producers found that finesse in Balcon's grandson.

Along with O'Connor, co-producer Susan Richards had auditioned more than half a dozen English actors known for their slapstick comedy. Daniel, however, fitted the comic bill better than any of them. 'They were all competent but predictable. Dan had absolutely no inhibitions,' remembered Richards. 'He reminds me so much of the great English character actors, such as Chaplin, Guinness and Sellers,' co-producer Sandy Lieberson enthused.

Daniel had not expected to get the job. He thought he was not the right age for the part – in the book Henderson is nearing forty. The young comic actors he was up against were much better suited, he thought. 'That probably brought me a kind of freedom I wouldn't otherwise have had. A gay abandon,' he said later.

Now, as he hurriedly prepared to slip into another skin, Daniel was comforted by the fact that the stuffy, repressed Englishman abroad was not such a draining leap as Tomas had been. If he had stayed at Sevenoaks, after all, he might have ended up in Henderson's immaculately polished, black Oxford shoes himself. 'This was a life that I understood more easily than, for instance, the life of Tomas,' he confirmed later. 'It was one I had been able to watch other people living, and so the distance to be travelled was not too great.' He admitted, however, that his fitness to step straight into a comedy was questionable at that time. 'I felt about as funny as a sick dog when we started!'

The movie, also due to star Harry Dean Stanton, was one of the first projects given the go-ahead in late 1986 by the then new chairman of Columbia Pictures, David Puttnam. The English producer, the inspiration behind the multi-Oscar winner *Chariots of Fire*, *The Mission* and *The Killing Fields*, had been installed on the Burbank lot in September in the hope that he had the Midas touch necessary to steer the studio, owned by Coca-Cola, out of a deepening financial crisis.

Puttnam had wanted to make *Stars and Bars* since Boyd's novel was first published. It had been embarrassingly turned down by Warners, with whom his Enigma company had a first-refusal deal. Now, with his hands on the Columbia purse-strings, he could finally bring the book to the big screen.

He saw the Anglo-Irish package of a best-selling Boyd

145

book, Irish director Pat O'Connor, maker of *Cal*, with Helen Mirren and John Lynch, and *A Month in the Country*, with Kenneth Branagh and Colin Firth, and the rapidly rising Daniel Day-Lewis as a dream team. It ended up a nightmare.

Daniel's stock had risen even higher at the beginning of 1987 as it was announced that he had won two major American awards. The 'double-whammy' he had delivered early in 1986 had not been forgotten. *My Beautiful Laundrette* had gone on to become one of the cult films of the year in New York, running for thirty weeks at one cinema. *A Room with a View* had gone one better, combining critical success with a blistering perform-ance at the box office. The £2 million Merchant–Ivory film had gone on to make $20 million at the US box office by the end of the summer of 1986. Along the way it became the first 'art house' English film ever to play in towns like Des Moines, Iowa and Boise, Idaho.

At the end of January Daniel was voted Best Supporting Actor in two of the most important turn-of-the-year polls that marked the run-up for the March Oscars. Both the New York Film Critics Circle and the National Board of Review of Motion Pictures made him their winner for the roles of Johnny and Cecil.

Kureishi was awarded the Best Screenplay award by the former body. He also won the National Society of Film Critics Prize. He went on deservedly to get an Oscar nomination, losing out to a slightly better-established though no less icono-clastic writer of socio-comedy, Woody Allen for *Hannah and Her Sisters*.

Daniel was unable to attend either of his award ceremonies, however. His next celebration was a subdued one. On 29 April 1987 he spent his thirtieth birthday in Atlanta, Georgia on the set of *Stars and Bars*. In keeping with the tradition of his Croom's Hill childhood there was a cake, a spectacular one, decorated with the Confederate flag. The choruses of 'Happy Birthday' were only a temporary respite, however. He was finding the pressure of once more being the star of a movie enormous. Even though *Stars and Bars* was a far less 'difficult' movie than *The Unbearable Lightness of Being*, the fact that

Columbia had high box-office hopes burdened the film's young star with a millstone the size of Stonehenge.

'In a film, particularly, you have a tremendous moral obligation because there's a lot of f---king money being spent. I'm told that's what they call the actors in films, "the money",' he confided in the magazine *American Film* afterwards. 'As you walk on the set, they say, "Here comes the money." It's appalling, but you have to accept that responsibility.'

His lack of rest began to tell. Reports of blown fuses surfaced. Daniel, normally unerringly polite, apparently erupted at a publicist. 'I disturbed him when he was in character and he started screaming at me,' the publicist confided to one visiting journalist from *Elle* magazine.

By the time filming had moved on to the streets of New York, Daniel was visibly approaching breaking point. As he filmed a late-night scene in which Henderson, dressed in nothing but a cardboard box, jogged on the spot waiting for the lights to change on the corner of Broadway and West 45th Street, he looked – and felt – little different from the strung-out street bums attracted by the warmth of the film crew's arc lights.

Hours later, after a nineteen-hour stretch of work, as he was interviewed by journalist Terry Minsky of *Elle* magazine, Daniel summed up his state of mind. He expressed his concern that because of 'a coincidence of timing' fame had come too quickly. 'I mean, it is totally unearned at this point,' he said, his head in his hands, his sentences fractured and faltering. He had not had the time others had had to make mistakes, he said. 'There used to be a system in England. You had a ten-year apprenticeship fucking it up time and time again, but just trying out anything possible,' he said. The twin triumphs of *My Beautiful Laundrette* and *A Room with a View* meant that he was no longer allowed that luxury. 'So I'm given a temporary period of time in which to make choices, and those choices will be drastically reduced when I fuck it up in a big way. In fact, I may have done it already,' he added.

The months spent relentlessly driving himself had clearly taken their toll. By the end of filming in June Daniel was drained. 'Dog meat' was his description of his state.

Back in London advance word on his performances in his two movies was strong. His agent Julian Belfrage's desk was groaning under offers of movies, television and stage work. After almost a year of continuous toil, however, Daniel once more felt trapped. The career that had been so liberating suddenly seemed constraining. 'I had a sense of being pressed in on.'

So once more he fled. Packing a bag with a little metal paintbox, some sepia ink, his running shoes and a thick roll of cash and Eurocheques, he took to the road. It was a time to seize some freedom again.

CHAPTER NINE

TRAVELLING LIGHT

'The heavier the burden, the closer our lives come to the earth, the more real and truthful they become.

'Conversely, the absolute absence of a burden causes man to be lighter than air, to soar into the heights, take leave of the earth and his earthly being, and become only half real, his movements as free as they are insignificant.

'What then shall we choose? Weight or lightness?'
MILAN KUNDERA, *The Unbearable Lightness of Being*

THE WALLS were bare apart from a torn-out newspaper picture of Keith Richards. The music swelling up inside them, however, was usually Bach. The ground floor housed a dining table, a cooker and a fridge, the second a racing bicycle and stereo. On the top floor lay a mattress. A hand-crafted bed would, eventually, join it. The only other fixtures and fittings, he said once, half serious, were 'bits of mould growing in the fridge'.

It was a house, not a home. A place to pass through, not a prison. It was a refuge, a hideaway, a bolt-hole in which to recharge run-down batteries. It was here, exhausted and once more a little confused, that Daniel Day-Lewis dropped anchor at the end of 1987.

The three-storey house in Ceylon Road, Brook Green, Kensington had replaced the Queen's Gate flat he had shared with Sarah Campbell as the place he made for when work allowed it. Since the couple's earliest days together in West Hampstead, friends had sensed that Sarah's hopes of making a life with Daniel might be dashed. They had watched as his work took him away for months on end, seen him pursue his ambition with a relentless drive. Sarah had waited stoically, but as

149

his roles absorbed him more and more, the distance had grown

'I think they were the great loves of each other's lives at that time. It was very sad, they were pretty settled,' recalled their friend and former flatmate Simon Dunstan. 'Sarah was a saint. She gave her life to him, she was never unfaithful, not that he was as far as I know, but the fact that he would go off for ages and not ring her or at least not communicate as much as one would have hoped meant it can't have been easy for her.'

Sarah had met Daniel's mother and, according to Sean Day-Lewis, was considered 'ideal marriage material'. All mothers' expectations for their sons are high. Sean recalled that over the years following the longest-running relationship he knew Daniel to have had, other romances foundered in the face of Jill's powerful influence. 'Dan went through the same thing that my father did, losing a parent young. My father was terrifically smothered by his father, and I guess it was the same with Jill and Daniel. There was that all-embracing love which is very difficult for parents to let go of. Or to acknowledge any of Dan's girlfriends as being worthy of him, which is something I have heard about quite a lot, that when he has had quite a long relationship it has been very difficult for the woman to stand up to Jill.' Sarah, however, had been an exception. 'She would have been an ideal wife if he had been able to settle down. She and Jill did get on.'

To his friends, however, Daniel simply seemed an unnatural candidate for marriage. 'From her point of view she definitely wanted it to be for keeps. But I don't think he would ever have committed himself. I don't think Daniel could do commitment,' said Simon Dunstan.

As Daniel's career had soared, work had become both a wife and a treacherous lover to him instead. 'I have always allowed the work to dictate to me, by necessity, the circumstances of my life. It's a marriage,' he confided to writer Sean French in 1989. Continuity in the real life that existed outside that marriage was almost impossible, he admitted. The depth of his immersion in lives like that of Tomas made the job of picking up the pieces of a normal, daily routine doubly difficult. 'You also have a life which very often bears no relation whatsoever to whatever life you lead outside of that film, depending on what you demand of yourself. And so whatever it is that you go back to when that film is over is almost invariably unrecognizable.'

His was a marriage riddled with infidelity, however. In many ways he had come to see each film and play as an act of adultery. 'Filming and theatre tend to involve an endless sequence of infidelities, and very, very disturbing infidelities because the love affair is a very passionate one, and therefore the betrayal in the aftermath is that much more painful,' he told the critic Richard Mayne in the film magazine *Sight and Sound* in 1989. 'I'm appalled by the process whereby one can fall in love, be part of the thing, be encouraged to be a part of it, and then no longer be of use to it – actually be discouraged from playing any part in its continued life, except in so far as one can appear in magazines and talk nonsense in interviews.' In at least one sense it seems that, like his father, he had already become a man 'better suited to starting affairs' than maintaining them.

By 1987 the die was cast. Since the break-up of the first, great love of his life, Daniel's disappearances into his roles appear to have mitigated against marriage and a stable, family life.

Tamasin had led the campaign to persuade him to invest his money in property. Before he had headed off to America to shoot *Stars and Bars* he had looked over the house in Brook Green, just a couple of streets away from his half-brother Sean's house on Caithness Road. While he was away, the wheels were put in motion; when he arrived back home it was his.

He had put up resistance. He had already seen his childhood home, Croom's Hill, dismantled. In February 1988 the Balcon family house in Upper Parrock suffered the same fate. His last surviving grandparent, Lady Aileen Balcon, passed away at the age of eighty-three. 'Those two places were home to me, I knew every corner, every crack in the paint. Every particle of dust I knew as well as I knew any person,' he recalled once. 'And overnight I saw those places disintegrate into nothing. Houses which had been apparently indestructible became nothing. That was tremendously shocking.'

At the age of thirty, he was realistically wealthier and more secure than his father had ever been at any time in his life. Both *Stars and Bars* and *The Unbearable Lightness of Being* had provided him with big pay cheques. Yet even though he was the owner of a place he could call that four-letter word, he was determined not to 're-create the concept of home again'. Instead, following the youthful example of Cecil Day-Lewis, he 'travelled light, unencumbered by the past'.

For months he had lived those words to the liberated letter. After finishing *Stars and Bars* in the summer of 1987, he headed back to England, crossed the English Channel and lost himself in the landscape of rural France. From there he moved on to Greece and then to Ireland. He wandered for three months.

He has shrouded his precise movements during those months in an enigmatic mist. His few clues about his time in the wilderness suggest a Byronic tour of the Continent, the travels of someone 'managing his pen with the careless and negligent ease of a man of quality', as Scott described the ultimate Romantic poet.

He spent some time 'hanging out' with students of the avant-garde director Patrice Chereau in the ancient, Holy Roman Empire citadel of Avignon. There he painted, ate, drank and philosophized under the stars, sometimes sleeping outside the walls of the Palais des Papes. 'Sometimes you need to go crazy, and it's easier to go crazy with strangers than with friends. I needed somewhere I could wander freely and be an idiot if I wanted to.'

By the time he felt ready to return from this 'idiotic exile', the house he had seen only briefly was his. Sean visited Daniel in his new home.

'It had been against the grain for him to have any luggage. But he was told to spend money on bricks and mortar,' Sean recalled. 'On the ground floor was the kitchen, on the middle floor he kept his bike and a record-player, which was usually playing an unaccompanied violin or cello suite by Bach, and the top floor was where he slept.'

152

The one-time aspiring cabinet-maker could not conceive of having any mass-produced furniture in his new home. 'Everything had to be specially made. That's why he was sleeping on the floor, he wanted a bed that was hand-made and bedded down upstairs while he waited for it to be delivered.'

His break had left him feeling physically rejuvenated. But once again he was emotionally muddled. The back-to-back strain of making *The Unbearable Lightness of Being* and then *Stars and Bars* had taken enormous tolls in different ways.

He had immersed himself so completely in Kundera's character Tomas that he found him impossible to shake off. By the end of the film Tomas's takeover was so complete that the director had voiced his concern about him. 'I think he went through a lot of torment with that character,' Philip Kaufman said as he completed the movie. 'He was trying to become Czech.'

'In a film that lasts six to eight weeks you can pace yourself – the end is always in sight,' Daniel conceded at the time. 'But six months is different, and I reached perhaps the lowest ebb I've ever reached.' He could have this conversation with himself many times in the future. As he adjusted to life in his new home in Brook Green, he began to question whether he wanted to carry on acting.

In April 1988, as *The Unbearable Lightness of Being* was readied for release in Britain, he dutifully helped promote it with a few selected interviews. In almost every one he publicly wondered whether he could bear the burden any longer.

'I'm privileged to be doing what I've dreamed of for many years, yet there are shameful moments, moments of exhaustion and despair when I feel I'm carrying an appalling burden up a very long hill,' he told *You* magazine writer Minty Clinch. The magazine, like many others that spring, saw 1988 as the year Daniel would emerge as one of the most potent forces in cinema. 'You may think this is my year of stardom. I think it's my year of nervous collapse,' he told Clinch.

He would not take on the strain of being 'the money' so lightly again. 'The pressure is that much greater when you are in the centre of a film. I wouldn't like to bear that responsibility four times a year, that would kill my enjoyment very quickly,' he told *Vogue* magazine.

He even had doubts about his right to assume other people's identities. 'There's the devil on your shoulder constantly reminding you of the inadequacies of the work, of the preparation, the ludicrousness of doing it in the first place, the nonsense of occupying another life. Who dares have the audacity to do that?' he worried in his interview with *Vogue*'s Katharina von der Leyen.

He lay on the floor of his new home 'brooding' over his future. And then one evening, as he remembers, there was 'a strange flopping' sound and the thud of something heavy landing in his letter-box. Inside he found a phosphorescent white script. He flicked to the first page and began reading. He felt a burden growing and lightening at the same time.

'It was a foot, this foot moving across, taking a record out of a rack, putting it back again, taking another one, moving across to a turntable, putting the needle on a very specific part, stopping the turntable, letting it go,' he was to recall. He flicked back to the front of the script and re-read the title. It said *My Left Foot*.

Later he recalled doing a jig of delight as he read the script. As it frequently had since the days when he was the most quixotic of Bedalians, Daniel's mood flicked from dark to light again. The Celtic twilight lifted.

As he read the script he realized it was telling him the same story he had heard delivered in a musical Dublin brogue a few months earlier. Daniel had met the theatrical producer Noël Pearson at a party held in Dublin in honour of Pearson's friend, the composer Elmer Bernstein. As the drink flowed, the snowy-haired impresario began doing what Dubliners do best. 'Noël began telling me a story, a quite incredible story about a man's life,' Daniel explained later.

My Left Foot was an adaptation of the autobiography of Christy Brown. Brown, who had died at the age of forty-nine in 1981, was one of twenty-two children, thirteen of whom survived, born to a poor Dublin family. He had arrived in the world with cerebral palsy and as he grew up was unable to speak or use his hands. His mother was told that he was a useless vegetable, who would be confined to his own world and a wheelchair for the rest of his life. Yet Brown overcame his appalling disabilities to become a successful painter and writer – in both cases working with the one functioning limb God gifted him, his legendary left foot. He lived life to the full, boozing and brawling his way around Dublin, eventually marrying a pretty young nurse called Mary with whom he had ten happy years. He wrote four novels, one of which, *Down All the Days*, stands unchallenged as one of the finest pieces of post-war Irish writing.

Daniel was overwhelmed by the power of the screenplay by two names that were unknown to him, Jim Sheridan and Shane Connaughton. It was not just the luminosity of the paper that lit up that murky early evening in Brook Green. So many of the scripts he was sent were formula-Hollywood. Plot-driven, predictable – pap. Even worse, they were badly written, to the poet's son the greatest sin of all. 'I can't ever bring myself to be involved with things that I don't find interesting or well written. I am far more likely to read something that's beautifully written with poor structure than something with great structure that is badly written,' he said once.

My Left Foot was written in a sparse, gritty language that gripped Daniel. 'The best screenplays I've read have been the most laconic. It's like poetry: if someone knows how to use very few words, it's far more effective than someone who uses a great many more to say less,' he told the magazine *US Film Comment* at the time.

That day Daniel binged on the script that broke this drought. He would later thank the strangers who had dropped it into his lap for 'rekindling my desire to work'.

Pearson, who had known Brown for almost twenty years, acting as his unofficial agent for many of them, wanted him to play the part of Christy. Daniel could see the film would be fraught with problems. Did it have an audience? Could he possibly play the part? Should an able-bodied man play a disabled man anyway? He contacted Pearson in Dublin and a meeting was set up. Pearson agreed to fly over to London to see Daniel.

Pearson and Jim Sheridan had become close friends in New York. The producer had based himself there in 1982, drying himself off after the latest expensive splash in a remarkable roller-coaster of a career. Pearson had worked with the legendary Brendan Behan and was acknowledged as one of Dublin's most charismatic theatrical producers. He had never been afraid of taking risks, however, and had had his fingers burnt on both sides of the Atlantic. In New York a ballet version of John Millington Synge's classic, *The Playboy of the Western World*, and another play called *Brothers*, with American TV star Carroll O'Connor, failed to ignite Broadway. The latter, an ambitious $850,000 production, had been 'slaughtered' by the critics. In 1982 a vast VAT bill from the Dublin tax inspectors had become Pearson's latest headache. As he licked his wounds, Pearson found himself in the city where every Irishman was assured a warm bath.

Sheridan had arrived in New York after leaving Dublin's Project Arts Centre, where he had created a vibrant alternative theatre, in 1980. He became the artistic director of the Irish Arts Center there and had also begun studying film at New York University. Sheridan and Pearson struck up a kinship, eating and drinking in O'Neill's, a popular haunt with Irish exiles opposite the Lincoln Center. Sheridan, like Pearson impatient to break free from theatre, had been inspired by the producer's telling of the Christy Brown story to write the script of *My Left Foot* with his friend Shane Connaughton in a frenetic fortnight.

Sheridan, wild-eyed and graced with a gift of the gab extraordinary even for a born-and-bred Dubliner, persuaded Pearson that he should direct the film, even though it was his first venture into movie-making. His experience on a film set extended to a six-week course on which, he admitted later, 'I did the sound on a film about growing tomatoes.'

Sheridan was in New York when he heard that Daniel Day-Lewis was interested in talking about the movie. Driven on by his wife Fran, he went straight to JFK airport and boarded a plane to London. He was not going to miss out. As he sat down and talked to the unlikely duo for the first time, Daniel, by now the possessor of hard-won and hard-headed insights into the brutal realities of the film industry, came to two instant conclusions. He summed up the first a year or so later: 'I didn't even think the film would be made. There was no financing. Noël had never produced a film before, Jim had never directed a film before. We were quite a threesome.' The second was that he was in.

My Left Foot appealed for reasons beyond the brilliance of its script and the possibilities of escape into another, extraordinary life, however. The draw of Ireland and its whispering roots had become powerful again. In the fifteen years since the last family holiday on their father's beloved west coast, both Daniel and Tamasin had made fleeting returns. Tamasin, by now married to John Shearer and the mother of two children, Miranda and Harry, was eventually to buy a place in County Mayo, scene of so many of her own happiest childhood memories.

Events in Britain in 1987 persuaded Daniel to tie himself closer to the land of his father's birth. He had grown increasingly depressed by the divisiveness of Thatcherism. When, that year, the Conservatives secured a third term of office, his heart sank. 'You know there is not a very good mood in this country at the moment,' he told the American journalist Graham Fuller in an interview at the end of 1987, hinting at the thoughts forming in his mind.

Even though he had carried a British passport, his father had been born in Ireland. Daniel discovered that this qualified him for an Irish passport. He applied and was given one.

It was not for a year or more that English newspapers picked up on the 'defection'. When they did, Daniel played down the protest vote, reportedly saying to *Today* newspaper: 'I am browned off with a lot of things here like a lot of people. It's more to do with the fact that I'm proud of my Irish connections than disgusted by my British.'

Over a meal at Sean's house in Caithness Road, Brook Green, however, Daniel confided that politics had been the main reason he changed his passport. 'It was at our house in Brook Green that he told me. There was a general feeling of gloom about the English electorate. He was very depressed at the prospect of more of the same,' Sean recalled.

In keeping with his father's socialism, Daniel was worried by the rampant capitalism that was then the defining force of eighties Britain. 'It was more a reaction against letting loose market forces and what Thatcherism stood for rather than Thatcher herself,' according to Sean.

During Daniel's early days at Brook Green, the distance that had existed earlier between the half-brothers closed. The two shared a passion for football, Daniel still following Millwall, Sean supporting their East London rivals, West Ham. Daniel regularly visited Caithness Road for dinner. 'He was a great appreciator of food,' recalled Sean. Daniel never invited Sean and Anna around for dinner, however. 'He was not confident enough to cook for us, I don't think.'

He was equally diffident when it came to his love life. 'Dan has this ability to compartmentalize which is very like our father.' Sean and Anna were never introduced to Sarah Campbell or invited over to the Queen's Gate flat, even though it was no more than two or three miles away. 'I never met her, that's odd, I suppose,' said Sean. 'Even when he was at Bedales he was like that. All the girls there were madly in love with him according to his mother, but he never said anything or presented any of them.'

Daniel's adoption of an Irish passport induced jealousy but little surprise. His half-brother sensed his rootlessness too. Brook Green was a phase, nothing more. 'Dan had a fixed home in Greenwich, but it was a home which did become difficult when he was young. There was also the schizophrenia of going to the state school and then being sent off to the semi-toffs. I think he was pretty rootless genuinely, but then who isn't who is sent away to boarding school?'

Ireland offered him another country, a romantic alternative home. He was, of course, repeating his father's behaviour. 'My father was rootless and in the end put on this Irish thing partly with genuine feeling and partly as an act of will. In the end he needed to have roots and that's where he tended towards. The old soft ts would come out when he was doing lectures or readings whereas when he was a young man he had a very public school accent.

'There is something about our temperament, insofar as Dan and I have the same, where we need to have something outside that which you are attached to that you can romanticize because you are dissatisfied with what you are living in. The definition of romance is that it is not earthy.'

As Sean got to know Daniel better, it struck him more and more that acting – with its cycles of intense passion, ultimate infidelity and escape – was the perfect conduit for this restlessness. It allowed a spirit reminiscent of his and Daniel's father to stay true to himself.

'Cecil was great at starting romances but not so great at marriages. Cecil said about himself, in general, he started things with enthusiasm but found it hard to finish them. Being an actor is terribly suitable for that. Once you have made it you can shrug your shoulders and go off to do something else.

'That's what would happen. We would see him and then he was working and he was incommunicado.'

Daniel's devotion to his work reminded Sean of their father too. He had the 'blade of ice' at his centre. There was also an unmistakable sense that success was expected of the youngest son of this illustrious father. 'There was always this feeling that he had to do well for our father even though he wasn't there, whereas anything he did would have been marvellous as far as Jill is concerned,' said Sean.

By the spring of 1988 the unlikely production that was *My Left Foot* had become the focus for Daniel's newest passion. Sheridan and Pearson planned to film the movie in Dublin. It would offer Daniel the chance to work in his newly adopted homeland. It also appealed for yet another reason. Playing a cripple might help deconstruct the image Daniel had by now acquired.

The release of *The Unbearable Lightness of Being* consolidated Daniel's reputation as the most versatile young actor in Europe. It also marked his emergence as a sex symbol for the cine-literate. The film was no mass-market blockbuster. Yet from the moment preview audiences heard Tomas whisper his mischievous mantra, 'Take off your clothes', to an attractive nurse in the film's opening minute, newspapers and magazines of all intellects realized that Daniel Day-Lewis was a matinee idol in the making.

In London, the tabloid *Daily Star* devoted two racy pages to the actor it described as Dazzlin' Dan. 'He's tall, dark, mean, moody and magnificent. He's Daniel Day-Lewis, Britain's latest heart-throb,' its piece began.

'Don't Call Me Dirty Dan', ran another headline, in *The People*. In an interview with the paper Daniel had asked writer William Hall to 'spare the thought' of comparing him to Britain's then most popular TV character, the philandering publican 'Dirty Den' in the BBC series *EastEnders*. The request not only provided the best quote, it wrote the headline too.

'People are always groping around for some label and this will no doubt turn me into a modern Casanova,' Daniel told *The People*. 'That's all right. But I like to think there is more to the film than bedroom frolics.'

In America reaction had been a notch more cerebral, but the message was the same. There were comparisons with *Last Tango in Paris*, Brando's controversial 'shocker' of the seventies.

Britain's more serious critics agreed that there were depths beyond the diverting sight of Daniel, Olin and Binoche's bed-hopping. Shaun Usher in the *Daily Mail* thought all three leading players 'faultless'. Daniel, he wrote, 'sparkles with mischievous lust'. The *Sunday Times*'s George Perry said Daniel's 'consistent well-judged performance establishes him as an international star'. 'He achieves the relaxed look of a man to whom life, sex and success come too easily.' Derek Malcolm in the *Guardian*, while finding Kaufman's direction suggestive of 'prose rather than poetry', said the acting of the main trio 'transcended' that heavy-footedness.

Meanwhile, however, *Stars and Bars* was suffering from the seismic after-shocks of a piece of Hollywood high drama. It had been in September 1987, a year after David Puttnam's arrival at Columbia, that the *Wall Street Journal* broke the news of his departure. 'Columbia Asks Puttnam To Leave Post' ran its headline, inaccurately as it turned out. Puttnam was desperate to leave after months of clashes with his bosses at Columbia and their owners, Coca-Cola. His $3 million pay-off was a compromise. He wanted out, they wanted him out.

The disastrous consequences of the 'experiment' of placing a visionary, internationally minded movie-maker at the head of a major Hollywood studio rumbled on for months afterwards, however. As the *Journal*'s prescient exclusive suggested, the end of 'the shortest tenure of a major studio chief in recent history' had spelled bad news for any of the projects associated with the Briton's regime. 'Dozens of projects he put into development may never see the light of day,' the *Journal* had predicted.

In the aftermath of Puttnam's departure some of the enemies he had made during his time in Hollywood seemed to extract their revenge. 'They are strangling my pictures at birth,' he protested at the time. Caught in the crossfire, *Stars and Bars* was reduced to the status of political pawn. It had been finished in October 1987, but at post-Puttnam Columbia the feeling was that it was 'a misfire, not funny'. O'Connor and Susan Richards had to fight off attempts to retitle their movie *An Englishman in New York*.

If there was one quality Daniel had acquired from his grandfather, however, it was tenacity. Mick Balcon's advice in such a situation would undoubtedly have been to fight for the film's release. With Pat O'Connor, Daniel took every opportunity to attack the new Columbia regime's decision to keep *Stars and Bars* in limbo. 'We are not going around saying this is a wonderful film which should be seen, because we are not in a position to judge in that way,' he told *Interview* magazine in America early in 1988. 'But we devoted a great deal of our time to it. Pat was on it for three years. I kept faith with it for two years before we were finally allowed to make it.'

'There's no way we can prove it has anything to do with David's departure, of course,' Daniel told the *Independent* in London. *Stars and Bars* was eventually released in the United States that month, April 1988. Its fate was sealed by the critics, many of whom seemed to use their reviews in part as a soapbox to peddle their own political take on the Puttnam saga.

'David Puttnam's film legacy *Stars and Bars* represents a major faux pas,' the *Variety* review began, setting the tone for what was to follow. It called the film an 'unfunny mix of farce and misdirected satire' with 'no conceivable audience apart from undiscriminating pay cable viewers'. 'Pic self-destructs rapidly.' It accused O'Connor of having 'no feel for comedy'. As for Daniel, the trade bible's review thought him 'downright embarrassing.'

In New York the *Village Voice* laid into Puttnam. 'David Puttnam . . . who commissioned the movie, must have thought the subject foolproof – a fish out of water comedy with something real to say about America. In the eighteenth century people were tarred and feathered for less – now they get the golden parachute. Who says the Yanks haven't been civilized?'

In America, the country where the film was made but ended up with few friends, *Stars and Bars* died. It was not even allowed to do so peacefully. Studios normally stop reporting films' takings when they drop below a certain level. Columbia, however, carried on issuing detailed figures for weeks of how little money *Stars and Bars*, and two other Puttnam films, were making. By the end of its run the film which cost $8 million to make had grossed $100,000 at the US box office.

Even before the final twists in the saga Daniel was adamant. 'After the way they've behaved I never want to work for Columbia again – but then they hated the film so much I can't believe they will ever employ me again,' he said in April 1988. Columbia would want to. Everybody would.

CHAPTER TEN

A HORNY CRIPPLE FROM CRUMLIN

'You always feel Daniel will inflict more damage on himself than anybody else.'

JIM SHERIDAN, December 1993

THE FOOTBALL scene confirmed it.

For days now cast and crew had whispered their wonder at the transformation, nodded reverentially in the direction of the twisted, twitching figure, sipping drinks through straws, heaving his contorted frame around as if it were some lumpen, lifeless, human sack of spuds.

'Christy' had been this way since day one of shooting, 18 July 1988. Not once had he broken out of his self-imposed confinement. Not once had he freed himself from the cripple's cage. Not even when some of the late writer's relatives had visited the set to see him. He had delivered a spittled, slack-jawed greeting. The faces of the relatives had paled, as if they had just seen a ghost. 'That wasn't a fellow playing Christy – it was Christy!'

'Madness or Method?' No one knew quite which it was. After the football scene they did. It was both.

'We set up the cameras and put Daniel in place,' Jim Sheridan explained later, the astonishment still etched on his face. 'The plan was to roll the ball towards him and he'd fall on his side and stop it with his head. When we were ready I gave the ball a real boot, as hard as I could to see what would happen.'

As the battered leather ball floated through the air, Sheridan and his crew watched Daniel, his face mangled in concentration, slide his body across the cobbled street. Arms fixed helplessly at his side, he arched his neck and with all the force he could muster swung his head towards the point on the floor where the football was headed. Miraculously the ball arrived to cushion his forehead from the cobbles. A fraction of a second sooner or later and his head would unquestionably have been split wide open.

'His brains could have been splattered all over the road,' Sheridan recalled afterwards. 'He's scary.'

From the moment he picked up the script, that luminous script with its grab-opening page, its air of impossibility and its wonderful title ('All the things I've been involved in I've been struck by the titles'), Daniel Day-Lewis had harboured an idea that he would one day inhabit the prison that was Christy Brown. 'I felt I understood Christy, knew what he was about, the bloody-mindedness, the sense of being trapped.'

At 'A' Stage, Ardmore studios in July and August 1988, he was tight in the grip of the late writer's chains. Only days before he arrived on the set, a pudding bowl haircut on his head, shrunken by his transformation, he had his opportunity to spare himself the pain. As he readied himself for the seven-week shoot, set for Ardmore and locations in Dublin and the Wicklow Mountains, Daniel had received a phone call from Noël Pearson, the producer.

Every since his first conversations with the silver-haired impresario, Daniel had been aware of the precariousness of the film's finances. Pearson had spent years touting the idea all over Ireland. He had approached anyone and everyone on whom he smelled investment money.

He had mixed luck. RTE, the Irish national TV station, had agreed to invest £150,000 of the £1.7 million they were looking for. Rehab, Ireland's leading charity for the disabled, had put up another £50,000. Assorted businessmen, including pop music figures like Rod Stewart's former manager Billy Gaff and U2's manager Paul McGuinness, had contributed too. For every offer, however, there had been a dozen refusals. One leading pop promoter had turned them down with the visionary view: 'Who would want to see a film about a horny cripple from Crumlin?' According to Pearson another businessman in Dublin had offered to pay him not to make the movie!

As his company, Ferndale, had ploughed ahead with plans to make the film, Pearson was still lacking a major investor. Virgin and Vestron, two companies he had interested, had said no. Many of the potential backers distrusted Pearson's choice of Sheridan as a novice director. A week into pre-production on the film only 40 per cent of the money was in place.

Salvation eventually came in the shape of Granada, the recently set up film-making arm of the English television company. The week before filming was due to start, however, their share of the budget had yet to be finalized. The credit line Pearson needed to finance the shoot was not in place.

So it was that the news had to be broken to the film's main stars: Daniel, and leading Irish-born stars Brenda Fricker, who was to play his mother, Ray McAnally, his father, Fiona Shaw, Christy's fictional mentor Dr Eileen Cole, and Ruth McCabe, his wife Mary. For Daniel, who had agreed to do the movie for £70,000 and a share of any profits it might eventually make, it made no odds.

'A week before we were due to begin shooting I had to ring Daniel and tell him we would not have the money to pay him,' the producer remembered later. Daniel's response was instantaneous: 'It doesn't matter,' he said. 'I'm arriving on Tuesday anyway.'

After months of inactivity and the frustration of seeing *Stars and Bars* locked in Hollywood limbo, he was burning to work again. He had no doubts about the project or the team Pearson had trusted to bring it to fruition. Christy was to prove the perfect part into which to pour the anger he felt, Sheridan the ideal man to bring it out.

Daniel had no fears about entrusting himself to the first-time director. Since their first meeting there had been a tentative bond. 'When you meet him, you know him almost immediately. I have rarely met anybody who has met him that hasn't wanted to strike up that rapport,' Daniel explained once.

Now, as he brought Christy Brown to life, he knew his instincts had been right. He would come to work with Sheridan again. He was exhilarated by his energy, encouraged by his occasional madness. He became the director's number one

165

admirer, De Niro to his Scorsese. 'I suppose I had never met anyone mad in quite the same way.'

As he prepared to play Christy he knew that self-consciousness would be death to the role. He could not be seen to be an actor playing the part of a cerebral palsy victim. He had to inhabit the role.

The bitterness of the 700 disabled members of British Equity made that all the more important. One actor, Nabil Shaban, had threatened to lead demonstrations against the casting. 'I find it incredible that an able-bodied actor has got the part when the whole point of the film is that he has got cerebral palsy,' he complained in the actors' newspaper, *The Stage*. 'Disabled actors never seem to get able-bodied parts – so why is it that Christy Brown's story is being played by Daniel Day-Lewis of all people?'

Pearson had tried to defuse the situation by summoning up the spirit of his old friend. Of course Christy would approve of a glamorous actor playing him, he would have expected nothing else. 'If Christy Brown was alive when we were doing this film he'd be looking for a young Marlon Brando to play himself, or Robert Redford or John Wayne,' he said. 'If you sent a guy in a wheelchair to play him he'd go mental. He considered that we are all the same.'

He had calmed Daniel's concerns with similar words months earlier. 'I did put it to Noël Pearson that it was a very odd thing for me to do and perhaps I wasn't the best person to do it.'

He had arrived in Dublin to discover no shortage of advice on how to play the hard-drinking legend that was Christy Brown. 'Every taxi-driver had a story about Christy, had been banned from a pub with him,' he explained later. 'It was everyone's story, their business as well as ours. We had to fight to make it our secret, because films should be secretive experiences.'

To study the realities of life as a cerebral palsy sufferer, Daniel went to the Sandymount School and Clinic in Dublin, Ireland's leading centre for the treatment of the disabled and home to 120 or so children and adults, many of whom faced the same problems as Christy. There he was helped by the head-master, Tony Jordan.

At first, however, Jordan was unsure of the tall dark stranger who presented himself unannounced in his office. 'I will never forget the day he turned up. There was a knock on the door and this tall gentleman dressed completely in black came in. He told me he was Daniel Day-Lewis, which didn't mean anything at all to me at the time,' recalled Jordan. 'He told me that he was over here to make a film on the life of Christy Brown. He wanted to know whether he could spend some time with us. There had been several efforts to do a life of Christy Brown in the past. I wasn't very interested in giving the man much time really.'

There was something about his unexpected visitor's clever-looking head and earnest frown, however, that made the head-master continue the conversation. His assurance that the film was being made by Noël Pearson, whom Jordan knew, and Jim Sheridan, whom he had heard of, softened him. 'That's when I knew it was a serious venture.'

Sandymount served up its first secret early on. He did not know it, but Daniel's past was inextricably linked with the school's.

Sandymount had been founded by the eminent Dubliner Dr Robert Collis. Tony Jordan had been in the process of organizing a memorial to Christy Brown – Collis and the school's most famous product – long before Daniel alerted him to *My Left Foot*.

'I told him that I was gathering all these people together, including most of Christy's brothers and sisters and three of the people who had known him best, Dr Patricia Sheehan, Catrina Delahunty and Dr Collis's widow, Han Collis. He was very excited about that. He asked permission to bring Pearson and Sheridan with him,' recalled Jordan.

On the day of the Memorial Daniel mixed with members of the Brown family, some of whom had already agreed to talk to him, and other star-struck guests. 'Eventually I got hold of him and said there's somebody here who wants to meet you, Dr Robert Collis's widow. They met and he was dumbstruck, he couldn't believe it. He was utterly knocked for six.'

Neither the headmaster nor Daniel knew that Han Collis was the same woman who, decades earlier, had come to stay at Croom's Hill with Cecil and Jill Day-Lewis. The Dutch-born doctor had just given birth to Dr Robert Collis's child. At the time, Collis was still married to his first wife. He wanted Han to be safe within a family atmosphere. In his hour of need he turned to his old friend Cecil Day-Lewis, the poet who often visited him in Dublin and Bo Island, in the shadow of the Wicklow Mountains, during the summer.

'She was a figure from his past. He couldn't believe it. All he kept saying was 'Wait until I tell my mother this'. It was an incredible coincidence,' remembers the headmaster.

There were further portents. On a visit to Dublin around 1949, Cecil Day-Lewis had gone to a party at Dr Robert Collis's house. There the famous Anglo-Irish poet had found himself collared by a crippled young writer called Christy Brown.

It was Christy's widow Mary who recalled the story later. 'Dr Robert Collis was a great help to Christy and encouraged him to have his work published. He used to hold soirées. One night Cecil Day-Lewis was there and Christy arrived with some of his poems. He was about seventeen and raging with enthusiasm, he had already been published in the *Irish Independent*,' she recalled. 'Cecil Day-Lewis read them through very quickly and said, "Yes, yes, but too many adjectives. Try again in ten or twenty years' time!" That really hurt Christy but he said it really spurred him on.'

The thought that in some small way, perhaps, he might make amends for his father's intolerance added yet more fire to Daniel's determination to play the role. He set to work.

Daniel did not arrive at Sandymount a stranger to the cruelty inflicted by nature on its pupils and patients. He had seen his mother once more lose the man in her life to the ravages of illness. Antony Brett-James had died in March 1984, after a long and courageous fight which had left him crippled and incapacitated. He had suffered from a rare wasting disorder. Daniel and his mother could only watch helplessly as the 'great scythe' once more claimed a loved one. James was only sixty-three when he lost his fight. His obituary in *The Times* made no reference to his illness nor to Jill, concentrating instead on his achievements as one of the outstanding military historians of his time.

Daniel rented a house near Sandymount. Most days for two months he cycled to the school to join in its routine. 'It was observational. We gave the full facilities for him to come and go and spend time round on the campus. There were one or two kids here who were using their feet to type with at the time. Mary Kiernan and another lady, Helen Curtiss, who has died since,' explained Tony Jordan.

'He never got in the way, he was very sensitive to the pupils and the staff, I could not praise him enough. He's a terrific guy, I was extremely impressed.'

With Kiernan and Curtiss at his side, Daniel began to experiment painting and writing with his own left foot. He was introduced to the disabled painter Gene Lambert and became a regular visitor to his flat in Dublin.

When the film was finished he would be asked whether doing such a thing was difficult. When he had recovered from what he felt was the offensiveness of the question, he would reply: 'I could say it was difficult or at the same time that's the easiest stuff. Anyone can learn to paint with their foot. But not everyone *has* to learn to paint with their foot.'

By the time he arrived on set, his head lolling hopelessly around, rag-doll-like, an ugly mixture of spittle and grunts spewing out of him whenever he attempted to speak, Daniel was prepared. From that moment he remained in character as Christy. So, unable to use anything other than his left foot, he had to be fed by crew members at meal-times and helped around the set when there were no wheelchairs around.

Soon the totality of his transformation frustrated as much as it thrilled. There were times when crew members cursed him as they were forced to carry his crunched-up frame over cables and other obstacles they knew he could easily have overcome himself.

In the evenings, after a hard day's filming, cast and crew would go out for dinner together. 'Christy' would come with them, drawing disdainful looks from restaurant diners with his vulgar behaviour just as the writer had done years before. For Daniel, however, it was all more fuel for his understanding of what it might be like to be incarcerated in the human wreckage of a cripple's body, to be mistreated by 'normal' people.

Gene Lambert watched the metamorphosis. 'He had this unique experience of being able to see it from both points of view, so when he went on stage and was angry, he was really angry. Because of the wires across the floor, because he was dependent, he had to be washed, fed, dressed, he had to experience the thousand little humiliations that occur, irrespective of your abilities,' he said.

In many ways Christy was an extension of Henderson Dores, Cecil Vyse and Tomas. Each was imprisoned by inarticulacy. Dores and Vyse were variations on the same suppressed Anglo-Saxon theme. Sex was not Tomas's problem. He simply could not bring himself to admit he was in love.

'One of the things I am most intrigued by is inarticulacy. And I don't mean the ability to put words together,' Daniel said once. 'Christy Brown's struggle – as it is for most of us – was to express himself. And that is the thing that I'm nearly always attracted to in a part; the difficulties, the personal problems people have in giving of themselves. Whether it's in words, in painting or passion.'

The more furiously he hurled himself into the part of Christy, the clearer it became that extraordinary things were happening. Ray McAnally was overwhelmed by the re-creation of the writer he had known himself.

'I knew Christy. He used to come to the Queen's Theatre a great deal,' the actor said. 'Daniel has caught the essence of Christy superbly. He has caught the whole feeling, the blind fury of being treated as a moron when you're more intelligent than the person talking to you.

'It's like the way actors normally feel. They are normally treated as if they were talented pets.'

The shoot lasted nine frenetic weeks. After visiting Sandymount, Sheridan organized for some of the pupils to appear in the movie. 'Some of the children got parts, about twelve or

170

fourteen of them were in it briefly, they appeared in the back of an ambulance,' remembered Tony Jordan.

As shooting came to an end, Daniel stepped free from his wheelchair. His last act as Christy was to sign autographs for visitors to the Ardmore set, with his left foot of course.

The difficulties he had already acknowledged in 'letting go' of his parts might have been more acute than ever before had he not, within days, had yet another role to immerse himself in.

This time he would adopt the approach of a deep-sea diver, emerging from the ocean bed. His decompression would be gradual. Within days he was on a plane to Argentina to play another high-spirited Irishman, one he would lace liberally with the spirit of Christy Brown.

Before leaving, Daniel returned briefly to a London weighing up his latest act of acting alchemy. As *Stars and Bars* finally opened in September 1988, the critics were divided on Henderson Dores and Pat O'Connor's troubled film.

'Day-Lewis, already a notable actor, emerges as a light comedy master. He sparkles throughout,' wrote Shaun Usher in the *Daily Mail*. 'He couldn't be bettered, sharing an entire biography in a vintage moment: about to kick a pile of bricks to smithereens in a tantrum, he remembers the old public school and compromises by side-footing just one loose.'

Philip French in the *Observer* had little praise for O'Connor or the rest of the cast but found some solace in Daniel's Henderson. 'Daniel Day-Lewis combines the exotic good looks of the young Olivier with the protean qualities of Guinness and Sellers, and he alone emerges with credit.'

Derek Malcolm in the *Guardian*, however, thought Pat O'Connor's film suffered 'for never knowing whether to go for subtlety or farce'. 'This puts Day-Lewis, looking saturnine and puzzled at the same time, into some of the most difficult acting spots of his notable screen career, and he doesn't always come out with flying colours.'

The *Financial Times*'s Ann Toterdell had the last, damning word, however. 'The usually excellent Daniel Day Lewis as Henderson seems so determined to give an impersonation of

Dudley Moore that one wonders why Moore was not cast in the first place.'

By the time his reviews had driven a final nail into the coffin of *Stars and Bars*, however, Daniel was 7000 miles or so away, lost in the lunar landscape of Patagonia, in Argentina. Like *My Left Foot*, *Eversmile New Jersey* had evolved into a drama within a drama.

Daniel had met the Buenos Aires-born director Carlos Sorin after seeing his debut picture, *A King and His Movie*, at the London Film Festival in 1986. Sorin and producer Oscar Kramer had then visited him in Paris where they talked him through the idea for their next movie. The story of a travelling dentist, administering to the poor of Patagonia, had originally been suggested as an idea for Donald Sutherland.

Finance in Argentina had been promised from Los Films Del Camino, but European money was less forthcoming. At one point there had been a prospective deal. Daniel had agreed to work on the film at the end of 1987. With his usual devotion to detail, he had even begun researching his latest medical role by boning up on dentistry textbooks. 'But we placed ourselves in the wrong hands and the money was not forthcoming,' he revealed later.

Eventually, however, Michael Ryan and J&M Entertainment in London had agreed to provide the finance. *Eversmile New Jersey* was the first Anglo-Argentinian co-production since the Falklands War. In autumn 1988, Daniel flew off to spend two weeks filming in Buenos Aires and a further seven weeks in Patagonia.

He had insisted on one major change to his character, an employee of a New Jersey charity. Rather than portraying him as a native American, Daniel suggested he play him as an Irishman. Sorin agreed and his character was renamed Fergus O'Connell.

As Daniel slipped into his new skin, sporting the same cropped hairstyle that the younger Christy had worn in *My Left Foot*, Fergus's manic behaviour and rich Dublin brogue echoed the part he had left behind at Ardmore studios. Christy Brown had hopped, able-bodied, out of his wheelchair and on to the back of a motor-cycle.

172

Patagonia's wastelands provided a spectacularly bleak backdrop. On the back of Fergus's mobile dentist surgery-cum-motor-bike and sidecar, Daniel and the crew could travel hours without seeing another soul. As a film-making experience the contrast with the pressures of Daniel's Hollywood-financed movies could not have been greater. At one point a giant bus hired by the crew to carry their equipment got stuck in mud in a particularly remote area. 'The bus was very heavy so we all had to push, even Daniel,' Kramer recalled later. 'That was the kind of spirit we had. Everybody pushed very hard to make this film.'

Daniel helped lighten the spirits by playing the tin whistle he now carried everywhere with him. Sorin was sufficiently impressed to let him play it in his movie. Daniel chose an old Irish favourite, 'Mise Eire'. Much of the sound was lost, however, against the wild winds of Patagonia. He had to post-synch much of his dialogue in a studio back in Buenos Aires.

He also admitted later that a kind of 'madness' set in on the wandering set. 'We all went quite round the twist in Patagonia – those phenomenal landscapes where you have no option but to confront yourself because there are no horizons,' he said. Sorin and his editor Bryan Oates would later have to re-edit the film, 'to get rid of some of the madness'. By the time they finished, Daniel would be deeply immersed in another kind of madness altogether.

CHAPTER ELEVEN

GHOSTS

'Be thou a spirit of health or goblin damned,
Bring with thee airs from heaven or blasts from hell . . .'
WILLIAM SHAKESPEARE, *Hamlet*

IN THE darkened hush of the Savoy Cinema on Dublin's O'Connell Street, different moments stirred different memories. The night was filled with a myriad emotions.

For Mary Brown, there was the memory of how she first looked into the darting, devil-may-care eyes of Christy Brown. It had been in London, at a party at his brother Sean's house. He had been bored, 'a bottle of Bacardi by his side'; he thought she had the 'beauty of a Botticelli'. They got on instantly, talked about Dickens, and fell in love. It seemed days rather than almost exactly twenty years since she had first met the man who was to be her husband. She would come to watch the film time and time again. 'I wanted to reach out and touch him,' she would say.

For Peggy Barclay, Ann Jones, Mona Byrne and Sean Brown, there were memories of the days when they dragged their brother around Dublin in the makeshift wooden wheelbarrow their father dubbed the 'auld chariot'. There were the sacrifices their Ma made for her beloved son. Most moving of all there was the sight of a reincarnation of their Christy, face contorted with concentration, chalk fixed between the toes of his left foot, scrawling the word MOTHER on the bare-boarded floor of their home.

And then there was the moment when their bricklayer father had recognized what his son would become, slung him over his shoulders like a sack of contraband coal and introduced him to his drinking friends as 'Christy Brown, my son, genius'. That reminded everyone of the greatness of Ray

McAnally. Months later, he died, just as his talent was finally being fully appreciated.

For Jim Sheridan and Noël Pearson, every moment was one to cherish. That the film they had fought for years to make was finally before an audience was a miracle. A smaller miracle than the life of Christy Brown, for sure, but a miracle in its own way nevertheless.

As he sat among them all at the world premiere of *My Left Foot* that night in Dublin, however, there was another, more richly resonant moment for Daniel Day-Lewis. Privately, only he appreciated its significance.

It came in an exchange between Christy and Eileen Cole, the fictional doctor Connaughton and Sheridan had written into their screenplay. Cole, played by Fiona Shaw, saw the genius locked inside the wasted wreckage of Christy's body. She encouraged him to broaden his mind, to read and to dream. One of her introductions was to Shakespeare, and to *Hamlet*.

'Well, what do you think of *Hamlet*?' Cole asks Christy in the film after leaving him alone with the play.

His reply is instant, acid and damning: 'A cripple.'

Two weeks earlier Daniel had walked into the concrete bunker that is the National Theatre on the South Bank of the Thames in London, his head filled with thoughts of that cripple. It was the first day of rehearsals for a new production of *Hamlet*, being directed at the home of English theatre by his friend Richard Eyre. The time for his own rendezvous with the darkest role in theatre had finally, inevitably, come.

In Dublin, as he watched himself as Christy, wrenching out Hamlet's 'To be or not to be' soliloquy that night, however, Daniel confined thoughts of the Prince of Denmark to the farthest corners of his mind. Instead he enjoyed the 'hooley' in his newly adopted homeland.

Dublin was proud to have been given the world premiere of the movie. Another feather in the cap . . . And on 24 February 1989, they celebrated in suitable style.

Before the screening there had been a reception at the Gresham Hotel. Afterwards a fleet of Mercedes swept Daniel,

Sheridan and company off to a lavish party at Powerscourt Townhouse Centre, South William Street. Eight hundred Dubliners had paid £50 a head to celebrate with Daniel, Brenda Fricker, Sheridan, Pearson and members of Christy Brown's family. Proceeds went to the Rehab charity. Bono of U2, there with fellow band members, The Edge and Adam Clayton, and manager/*My Left Foot* investor Paul McGuinness, made a brief speech, as did Daniel.

The man who had astonished his fellow revellers with his transformation into Christy paid tribute to the family that had taken him into its heart. 'Many families could have been less kind to me, but the Browns took me in like their own,' he said shyly. 'I received tremendous help from everyone involved, it was a great experience working with actors of the calibre of Ray McAnally and Brenda Fricker. Dublin is a marvellous place to work.'

Tony Jordan of Sandymount was there with some of his pupils. He had already seen the film once. At an earlier, sneak preview, Daniel had sought him out. 'There was a special showing before the premiere, most of our kids were at it and he was at it,' remembered the Sandymount headmaster. 'I was standing at the very back and I remember him coming down to see me. He was dying to know what I thought of it.

'I said, "Fantastic, completely authentic." He was so relieved. He said that the judgement of the people he had spent time with was the most crucial from his point of view.'

Daniel spent much of his night talking to cerebral palsy sufferers. One, a thirteen-year-old girl, Davoren Hanna, had moved many to tears with a poem she had written. Inspired by Christy Brown and dedicated to his memory, it was called 'Seas Damned Shall Take the Arid Earth by Storm'. She gave an emotional Daniel a copy after her reading. Another young girl who had learnt to write with her feet, Mary Kiernan, one of those who had helped Daniel during his time at the Sandymount School Clinic, posed for photographs with him.

The event was the first time since Christy's death that all of his brothers and sisters had been together. One of his sisters, Anne Jones, summed up their feelings. 'It triggers such emotions. For me Daniel is Christy,' she said.

Mary Brown's reaction was equally effusive. She and Daniel talked quietly in a corner together. Afterwards she said, 'I looked right into his eyes and he looked back into mine and he knew that I thought he was Christy.'

Daniel had given a handful of interviews in Dublin to help promote the film. He had been unsure about taking on *Hamlet*, he explained. 'I thought about it for a long time before I decided that it might be a good idea,' he told Deirdre Purcell in the *Sunday Tribune*.

He admitted that he had never studied the play. Rachel Fields had introduced him to Shakespeare at Bedales. Bristol and the RSC had left bitter-sweet Bardic memories. He had seen Bergman's Swedish-language version at the National Theatre the year previously. But *Hamlet* had never been an obsession, he said. 'I know some people carry around the idea that this is something that they have to do at some stage in their lives, that was never part of mine,' he told Purcell.

He also hinted that returning to the theatre had been less of a happy homecoming than Dublin. 'There is a lot about the theatre that I find tremendously depressing,' he said enigmatically, trailing off before he explained further, the old wounds of the RSC raw still.

Hours after the last Mercedes had dropped off its champagne-filled cargo on the night of the world premiere, however, Daniel was back in London, in the bowels of the National Theatre. He admitted later that architect Denys Lasdun's pre-cast concrete creation was a depressant in itself. For him, simply walking into the building was a profoundly upsetting experience. 'It's the ugliest fucking building you have ever seen in your life,' he said, suddenly back on the Millwall terraces. 'The dressing rooms are nasty, horrible concrete pillboxes – like those things left over from the Second World War along the beaches. Sometimes I think, "How long would I be prepared to go to prison to have the pleasure of razing this place to the ground?"'

If he had barely a kind word to say for the cold concrete National Theatre, however, he felt nothing but warmth for its recently installed director. Since he had worked with Eyre on *The Insurance Man* and *Futurists*, he had been an admirer. Soon after they had met, Eyre had suggested *Hamlet* to Daniel. He had always seen him as the perfect embodiment of Shakespeare's description:

> The courtier's, soldier's, scholar's eye, tongue, sword,
> Th'expectancy and rose of the fair state,
> The glass of fashion and the mould of form,
> Th'observed of all obervers.

Bringing Daniel, now an established movie star, to the South Bank to perform his first Hamlet was a coup for Eyre in his early days as the new head of the National. His production was a hugely ambitious one: nine months and more than 110 performances. There was to be a visit to Dubrovnik, Yugoslavia, where a historic staging of the play would be held inside the city's battlements.

The punishing schedule demanded a high-quality cast. Dame Judi Dench was there to play Gertrude, John Castle was Claudius, David Burke the Ghost, Michael Bryant Polonius, Stella Gonet Ophelia.

Read-throughs began in February 1989. Early on it was apparent that the actor who would occupy the troubled soul of the production was somehow approaching the play from another direction.

The first sign came when he arrived at the first read-through with a different edition of the text to his colleagues. Everyone else walked into the rehearsal clutching a buff-coloured, specially typed edition of the play. Daniel, colleagues recall, had his own version. 'I found it absolutely bizarre, part of him seemed wilful to do something different,' one member of the production remembers.

As rehearsals got under way, Daniel unveiled a dynamic, masochistic Hamlet. He gave the impression of a man who was ready to throw himself at the walls of Elsinore every night. It was exciting stuff. One member of the cast recalls how he 'charged around like a lunatic horse on the loose' after the play-within-the-play scene. 'It was enthralling, and totally spontaneous,' the actor recalls.

It was soon clear, however, that Daniel was suffering from having pushed himself to the physical limits once more. *My Left Foot* and *Eversmile New Jersey* had clearly taken the same toll as the prolonged workload of *Unbearable Lightness* and *Stars and Bars*. One member of the production remembers hearing him talking to colleagues in the National Theatre canteen about the strain of back-to-back filming. 'He was saying that it was a big mistake. When he had finished *My Left Foot* he had had two days off to do some laundry and then he was on a plane to Argentina. He acknowledged that at the start,' the production member says.

By the time the first night arrived, anticipation was enormous. The return of the conquering Hollywood hero is a rare and bloodthirsty ritual in the English theatre. Suspicion, snobbery and jealousy are often its dramatic subtext. When Richard Burton returned to the Old Vic in 1953, Hollywood at his feet, queues snaked around the streets of Waterloo to see his Hamlet. The critics stood in line too, poison pens poised, itching to prick at any signs of inflated ego. And prick some did. Gielgud defined the divide in his famous exchange with Burton. 'Which do you want to be, dear boy, an actor or a movie star?' 'Both!'

Daniel had supplied a similar answer when asked the question a year earlier by the magazine *American Film*. 'I'm greedy, I prefer both.' That greed would soon be diminished.

On 16 March he emerged from the dry-ice mists swirling around the castle, a vast, domineering statue of his recently departed father the King towering over him; his hair was conservatively cut, Tomas-style, and he was dressed in sequined, funereal black. As he had promised to do in rehearsal, he threw himself athletically around the ramparts of Elsinore. At the end of the three-and-a-half-hour performance there was a rapturous ovation.

Afterwards, he dutifully shared a first-night drink with his company members and waited for the first notices to arrive. In the run-up he had admitted that he dreaded the experience. 'I am not brave enough not to read reviews, not resilient enough to take no notice of them, not sensible enough to take the praise with as much scepticism as the damnation. I just take them to heart really and sometimes they are incredibly unpleasant.'

The damnation came in waves. Early editions of the newspapers arrived by midnight, other reviews followed the next day. More would follow at the weekend. Quickly, however, it was clear that the production had few fans among the critics.

There was universal praise for Daniel's dashing good looks, but his high-octane interpretation was widely criticized. In particular, many critics felt that the poet's son had lost the poetry of the play by flying full-throttle through many of Hamlet's soliloquies.

'Hamlet needs more than a handsome figure, intelligent reading and a graceful athleticism,' wrote Milton Shulman in the *Evening Standard* the next morning. 'Listening to Day-Lewis, one felt one was in the presence of a keen young barrister who occasionally lost his temper over an error in his brief.' The veteran critic, perhaps influenced by the fact that the production was sponsored by the bookmakers Ladbrokes, saved a horse-racing analogy for his most withering attack. 'Since his only previous theatrical experience seems to have been in what in racing parlance might be called sellers, it is rather surprising that Richard Eyre believed he had the qualifications for an attempt at the Grand National of English drama.'

The *Daily Telegraph*'s Charles Osborne was equally cruel. He praised Judi Dench and Michael Bryant but said he had 'seen better acting on the London fringe this past week . . . the play stands or falls with Hamlet, and it is with Daniel Day-Lewis's Hamlet that, this time, it falls. I used to think that this was a role in which it was impossible completely to succeed or to fail, but I may have to revise my opinion.'

Both the *Daily Mail* and the *Daily Express* were equally unimpressed. 'Alas, poor Daniel Day-Lewis,' wrote Shaun Usher in the *Daily Mail*. 'His Hamlet has fire, rather too much of it . . .' he added. He said the performance 'must be one of the most manic, physically active performances this generation'. But 'one had little sense of a tormented intellectual'.

'Hamlet has to be more than just a handsome, physical jerk,' wrote Maureen Paton of the *Daily Express*. 'Daniel has placed himself in the lion's den with this notoriously demanding role and misses the sense of danger.'

Members of the production remember the mood the following morning as 'mild hysteria'. Daniel told colleagues that he had had a big breakfast on the way in that morning. 'I've fed myself up,' he said. It was clear, however, that he was consumed by anguish.

'I have never seen anyone take notices so personally. It was like he had been kicked in the head,' said one veteran actor there to witness the morning after.

Judi Dench, consummate, indestructible professional that she is, attempted to rally the troops. 'She was walking around saying, "Never mind, there's a long way to go, don't be so gloomy."'

More reviews arrived over the weekend, some offering welcome relief from the earlier savagery. A few critics felt that Daniel had shown great potential. He might grow into a great Hamlet, they thought. 'It is a performance of much promise, still in awe of the play and the role,' wrote Michael Ratcliffe of the *Observer*.

Another weekend reviewer, Peter Kemp of the *Independent*, gushed praise. He thought Eyre's production 'a triumph of intelligence' and Daniel 'genetically typecast for Hamlet'. 'In a performance that perfectly complements this physical persona, Day-Lewis never lets you forget the central fact about Hamlet: that he is a young intellectual, someone whose mind is more developed than his emotions.'

In general, though, the verdict went against the young Prince. 'Day-Lewis's attitude to the verse is one of furious attack alternating with hasty withdrawal. The brusque, almost icy manner is reflected in verse-speaking which is fast and poorly articulated: we lose the poetry, and with it a vital element of the play, which is that Hamlet is a real intellectual,' wrote John Peter of the *Sunday Times*, 'his headlong delivery leaves him no time to give the words their flavour and breathing time.'

'Day-Lewis comes nowhere near solving the contradictions of Hamlet, manipulator and victim, sometimes spider, sometimes fly. He often fails to find either rhythm or sense in the soliloquies,' commented Kenneth Hurren in the *Mail on Sunday*.

Richard Eyre tried to console his cast. He often veered to the view that 'the appropriate fate for the critic is what they did to the dead Pharaohs before embalming them – having their brains drawn out with a long hook'. But he was calmer in this crisis, putting the panning down to jealousy of Hamlet's Hollywood alter ego. He accused the critics of 'a squalid display of envy'.

If the critics' intention had been to drive Daniel Day-Lewis back to a life before the film camera, however, they failed miserably. As he had done years earlier at the Bristol Old Vic, after his Jimmy Porter had brought him his first acid taste of personal criticism, he fought back.

Leading members of the cast had been offered the option of leaving the production halfway through. Soon after his first-night mauling Daniel told colleagues that he intended to fight on. 'Fuck them,' he had said.

He immersed himself even more deeply in the role, in the process cutting himself off further from outside influences. One night Stephen Frears turned up to see him. Daniel passed on a message that he did not want to be disturbed. Janet Maw arrived another night but got the clear impression that Daniel did not want to be disturbed afterwards.

A friend from the National Theatre visited him at his house in Brook Green one Saturday afternoon when Daniel was off. According to colleagues at the National, he found Daniel sitting surrounded by bare walls, poring over the script of *Hamlet*.

The totality of his immersion in the part was obvious to his half-brother Sean when he saw him in the street in Brook Green. Sean's admiration for Daniel's application was already established. 'When he gets a task it is tunnel vision, it is his way of compartmentalizing. My father used to talk about the blade of ice in your centre which means you can detach yourself from everything else to concentrate on something.' This time that concentration was so absolute that Daniel did not even acknowledge Sean. 'We walked past each other in the street. He was lost in Hamlet. He did say afterwards that he always put his head down, but when he was "in" a part he was incommunicado.'

At the National, Richard Eyre was accepting some of the blame for the poor notices himself. In his autobiography, *Utopia and Other Places*, he had taken issue with Olivier's argument, 'Scratch an actor and you find an actor.' 'What is true, I think, is that if you scratch an actor you will find a child,' he wrote. 'Not that actors are inherently less mature than politicians, priests, etc., but actors must retain a child's appetite for mimicry, for demanding attention, and above all for playing. They must see with a child's heart, innocent of judgement.' It was an opinion Daniel shared and voiced himself. 'A lot of acting is trying to get back to how we were as kids, a process of unlearning, of retrieving innocence.'

During the run-up to that laceratory opening night, Eyre admitted later, he failed to be the paternal influence that Daniel, in his child-like search for the heart of Hamlet, needed. 'I wasn't sure-footed myself,' he admitted. 'I had just taken over the National Theatre and was not in the right state to be Daniel's surrogate father.'

In the absence of that fatherly influence, Daniel had drawn on the memory of Cecil Day-Lewis to guide him through the performances. A huge blow-up photograph of the late Poet Laureate was stuck on his dressing-room wall. He described it later as 'a big, beautiful one, staring very directly, alive, a really living photograph'. As he prepared to go out on stage each night to face the ghost of Hamlet's father, Cecil's gentle smile watched over his own son.

Daniel had come to talk more and more about Cecil. In 1988 he had admitted feeling he had let his father down in some ways. 'I regret my father's death more now than at any time,' he said then. 'I also regret that he never had the chance to see me do anything worthwhile because he had more than enough chances to see me screw things up.'

In beginning to use his memories and unresolved feelings

for his father as an acting tool, however, Daniel was also unleashing forces that had lain dormant since his troubled adolescence. By dwelling on his own loss he provided himself with a key to the mind of Hamlet, the most tortured of all grieving sons. But at the same time he unlocked the demons of his past. Those forces would ultimately destroy his Hamlet.

In July, four months into the run, Daniel and the company flew to Yugoslavia for the Dubrovnik performances. The historic walled city, then still the shining jewel of the Adriatic coast, despite the growing ethnic tension in Yugoslavia, had invited the National Theatre to perform in the fourteenth-century Fort Lovrjenac, site of a stunning, 400-seat open-air stadium overlooking Dubrovnik.

The blazing sunshine lightened the company's mood. The production's twenty-foot-tall, moulded plastic statue of Hamlet's ghost added a touch of comedy during rehearsals. Stagehands could not pass the statue through the six-foot doorway to the theatre. After two days on display to the entire city, helicopters flown in from Sarajevo lifted the spectre into position. 'I saw it hovering in the air – it was spectacular, a kind of pagan rite,' Daniel said.

The opening night could not have presented a greater contrast to London. The castle was a perfect setting, its cold stone, whipped by the Adriatic winds, and imposing shadows combined to add an eeriness to the setting that complemented Eyre's dark vision of the play. During one soliloquy a bat hovered over Hamlet's head.

Daniel admitted that he had had to strain to be heard when he was aloft the blustery battlements. 'I gave it some welly,' he explained afterwards. His one regret was the spontaneous head-butt of the twenty-inch-thick stone walls he produced during one of Hamlet's deepest rages. 'I will not be doing that again.'

As the dead Hamlet was carried off stage, spectators in the front rows wept openly. 'We are a people who can still cry at Shakespeare. Hamlet speaks directly to the Slavic soul, half in love with melancholy,' the director of the festival, Misha Mihocevich, said. After four curtain calls the ecstatic audience let the cast leave the stage at 2 a.m.

The success seemed to lift Hamlet's gloom. During the run Daniel admitted he had been wounded by the opening night. 'I felt quite comfortable in the rehearsal room but going on stage was quite a shock,' he told writer Michael Owen of London's *Evening Standard*. He said he thought he may have been 'a bit over-eager' that night but played down the effects of the notices.

'I was kind of prepared for the aftermath from the critics. I have been quite affected by the brutality of that stuff in the past but I was more able to deal with it this time than ever before,' he told Owen.

Dubrovnik's triumphs soon faded, however. And as Daniel returned to London to complete the final two months of his run, his energy levels were dwindling visibly. On days when he had to perform both a matinee and an evening performance it looked as if he might grind to a halt under the Olivier's spotlights.

'He was throwing himself into the part so hard that on matinee days come the start of the second show you thought there was no way he was going to get through it. It was mad, weird, frightening, the whole thing. It was like an exorcism going on, it was like a personal thing he had to get out of his system,' recalled one National Theatre actor.

At one stage Daniel's understudy, Jeremy Northam, was asked to take over the matinees. The actor asked for an announcement to be made to avoid disappointing Daniel's admirers. Despite the poor opening notices, most performances were filled with fans of his movies. Groups of women hung around the stage door each night, at one point forcing the reluctant idol to start leaving by the public entrance instead.

'Twenty-four hours after it was arranged, it was off because Dan would not allow it to be announced to the public,' a company member confided. Eventually, however, Daniel agreed with Richard Eyre that he was exhausted and that he should leave. A company meeting was called and the news was announced.

In August *My Left Foot* was released in England. *Hamlet*

brought the worst reviews, now the *Hamlet*-hater Christy brought the best.

The *Guardian*'s Derek Malcolm thought Daniel would have been a near certainty for the Best Actor award had the film not fallen victim to the politics that lie behind the Cannes Film Festival and been accepted as an entry there by its director Gilles Jacob. 'The fact that he didn't . . . would be shaming if those who run the world's premier festival ever thought they could do anything wrong.' 'If I was asked which was the better performance between that of Dustin Hoffman in *Rain Man* or Day-Lewis here, I would undoubtedly choose the latter. It's that good and necessary to see.'

'If you are American and you want to win an Oscar there is no better way than to play someone disabled,' Christopher Tookey wrote in the *Sunday Telegraph*, picking up the same thread. 'As Christy, the British actor Daniel Day-Lewis makes most of these performances look shallow.'

'The problem is: which part of Daniel Day-Lewis do I praise most?' wrote Alexander Walker in the London *Evening Standard*.

Daniel took three weeks off from *Hamlet* to help promote the movie. The pent-up anger poured out. In his interviews he was the opposite of the talk-a-lot-say-nothing Prince of Denmark. He was short, sharp and shockingly honest. On critics: 'Some of them were appalling. One or two made me seriously consider getting a sledgehammer and paying a couple of visits. There are one or two people who need to learn some manners.'

On the film business: 'It's wrapped up in all this bullshit and I really can't live with that. I can't stand all those fucking fat people who smile and shake your hand because you're worth a few bob.'

On England: 'I'm shocked at the total depression I sense. I have a really tangible sense of this country's seclusion and that psychology has profoundly diminished opportunities in art.'

He spent part of his break in the south of France but returned in time for a Royal Premiere in the presence of Princess Alexandra at the Curzon, Mayfair. At the premiere Daniel talked to Michael Dwyer of the *Irish Times*. He said, hardly surprisingly after *Hamlet*, that he had not read the English reviews of the film and had no plans beyond seeing through his commitments at the National. His words were portentous. 'As soon as I have finished *Hamlet* at the National I'm planning to collapse for an indefinite time.'

When he returned to the National Theatre it appeared that the break might have saved him from driving himself over the edge. Colleagues remember him returning looking tanned, healthier, and well-fed. The first of the eleven remaining performances he was contracted to give, the sixty-fifth of the run, went on without any hint of a problem.

The night before the sixty-sixth performance, on Tuesday, 5 September, Daniel spoke to the man who would replace him as Hamlet. Ian Charleson, whom he had first met in India on *Gandhi*, had been hired to take over by Richard Eyre. The director was one of the few people who knew that Charleson was HIV positive. In his final public appearance, his Hamlet would carve a unique place in stage history, his dying Prince leave a memory none who saw it would forget. He died months later.

Charleson and Daniel had chatted before. Daniel's replacement had confessed his admiration for his colleague's portrayal of the role. But he had very different views about playing the part.

Charleson had admitted that he had fears about whether he was strong enough to survive the three-and-a-half-hour marathon. That night he and Daniel had talked briefly about how to negotiate acting's great assault course. 'He told me he always felt if you could get through the first scene with the father's ghost, you'd be all right for the rest of the play,' he remembered later.

Three-quarters of an hour into the play that night, Daniel approached that moment, Act One, Scene Five. David Burke, whose performance as the Ghost had drawn praise, led Hamlet into the scene. As he had done each night, he told Hamlet, 'I am thy father's spirit', and went on to describe how he had been the victim of 'murder most foul'. As Burke delivered his final lines, 'Adieu, adieu, Hamlet. Remember me', and began to make his exit, however, the audience saw Hamlet follow in his wake. What should have followed was one of Hamlet's most impassioned soliloquies, 'O all you host of heaven! O earth! What else?' Instead there was silence on the Olivier stage. Behind the scenes Daniel had slumped to the ground, sobbing uncontrollably.

One eye-witness remembers walking along the network of corridors behind the stage and hearing unscheduled applause come across the tannoy. 'I thought, that's a bit odd,' he recalls. As he turned a corner he saw the explanation for the unforeseen break.

'I came round the corner and Dan was slumped down the corridor with David Burke rather kind of surreally dressed as this ghost all in white and silver leaning over him saying, "Dan are you all right, are you all right?" He was obviously not in a good state. He was kind of sobbing, saying, "I can't do it, I can't do it, I'm not going back on."'

Burke and back-stage staff helped Daniel to his dressing room where he was placed in a chair. In the meantime understudy Jeremy Northam was asked to get ready in case it was decided he would have to go on that night.

'It had been five months since we had done a word-run or anything, so I went to my dressing room to look for a script. I was doing other scripts as well at the time,' the understudy recalls. 'I knew that Ian Charleson was taking over, I was rehearsing with Ian to take over as Laertes, because Laertes was leaving.'

While Northam waited for news of what was going on, more surreal scenes were unfolding in Daniel's dressing room.

'There was this bizarre scene in the dressing room, he was dressed in his garb feeling wretched and sobbing. There were all these people around him, the company manager, the assistant director, Stephen his dresser, Judi Dench,' recalled a member of the company.

'Judi kept saying, "Do you want a break of about ten minutes and then we'll go back on?" And he was saying, "No, no, I can't do it." "Well, how about if we leave it twenty minutes?" and again he said, "No." So then somebody said,

188

"Well, give us your boots then!"' If Daniel was not going to continue, then his understudy would need his boots. Professionalism overrode all.

As drama and bleak, black comedy unfolded back-stage, an announcement was made to the audience. Jeremy Northam stepped out on to the stage to pick up the play. 'O all you host of heaven,' he began, and that night's performance was completed.

When Northam returned to his dressing room he found a handwritten note from the man he had replaced. It read: 'I am sure you would have been wonderful.'

Daniel was taken off to stay with a friend in London. The next day, as news of his collapse percolated out, Richard Eyre and the rest of the production tried to play down the drama. Initially the National told reporters that 'technical problems' had been the cause of the star's disappearance. But by the next morning the *Evening Standard* reported that he was feeling unwell and would not be appearing again that night either. 'We're crossing our fingers that whatever is the matter, he'll be all right. He's a brilliant actor and a terribly nice man,' a National Theatre colleague was quoted as saying.

Behind the scenes, however, it was quickly emerging that Daniel was in no fit state to continue. He was sent to see first a doctor and then a psychiatrist. 'He had to go in order to confirm what was wrong. That way the National would be sure to get the insurance on the production for any lost ticket sales,' a senior member of the production explained.

The diagnosis was that he was suffering from 'stress syndrome'. It was accepted that he was in no condition to continue and a statement was prepared. A week after he had followed the spectral figure of David Burke off the Olivier stage, it was announced that Daniel would be leaving the production permanently.

'He is naturally very upset at having to withdraw so near the end of his scheduled run and we are very sad that he is not returning,' the National Theatre's spokesman said. 'He pours everything he has into all his roles and does nothing by halves. That's presumably why he is in such a state.'

Judi Dench added her reaction. 'It's a great shame Dan won't be with us. We are all very sad about what has happened,' she said.

The news sparked feverish speculation about what had led to his premature departure. There were rumours that he had seen his father's ghost on the stage that night. The spectre of Cecil Day-Lewis had apparently chided his son for 'frittering away' his talents on the stage, according to some. He had appeared to tell his son 'not to fret', according to others. Elsewhere there were suggestions that Daniel's collapse was delayed reaction to the critical mauling he had received. He could no longer live with the sense of failure instilled in him, the theory ran. The note he had left his understudy, with its hint that he might have been better suited to the part, buttressed that view. Many simply put it down to exhaustion. This time he had simply pushed himself too far.

There was sympathy, comparisons were made with the experiences of other great names, from Olivier to Anthony Hopkins to Dame Judi Dench herself. Olivier had been taken to the brink of a breakdown by *Othello* at the National in 1964. The greatest actor of his time could not bear to be left alone on stage to deliver his soliloquies and insisted that his Iago, Frank Finlay, stay in the wings where he could see him. He also became paranoid that he would dry up on stage after discovering that his mind was running through lines from another play, *Richard III*, on the train up to London one day. Hopkins had been forced to leave a National Theatre production of *Macbeth* in 1972 while Dench had found the part of Regan in *King Lear* unbearable and given up too.

The peculiar demands of Hamlet were blamed. Kenneth Branagh, who had played the part the year before at the National, admitted that 'the stomach-wrenching sick feeling that overtakes one as the first soliloquy begins is truly terrifying'. So too were the demands of a theatre that asked an actor to perform six nights out of seven, sometimes twice a day.

Daniel's colleagues at the National recognized truth in all the arguments. 'Dan was on this realism kick, which was pointless. He got himself more and more fired up, it became an athletics event rather than a play,' said one colleague. 'You can't do *Hamlet* like you are living it, otherwise you go around killing people.'

Daniel's understudy fully understood how his colleague could have come to be immersed in the role, however. He also saw nothing unusual in the idea of being confronted by a ghost. He too had once been haunted in that way. 'When I played Hamlet I saw the ghost of my currently alive father, you feed off whatever it is.

'With Hamlet it is the personality of the person playing in it that is the part, you can sink yourself absolutely into the part. It is the ultimate role in many ways,' said Jeremy Northam.

'It is also boxes within boxes within boxes. At the time you emotionally get involved in peeling back layers and at the centre of the play it's about having the nerve to be yourself. You can't hide behind bits of business, you have to bare your heart, it has huge technical demands, its length, the various forms of language in the text, the prose, the blank verse, the huge soliloquies, the complicated relationships Hamlet has with everybody in the play. And if you get all that right it releases you even more to be yourself.'

Afterwards, Richard Eyre questioned his casting of Daniel as Shakespeare's eternal outsider. Hamlet's world of shadows and ghosts, suspended as it is between fact and fiction, can be an unsuitable place for any actor intent on inhabiting his parts. But Eyre also realized that so much of Hamlet, his brooding brilliance, his contradictions, his constant role-playing, even his mission to grant eternal peace to his father's restless spirit, was Daniel too. 'It was like asking him to stand centre stage and do archaeology on himself. In retrospect, Hamlet was the last part I should have asked him to play,' Eyre mused afterwards.

Judi Dench admitted later that she too felt he was consumed by the role. 'Hamlet for most actors is a very private role,' she told the arts and theatre magazine *Connoisseur*, soon after Daniel's departure. 'For Dan, in a way, it's a way of life.'

At the National Theatre the company was left with mixed feelings. Some felt Daniel had been let down. His casting as

Hamlet had given a new regime at the theatre a suitably high-profile launch. But he had not been supported by Eyre and his staff. 'Dan drove himself into a hole, Richard did not know how to help him fake it,' said one company member.

Most felt a 'there but for the Grace of God' sympathy. As actors, however, they all knew that in many ways the departed Hamlet's troubles lay ahead of him rather than behind at the National.

'The thing that absolutely struck us all immediately was that if you do something like that – and every actor's bottle goes, every actor you have ever seen either in the past or in the future it has gone or it will go – the spin-off will be when will you ever get the nerve to go back on?

'It is a very frightening business, no doubt he will do it, but every actor knows that that is more frightening than any fear you could possibly feel on the stage.'

It took Daniel two and a half years to offer an explanation. In a piece he wrote himself, in the *Observer*, to mark the publication in May 1992 of the *Complete Poems of C. Day-Lewis*, he answered the rumour that he had been confronted not with the ghost of Hamlet but with that of his father.

'Well, of course I was talking to my father, as I do every day. Wouldn't it seem stranger not to have been?' He went on to say that what his father had said to him 'seemed particularly hard to bear'.

He later amplified his explanation by telling American writer Joan Juliet Buck of the role his father played at the National Theatre. As any actor would, he had brought his own experiences to the role. But as the strain of that role became unbearable, what had been a tool to aid his Hamlet became a weapon of destruction. That night, particularly after his conversation with Ian Charleson, his mind was in turmoil. He imagined he was talking to his father.

'The ideas I had explored when I was working on the play began to torment me once my resistance had disintegrated. Images of my childhood, of my father,' he told Buck in the *New Yorker* magazine.

'Before going onstage every night, in the transition between

192

the darkness of the wings and the light of the stage, I had to run a gauntlet of strange, fleeting images of myself as a child. My father had become a remote hovering figure, not unaffectionate but slightly threatening.'

That night, on the stage of the Olivier, his father's twin legacies conspired to drive him over the edge. Cecil bequeathed him an artist's vision, an 'irrevocable sense of decay', a dreadful, perfect gift. But in leaving too soon, Cecil also left his son with a need to prove himself worthy, a desire to hurl himself headlong into his art in the same way his own father had done. During *Hamlet* the two forces converged. In the heat of the nightly battle with the demons within, Daniel grew too weak to see the damage he was causing himself.

By the time he began to explain the events of that night, however, the tragedy of *Hamlet* had been woven into the fabric of his own legend. Within months of his departure from the Olivier stage, his career was offering 'more things in heaven and earth . . . than are dreamt of in our philosophy'.

CHAPTER TWELVE

A SILLY BINGO GAME

'I don't care what they say to the press, I've never met an actor in my life who doesn't have an acceptance speech going through his head every day.'

JAMES WOODS, 1980

ELSEWHERE in the City of Angels, the word was that the demonically driven Harvey Weinstein had sent out 4700 video-cassette copies of his film. The head of *My Left Foot*'s American distributors, Miramax, winged each one on its way complete with copious notes on Sandymount Clinic, the preparation, the submersion in the soul of Christy Brown, the blood, the sweat, the spittle, everything.

In Los Angeles' restaurants, hotel lobbies and reception rooms he was being backed up by Noël Pearson. Silver-haired, silver-tongued, he was flitting around like a Tammany Hall hustler, an Irishman in America, chivvying, charming everyone into voting for his man and his movie.

For the PR people pushing her film the hyperbole was more Gallic than Gaelic. How she had battled for years to get *Camille Claudel* made. The electricity between her and Depardieu's Rodin. How she perfectly captured the spirit of one of the most remarkable women of her time.

Their targets were, according to LA legend, 'as old as God', actors and actresses who hadn't seen a movie lot in twenty years. But once more they were the nearest thing this town had to God. It was a time for high visibility, a time to be noticed. The Irish and the French would have spoken to every voting member of the Academy of Motion Picture Arts and Sciences had they been able to. There were votes to win, 4700 of them.

Yet as they sheepishly took to the sidewalks, far from the crowds already gathering outside the Dorothy Chandler

194

Pavilion, days in advance of the 1990 Oscars, both the objects of all this desire yearned to be invisible. He wore jeans and a billowing, baggy shirt. Clean-shaven, his hair grown long, he was unrecognizable from the posters of tortured, twisted Christy up on Sunset Boulevard. She wore the dark Raybans she favoured whether she was in California or Somerset. It was, he would come to say, 'the most on–off relationship in the world'. For now it was supposed to be the most secret.

In March 1990, Daniel and Isabelle Adjani, the beautiful French actress whom he had been seeing since the summer of 1989, eased their way into Los Angeles for the Oscars. Both, full of hope, were nominees for major awards, he for Best Actor for Christy Brown, she for Best Actress for her performance in *Camille Claudel*. They had hoped to spend their time in LA undetected. Escaping the most high-profile week in the most high-profile city in the world was the one hope forlorn from the very beginning.

Talk of a relationship between the two had first surfaced in Dublin while Daniel had been completing filming on *My Left Foot*. The publicity surrounding his collapse at the National Theatre in *Hamlet*, however, had relegated the rumour to a sub-plot in a more intriguing Shakespearean drama.

During those traumatic first days after his collapse as Hamlet Daniel had in fact turned to another woman, his sister Tamasin. The inseparable bond formed between brother and sister in childhood and adolescence had continued to deepen. As he had done before, Daniel sought out Tamasin, the 'toughie', when he once more found himself in trouble.

After seeing a doctor and a psychiatrist in London he exiled himself at her home in Somerset to rest and recuperate as speculation about the reasons for his disappearance filled end-less column inches. The peace and rural routine of life there proved a perfect antidote to the self-obsession of his nightly disappearance into the abyss of Hamlet.

'He was here for some time, there was nowhere else he could have gone,' Tamasin explained later. At the mill house where she now lived with her husband John and three children – a second daughter, Clarissa, had joined Miranda and Harry that year – Daniel was left to recover his strength at his own pace. 'There's no pressure for him to do anything here, even the washing up,' Tamasin said. He spent his time watching Clint Eastwood videos, indulging the passion for chocolate both he and his sister inherited from their father, and playing with the children.

Both Tamasin and Daniel's half-brother Sean talk of him being a natural with children. 'He was very good with the children. He would always ply them with too many chocolates,' recalled Sean, father of two children, Keelin and Finian. Daniel had spoken intermittently of having children of his own – sooner rather than later in life, so as not to repeat the experience of his own childhood when Cecil had been a fleeting influence. 'I would like to have children while I've got the energy,' he said in 1988. 'While he was a very affectionate father – he was – it was difficult. His age certainly created a distance which I would not choose for my children.'

His sister's children came to call their relative 'wicked Uncle Daniel'. 'He makes the kids do utterly mad things like leap into the sea on freezing days when there is a gale force wind,' Tamasin revealed once.

To help him recover, Tamasin suggested her brother see a herbal healer she had met. He advised Daniel to go on a strict diet, cutting out starch, sugar, coffee, tea, meat and alcohol. Cigarettes somehow slipped through the draconian net. 'They didn't mention smoking, so I didn't.' More important, as far as his sister was concerned, Daniel dosed himself on fresh air and real life. The 'toughie' gave him back his strength. 'I sussed that in a sense it would bring him back to life.'

Isabelle Adjani played her part in his rehabilitation too. Tamasin and Adjani shared qualities that went beyond darkly exotic beauty. The actress, the daughter of an Algerian Moslem father and a German Catholic mother, had a reputation for courage, determination and intelligence.

Isabelle Adjani rose to international heights in 1976 at the tender age of twenty. Her performance in the late, great François Truffaut's *The Story of Adèle H*, the story of the journey Victor Hugo's daughter Adèle took in following her lover from France to Nova Scotia, earned her a Best Actress Oscar nomination. In 1990, she was still the youngest actress to win the accolade. '*Elle crève l'écran*: she burns up the screen,' Truffaut said of her.

Adjani had a brief flirtation with Hollywood, starring in two disasters, *The Driver* in 1978 and the infamous *Ishtar* with Warren Beatty and Dustin Hoffman in 1987. The latter, of which she said, 'Oh, I took it the way Dustin Hoffman did, as a nice holiday in Morocco', also brought a brief fling with Beatty according to the rumour mill.

Neither Beatty nor Hollywood wooed her permanently, however. She returned to France, uninterested in being a bauble, to make films that she cared about. *Camille Claudel* had been her greatest triumph of will. Like *Adèle H*, the eponymous heroine of the story was a real-life character, this time the nineteenth-century poet Paul Claudel's sculptor sister Camille, who had conducted a passionate, but ultimately doomed, affair with the great sculptor Rodin. The loss of his love sent her spiralling into depression and mental illness.

For years Adjani had fought to bring the tragic love story to the screen, first overcoming the resistance of Claudel's family, then raising the film's budget, partly out of her own pocket, and then moving heaven and earth to cast France's charismatic Gérard Depardieu as Rodin. She also enlisted the help of a former lover, director Bruno Nuyteen, with whom she has a son, Barnabe.

'Her strength of will is unbelievable. She wanted to play Camille Claudel, so she went out and got the whole thing together,' Depardieu said admiringly of her. In 1989 her persistence was rewarded with Best Actress prizes at the Berlin Film Festival and France's César awards, where *Camille Claudel* was also voted Best Film.

Adjani possessed fire as well as icy determination, however. Her indomitable willingness to speak her mind regularly got her into trouble. The French press, with whom she conducted an ongoing war, once awarded her a special prize, the Prix Citron, roughly translated as 'the acid prize', for her less than co-operative behaviour in interviews. She guarded her privacy passionately, refusing to give interviews or comments even when she might have been better advised to do so. For years she was the subject of rumours that she had AIDS. She refused to deny them even though they were false. When she eventually broke her silence, after TV and radio stations had started broadcasting reports that she was dead, she said: 'It's terrible to have to announce you are not ill, as if I were saying I was not guilty.'

If she had much in common with Tamasin, she was even more of a soul-sister to Daniel. Like him, she had been unable to settle down to marriage. 'I worry so much, it would probably take centuries before I could make up my mind that he was the right person,' she once said. Like Daniel, too, she had had a difficult relationship with her father. She ran away to the Comédie Française when she was just seventeen. A troubled childhood had left her with a wanderlust, an unwillingness to be pinned down. 'I believe you can't be an actress or actor if you haven't had the feeling of being abandoned as a child,' she said once. 'I've never had any roots or rather I have got flying roots. I plant myself as best I can and then I plant myself somewhere else.'

Even her feelings for film-making, and the difficulties in breaking away from parts, were echoes of Daniel's own. 'Movies are completely ephemeral. All that is very painful because you can't hang on to anything,' she said once.

A friend has said of Daniel, 'He likes his women dark and mysterious.' Adjani had both qualities – and more – in irresistible abundance.

In France, where privacy laws prevent paparazzi photographers from taking the sort of *in flagrante* photographs that fill magazines and newspapers in Britain, Italy, Germany and America, the publicity-shy couple had been able to conduct their romance quietly. Parisian friends of Adjani's like the portrait photographer Brigitte Lacombe, whom Daniel, a reluctant subject at the best of times, sat for, and the writer Marilyn Goldin kept the romance confidential.

Whenever they travelled together elsewhere, however, their desire for secrecy bordered on the obsessional. Isabelle stayed with Tamasin and her family in the West Country. 'She's not a name to conjure with in this country, even in

London. But even in Taunton she wears dark glasses so as not to be recognized in the streets,' said Sean Day-Lewis.

Adjani had introduced Tamasin to her friends Katia and Marielle Labèque, France's famous pianist sisters. Daniel had come to know them through his passion for the music of the guitarist John McLaughlin, Katia Labèque's boyfriend. Tamasin went on to make a documentary for the BBC on the remarkable duo.

Daniel had resisted all pressures to return to work during the end of 1989 and the early part of 1990. As he disappeared from the public gaze, however, both *My Left Foot* and *Eversmile New Jersey* were released in America.

Eversmile New Jersey had been given a lukewarm reception at the London Film Festival: only the *Guardian* had a good word to say about it. It praised the Anglo-Argentine production for showing 'the more positive face of hybrid film-making', but said nothing in particular about the performances. In New York weeks later it fared equally poorly, only the *Village Voice* finding a place in its heart for Sorin's off-beat road movie. Critic Manohla Dargas called the film 'outstanding' and Daniel 'inspired'. The underwhelming reviews left the British investors with a problem. A question mark was placed over whether it should even be released in cinemas.

My Left Foot, however, was winning friends in the highest of places. At its debut at the New York Film Festival in October, America was uncontrollable in its praise. Five years after questioning whether Daniel Day-Lewis could act at all, Pauline Kael performed a *volte-face*. She was moved as she had never been before at the cinema. She wrote that the restaurant scene in which Christy learns that Eileen Cole, with whom he had fallen in love, is to marry another man, 'may be the most emotionally wrenching scene I've ever experienced in the movies'. Daniel, she enthused, 'seizes the viewer, he takes possession of you'. Suddenly even Olivier was being mentioned in the same breath. 'His interpretation recalls Olivier's crookbacked, long-nosed Richard III. Day-Lewis's Christy Brown has the sexual seductiveness that was so startling in the Olivier Richard.'

The *New York Post* described Daniel's performance as 'passionate, unsentimental and technically astounding'. Vincent Canby in the *New York Times* thought it 'exemplary'. 'At first he is so explicitly deformed that it seems rude to stare at him, which might just be the sort of reaction Christy would use to gain an advantage over a stranger.'

The reviews left *My Left Foot*'s American distributors – the brothers Bob and Harvey Weinstein of Miramax – in no doubt that Daniel would figure strongly in the New Years's awards season. There might even be a whiff of an Oscar.

In Hollywood everything has its price. A Best Picture Oscar, for instance, is reckoned to be worth, on average, $30 million at the box office. Marketing millions are poured into campaigns that can subliminally manipulate the minds of the voting members of the Academy. The Weinsteins, among the sharpest marketing men in Hollywood, went to work.

The brash, bearded Harvey Weinstein did not hit it off instantly with the star of the vehicle they planned to drive all the way to the Dorothy Chandler Pavilion, the home of the Oscars, however. According to one account, their first meeting almost came to blows.

Punctuality, a discipline instilled deep in Daniel by life at Croom's Hill and the regimental Nanny Bowler, was not Weinstein's strongest suit. When they first met for lunch in London the American arrived thirty-five minutes late. As Daniel made his displeasure clear there had been an uncomfortable moment when he and the abrasive Weinstein had glared menacingly across the table at each other. 'I thought those two guys were going to kill each other,' Miramax executive Susan Slonnaker recalled later after the temperature had dropped.

Weinstein eventually won Daniel over, however. Just days before Oscar voting closed in early February 1990, Miramax subtly insinuated their film into the minds of the most socially aware Academicians by organizing a screening of *My Left Foot* in support of the Americans with Disabilities Act, a worthy new piece of legislation being steered through Congress. The viewing was held in Washington, DC, where senators Edward

Kennedy and Robert Dole joined an audience including many blind, deaf and physically disabled people.

As well as drawing the interest of the Washington press corps, the screening was covered by the coast-to-coast American TV show, *Entertainment Tonight*. Viewers saw Daniel Day-Lewis win an ovation as he made a brief but impassioned speech explaining how his experience in playing Christy Brown had opened his eyes to the plight of the disabled. To cheers he promised to toast the Americans with Disabilities Act in a Dublin pub.

Daniel's genuine commitment to helping the disabled has not wavered since he first walked through the door of the Sandymount School. Over the years he has done much good, quiet work for the institution that took him to its heart. During his time in America he told reporters that it was only his feelings for the cause of cerebral palsy that had brought him across the Atlantic.

As far as Miramax and its vice-president Russell Schwartz, interviewed afterwards in *Variety* magazine, were concerned, however, the event was a shrewd piece of Oscar election-eering. 'It wasn't too Hollywood and it did create aware-ness.'

Exactly a week later, on St Valentine's Day, as the Oscar nominations were announced in Los Angeles, that awareness had been alchemically turned to gold. The Academy had fallen in love with Daniel Day-Lewis and *My Left Foot*. To the astonishment of even Sheridan and Pearson, their film was nominated for five Oscars.

Daniel was nominated for Best Actor. The other four nominees were his fellow graduate of *Another Country*, Kenneth Branagh, for *Henry V*, Tom Cruise for *Born on the Fourth of July*, Robin Williams for *Dead Poets' Society*, and Morgan Freeman for *Driving Miss Daisy*.

If its star's selection had been predictable, *My Left Foot*'s four other nominations were less so, however. The little miracle of a movie, a film that had almost never been made, was in company with Bruce Beresford's *Driving Miss Daisy* and Oliver Stone's *Born on the Fourth of July*, one of the three most heavily nominated films of the year. Brenda Fricker was nominated for Best Supporting Actress, Jim Sheridan for Best Director, Sheridan and Shane Connaughton for Best Screenplay, and best of all, producer Pearson was cited for Best Picture.

Daniel travelled to Dublin to join 'Shay' Sheridan and company for the celebrations. Back in London, days later, he admitted that the contest would be tight. 'I haven't seen *Born on the Fourth of July* yet, but I've heard from several friends that Tom Cruise is very good in it,' he said. 'I'll have to see it soon, because when I go out to LA everybody will be talking to me about their own films and will assume I've seen them, so I better get moving on that one.'

He was full of admiration for Morgan Freeman, 'a truly great actor', whom he had met when he presented him with a New York Critics Circle prize. 'The competition couldn't be tougher. The betting for most of the categories is extremely tight this year.'

In Hollywood Daniel was joint favourite with Cruise. 'His work is known and Academy voters like British actors,' *Variety* said. Daniel's odds shortened with each of the awards he began picking up. While Cruise beat him to the Hollywood Foreign Press Association's Golden Globe award for Best Actor (Drama), Daniel walked off with three of the other 'major' American awards, The New York Film Critics Circle, The Los Angeles Critics and The National Society of Film Critics.

Sheridan and Pearson had done much of Daniel's donkey work. The duo had been working hard in Hollywood and New York since December. With the cinematic spin doctors of Miramax at their side, they launched a charm offensive that many Americans found irresistible. It was almost a decade since Colin Welland, collecting his writing Oscar for *Chariots of Fire*, had told Hollywood the 'British are coming'. Now the Irish were on the march.

The rest of the emerald army rolled into Hollywood in early and mid-March. While most of the Irish contingent was divided between the Four Seasons Hotel, the Bel Age Hotel and apartments near the Beverly Center, Daniel and Adjani had kept themselves hidden away. Soon, however, they were photographed out walking together in Beverly Hills. Despite Adjani's *de rigueur* dark glasses, pictures of the new couple appeared in Dublin. They were also seen in each other's arms in the bar of the Four Seasons Hotel. Cynics could say, of course, if there was a time and a place to blow your cover, this was it.

Whether accidental or contrived, however, news of the romance between two of Europe's most enigmatic stars would now have little influence on the outcome of the Oscars. By the time Daniel arrived, much of the hard hype work was almost over. During the final run-up, however, he helped Pearson, Sheridan, Connaughton and Brenda Fricker ride the breathless media merry-go-round, each of them telling and retelling, in their best blarney-lined lilts, the remarkable stories of Christy and *My Left Foot*. Six months after his collapse as Hamlet, Daniel was still not recovered and was spared as much as he could be. Anyhow, according to Miramax's Russell Schwartz, 'it's not the stars' place to do parties'.

From the moment their nominations had been announced, Sheridan and Pearson had been courted like kings. In the week before the Oscar ceremony, they went along to the Independent Spirit Awards at the Roosevelt Hotel. *My Left Foot* collected the prize for Best Foreign Film.

As Oscar mania mounted, congratulatory presents poured into their hotel suites: leather jackets, Easter bouquets, bowls of fruit. And there were lunches with the most potent figures in town. Pearson was a guest at the table of Mike Ovitz, head of the all-powerful CAA agency. He sat next to actress Mimi Rogers, the soon-to-be-ex-wife of Tom Cruise, Daniel's arch-rival for Best Actor. Pearson delighted in telling his fellow-Dubliners how she was backing *My Left Foot*.

The men who had had to beg their way around Dublin to finance their film were suddenly being offered money even the wildest, Guinness-fuelled Irish imagination would not have dreamed of. Sheridan was offered a $1.2 million 'hello' to sign up with one studio. There was talk of a deal to make six $10-million pictures with Columbia.

In the run-up all the nominees, Daniel included, had been

invited to a lunch for Oscar contenders held at the Beverly Hilton Hotel. There the format of Hollywood's most elite evening was laid out before them. They were warned against waffling if they made it up on the stage. Gil Cates, producer of the show beamed live to an audience of one billion around the world, told the gathering that speeches would be kept to a forty-five-second minimum. 'Long speeches make a few people happy and 999,999,999 very bored,' he japed. A fifty-inch monitor thirty feet from the stage would count down the seconds. After that, Cates warned, 'a hook would come across and the orchestra would start up'.

Opinion was wildly divided on whose speeches would be supervised by Gil Cates and his hook. Brenda Fricker had emerged as a clear favourite for the Best Supporting Actress Oscar. Her main competition was seen as Daniel's *Unbearable Lightness* co-star Lena Olin for her role in *Enemies, A Love Story*.

The Best Actor award was being billed as a 'battle of the wheelchairs'. Tom Cruise, whom many had thought deserved an Oscar for his performance alongside Dustin Hoffman in *Rain Man* a year earlier, had come of age as Ron Kovic, the real-life Vietnam veteran who overcame disability to become a prominent anti-war campaigner.

Morgan Freeman, in line to be the first black Best Actor winner since Sidney Poitier in 1963, was the outsider best placed to benefit from a split vote, particularly as his movie, the Bruce Beresford-directed *Driving Miss Daisy* was emerging as a likely Best Film winner. Williams and Branagh – whose film had barely been seen in middle America – were seen as rank outsiders . Equally Sheridan, Connaughton and Pearson were regarded as long shots for the Best Director, Best Screenplay and Best Film awards.

As they left Dublin, the Irish had tried to dampen expectations by declaring the five nominations triumph enough. 'I just feel we've won already,' Sheridan said. 'Anything else will be a bonus,' he added, slipping into the sort of Saturday afternoon sportspeak normally reserved for footballers. As the Big Day approached, however, the director admitted that he would be disappointed if Daniel did not emerge the winner.

By Friday all the votes had been cast and delivered to the Wilshire Boulevard offices of the accountants Price Waterhouse. They would remain there under lock and key until Monday evening's ceremony.

Over the weekend, as the Hollywood hopefuls resigned themselves to the fact that they could do no more, there was still no consensus. Three of the *Los Angeles Times'* four film critics backed Daniel for the Best Actor award. The influential TV critics Gene Siskel and Roger Ebert, however, predicted Morgan Freeman would get the nod. They thought Cruise was his main competition.

In one of the most open Oscar races for years, pundits even looked at the seating arrangements in the 3000-seater pavilion at the Los Angeles Music Center for tips. Few clues there: Daniel, Cruise and Freeman were each in prime position to bound on stage.

Oscar morning arrived and with it more gifts. By now there were no wide-eyed innocents to receive them in the Four Seasons. As he surveyed an Easter basket from CAA, resplendent with a plaque reading 'for the luck o' the Irish' and a handwritten note from Peter Guber, on his way to the headship of Columbia Tri-Star, the director wondered out loud 'whether the other four had the same note'.

The show would start at 6 p.m. precisely LA time, 2 a.m. Dublin time. The stretch limousines rolled up at 3 p.m. to collect the *My Left Foot* contingent.

The fashion parade was a mixture of style, sobriety and superstition. Shane Connaughton was wearing a tuxedo he had borrowed from actor friend Peter Egan. Apparently, Connaughton told his friends, Timothy Dalton had worn it for his audition to play James Bond. A lucky suit. Brenda Fricker was dressed in a sequined trouser suit by designer Frank Usher, Fran Sheridan in a Louis Féraud number, Daniel in a sweeping black dress-coat, white silk shirt and a Mississippi riverboat gambler's bow tie. The effect was Byronesque Beau Brummell or Brett Maverick, depending on which side of the Atlantic you came from.

Soon they were stuck in the most valuable traffic jam of Los

Angeles' year. The ten-mile trip from Beverly Hills to the Dorothy Chandler Pavilion passed at a snail's pace, cars grid-locked together along most of the approach roads. Daniel, Sheridan, Pearson, Connaughton and Fricker shared the same capacious auto, their conversation a mixture of nerves and nonsense, they admitted later.

In another limousine a red-eyed Kenneth Branagh was recovering from a 6000-mile flight from Tokyo. He had left the stage in the Japanese capital where he had been playing King Lear and hopped straight on a pan-Pacific flight. As, to his annoyance, everybody was comparing him with Olivier, whose 1944 version of *Henry V* had been nominated for four Oscars and won none (he was given a special award instead), he was reminded of the great man's excuse for boycotting a later Academy Awards night. 'It's an awfully long way to come and my face isn't going to look any prettier with egg all over it.' Like the *My Left Foot* party, however, the effortlessly savvy Branagh knew that the worldwide exposure his film would get that night – win or lose – was worth millions in audience receipts.

Britain's other contender for a major prize, Pauline Collins, nominated for Best Actress for her part in Willy Russell's acerbic comedy *Shirley Valentine*, lounged in yet another limo with her actor husband John Alderton.

Outside the Dorothy Chandler Pavilion it was the annual flash-blazed bun-fight. The walk along the 200-yards of red carpet took an eternity, America's box-office aristocracy either loving or loathing every moment, depending on their disposition. Robert De Niro, there to present the Best Director award with his friend Martin Scorsese, grimaced. Jack Nicholson, there to present the Best Picture Oscar with his pal Warren Beatty, grinned wolfishly. Jessica Lange, nominated for Best Actress in *Music Box*, smiled politely. Two new super-couples, Cruise and Nicole Kidman, Kiefer Sutherland and Julia Roberts, star of the just-released hit *Pretty Woman*, flashed mega-watt smiles. Daniel negotiated his first taste of Holly-wood's grossest display with the sort of fixed, Cheshire Cat smile he had used as a boy. Once he was past the final hurdle, the TV interview stand of *Variety*'s veteran reporter Army Archerd, and into the shadows of the pavilion, the smile faded with the early evening Los Angeles light. He was alone in the dark with his thoughts.

The woman who would present that night's Best Actor prize, the previous year's Best Actress, Jodie Foster, once said of the annual ritual now unfolding: 'As much as I love Oscar night and all its pageantry, it's a silly bingo game.' As he made his way to his seat, Daniel was acutely aware of what was at stake if, in that night's bingo game, his number came up.

His career was at a crossroads.

Since the dole queue days and his dreams of becoming a new Gielgud, he had not hidden his desire for success at the highest level. He abhorred much within the industry, the 'fat people', their handshakes, having to display himself outside his roles. But film was still a world of infinite possibility. He wanted an invitation to sit at a grander table, the best roles, the best opportunities for escape. The *Stars and Bars* imbroglio, the uncertainty already surrounding *Eversmile New Jersey*, and, of course, the *Hamlet* headlines had conspired, however, to place question marks over his career. Had he been less than sure-footed over the last few years?

That he was the most chameleonic of character actors was in no doubt. But did he have the nerve to go with his dashing good looks, did he have the judgement to go with his ability? Did he really have the makings of a matinee idol, as everyone had imagined he had since March 1986?

Once a year, such doubts can be erased in the time it takes to unseal an envelope. Lazarus-like, dead or dying careers can come back to life. Virtual unknowns can become box-office bankers, lightweights can become heavyweights, losers can become winners. If there is a magic to the Oscars, it is in that trick. Daniel knew that, and so did his rivals, each of whom had their own reasons for craving a win. A few yards away, Tom Cruise yearned to be taken seriously as an actor, Robin Williams was desperate to break free from his comic cocoon, Kenneth Branagh hoped to lift the yoke of the 'new Olivier', Morgan Freeman wanted a small sign that the racism of the

Academy was a thing of the past. The quintet sank into their seats. The numbers would be up shortly.

Soon there was cause for optimism. Within an hour or so, by the time the fifth of the eighteen awards was announced, Ireland's latest exodus to the American continent had proven worthwhile. Brenda Fricker, Olin, Roberts, nominated for *Steel Magnolias*, Anjelica Huston for *Enemies, A Love Story*, and Dianne Wiest for *Parenthood* watched stone-faced as Kevin Kline peeled open the envelope containing the name of the Best Supporting Actress winner. Fricker visibly mouthed 'I don't believe it' as Kline read out her name.

Her speech was a model of effusive efficiency. She thanked her *My Left Foot* colleagues, the late Christy Brown 'just for being alive', and his mother – 'anyone who gives birth to twenty-two children deserves one of these' – then headed, face flushed with emotion, back-stage for her appointment with the 638 assorted media folk in the interview room. There had been no need for Gil Cates to reach for either hook or stopwatch.

Still, however, there were few clues as to which direction the big prizes were headed. As the time for the Best Actor award arrived, no one film was sweeping up in the manner of *Gandhi* in 1983 or *The Last Emperor* in 1988. *Driving Miss Daisy* had collected Best Make-up and Best Screenplay. *Born on the Fourth of July* had won Best Film Editing. So many Oscar ceremonies in the past had taken on a mood of momentum-induced inevitability. Not this one.

Jodie Foster, draped in black, arrived on stage to announce the recipient. The five nominees sank deeper into their chairs to watch clips from their films. Branagh smiled at his Agincourt speech, Cruise joined in the applause for his anguished vet, Daniel appeared to be holding his breath as his clip came up. Morgan Freeman and Robin Williams nodded and smiled as humbly as they decently could as their finest moments followed.

Foster recited the time-honoured words: 'And the Oscar goes to . . .' and, as she emptied the card from the envelope, let her face wreathe itself in a warm smile. 'Mmmm,' she said with relish, 'Daniel Day-Lewis.'

All around him the audience was rising to its feet. Branagh let loose a yell of delight at the announcement. Cruise, Williams and Freeman were standing, smiling and applauding generously. Daniel flopped forward. Later, he would claim, someone projected him out of his seat.

He walked rigidly up the steps to collect the 30-inch, 24-carat-gold-plated piece of pewter alloy that had in that instant dispelled the doubts and transformed his life. For a moment he simply acknowledged the applause. Later, as he struggled to describe the thoughts coursing through his head, he would remember feeling drained of blood, light-headed, hallucinatory, even.

He had prepared a few words, as everyone does. Visibly drawing a deep breath to compose himself, he began to say them. The son of the Anglo-Irish poet, at this instant the provider of one of the finest feathers ever to be placed in the old country's cap, began by committing a city to one of the great parties in its history.

'You have just provided me with the makings of one hell of a weekend in Dublin,' he said, his vocal cords, as his father's had done, misting an impeccable Englishness with a distant echo of Irishness. There would be other moments to think of his father. For now, thoughts of him watching, smiling somewhere, took second place to those of another heaven-sent writer. 'I am truly grateful to you that, in giving me this award, you are encouraging Christy to carry on making his mark,' added Daniel, to more applause.

He said 'Thank You', made the last wrong turn of his life by starting to walk the wrong way off the stage, spun on his heels, took Foster's, his 'back-stage wife's', hand and walked off to face the media mêlée.

Arriving, still dazed, in the interview room, he received the biggest ovation of the night. The questions were stock cub-reporter standard: 'How do you feel?' 'What does this mean?'

There was a question about the disabled actors' protests in Britain. 'More than once disabled actors have made it clear they don't like the fact that I made this film,' he said. 'And in the end they're right, there's no argument. But the film wouldn't have been made with a disabled actor. I did it for selfish reasons, I wanted the film made.'

One voice, however, had clearly researched the Oscar winner in advance. 'Daniel, have you ever thought of not acting any more?' it asked. Through a stiletto-thin smile he replied, 'Every morning.'

As he dealt with the banalities of his newborn celebrity, his friends Sheridan and Pearson were being disappointed back in the auditorium. So too was Isabelle Adjani. English-born Jessica Tandy, star of *Driving Miss Daisy*, beat Adjani, Collins, Lange and Michelle Pfeiffer for *The Fabulous Baker Boys*, for Best Actress. Oliver Stone collected the Best Director award for *Born on the Fourth of July*, producers Richard D. Zanuck and Lili Fini Zanuck took delivery of the Best Picture prize for *Driving Miss Daisy*, in the end the most successful film of the night with four awards.

As Daniel headed off to his first party of the night, Hollywood was already weighing up the new star suddenly in its midst. The 'fat people' smelled great things. They would smile even harder, shake his hand even more firmly. He was worth a 'few bob' more.

The first celebration was the Academy Governors' post-Oscar ball. Over canapés, caviar terrine and veal chop, winners and losers mixed, swapping tales of what might have been. The *My Left Foot* team was told that the film had come within a whisker of winning the Best Picture award. One actor, admitting he had voted for Daniel, bared his soul with un-Hollywood honesty: 'I saw someone up there doing something I could not do myself.' The word was that Oliver Stone was 'pissed' that Tom Cruise had been beaten by Daniel. He had blamed his film's failure to pick up more than two Oscars on 'the right-wing media'. 'It's political, it made a lot of people angry,' he complained.

Isabelle Adjani was there, disappointed but dazzling in a white organza dress designed for her by Dior's Gianfranco Ferre. Hollywood's new Best Actor stayed away, however, as the couple were determined not to flaunt their relationship under the noses of the world's press. Instead, members of the

Irish party, keeping the secret, had to look on as the empty-handed French star was outrageously courted by her old flame Warren Beatty. Afterwards one member of the loyal *My Left Foot* contingent confessed he had felt like 'nutting' Hollywood's incorrigible Don Juan as he toasted Adjani over Waterford Crystal flutes of vintage champagne: 'He was moldering her.'

Daniel had headed for the celebration that was being thrown mainly in his and Brenda Fricker's honour, organized by Miramax at the Beverly Hilton. There *My Left Foot* colleagues like line producer Arthur Lappin and publicist Gerry Lundberg were already in full flight. Bono and his wife Ali, Bob Geldof and a raft of other Irish supporters joined the champagne frenzy. Fricker arrived clutching her statuette and feeling 'confused, elated, hyped-up, shocked and inarticulate'. Like Daniel, one of her few regrets was that one of her parents was not alive to see her triumph. Her late mother had started her in showbusiness young. 'Oh, if only she had been alive to see her dream come true,' she said sadly.

As he swept into the party, a still dazed-looking Daniel was collared by reporters and an RTE television crew. 'Your ears are just expecting to hear anyone else's name but your own,' he said beaming. 'And when I heard my own I think someone had to push me out of my chair, all the blood just drained out of me, you know. I felt quite overwhelmed.'

Agents, producers and studio executives wasted no time in seeking out the Irish winners. Brenda Fricker's American agent Russ Tyler announced that his client would be looking for comedy roles. Jim Sheridan and Shane Connaughton were adamant that they did not want to move to America full-time. Daniel's American agent, Gene Parseghian of Triad Artists, was presenting a similar message.

After leaving the Beverly Hilton at 1 a.m., Daniel, Pearson, Fricker, Sheridan and company headed off into the Hollywood Hills to the home of one of *My Left Foot*'s investors, Billy Gaff. There the party went on until dawn with Branagh, American director Steven Sodebergh and one of Gaff's old friends from Rod Stewart days, Britt Ekland, joining in.

'Daniel was keen to come along because there were a lot of crew members from *My Left Foot* there,' one reveller remembered. He recalled seeing Daniel, exhausted by the events of the evening, slumped in a huge white armchair, cradling his Oscar. 'He was drained by the emotion of it all that night, we all were.'

The sun came up accompanied by Sheridan and Pearson singing an Irish ballad, 'The Foggy Dew'. Brenda Fricker and Gerry Lundberg were waltzing in the thin daylight. There was Irish stew and more chilled champagne for breakfast.

Next morning one of Daniel's first calls was to his mother back in Hampshire. 'He said he couldn't believe it,' she told local newspaper reporters at home as she posed for photographs alongside a self-portrait of her son painted while he was at Bedales. 'He almost keeled over. He said he got on the stage and thought he was hallucinating.' Jill said she had received messages of congratulations from neighbours Sir Alec Guinness and Dame Peggy Ashcroft among others.

Back in Hollywood, Daniel had told reporters that he would be returning to London after recovering from the partying. His mother let slip, however, that he had mentioned other plans. He was off to Paris, she said. *My Left Foot* was due to premiere there that week.

Daniel headed off to Adjani's home city where Noël Pearson also attended the premiere. Days later the two men flew into Dublin airport in time for the beginning of the 'hell of a weekend' Daniel had anticipated on the Oscar podium. The full impact of his Oscar had yet to dawn on him. Greeted by RTE at the airport, he said, 'You can't start talking about what it means, nobody knows what it means.'

Dublin was determined to treat its conquering moviemakers with a reception to outdo even those laid on for two favourite sporting sons, Stephen Roche the cyclist after his win in the Tour de France and world champion boxer Barry McGuigan.

Daniel met Tamasin at the Shelbourne Hotel where they would stay during the weekend. Isabelle Adjani was to join them there. With his sister at his side, Daniel's first stop was

Sandymount Clinic. He arrived unannounced and spent hours talking to the friends he had made there a year earlier.

'He, his sister and Oscar arrived unannounced on the Friday morning,' Tony Jordan recalled. 'He had the Oscar in a duffel bag over his shoulder. They spent several hours seeing everybody, signing autographs and posing for photographs. In the junior class one tiny tot identified Daniel: "He's my left foot." '

The official party began that Friday night with a grand civic reception at Dublin Castle's St Patrick's Hall. There Daniel, Fricker, Sheridan and Pearson were presented with Cavan Crystal cups by the Lord Mayor, Sean Haughey.

'I am so happy the weekend in Dublin has finally started,' Daniel said in a short speech in which he again thanked the Brown family for all their support. He also spoke of the growing affection he had for the city and hinted that he was thinking of making it his permanent base. 'I am consistently astonished by the amazing welcomes I have had in this city,' he said. 'I never make plans to leave Dublin.' He joked that he had left his Oscar on a chest of drawers back at the Shelbourne Hotel.

One of Christy Brown's sisters, Mona Byrne, told the gathering that the spirit of her brother would want them to enjoy the weekend. 'Christy is in heaven saying, "Have a great time and have a sup on me." '

Adjani jetted in from Paris to join the celebrations. She and Daniel once more attempted to shy away from the cameras, however. They had been pictured together again arriving in Paris. After the photographs had been published in France, Adjani sued the magazine for printing them without her permission.

In Dublin she refused to leave the limousine which delivered her at the Shelbourne. According to later reports, Daniel stepped out of the car and asked the waiting banks of photographers to leave. 'She won't come in if you're all here. Kindly leave so we can go in and enjoy the party,' he supposedly said.

News of the romance was everywhere by now. In London Baz Bamigboye, the *Daily Mail*'s impeccably connected show-business columnist, ran a piece on the 'secret passion'. 'There's something going on between Daniel and Isabelle but you know what he's like: he'll be mortified that people are talking about him,' one friend was quoted as saying. 'You can never tell with him whether it's a fully-fledged romance or just a fling that may last a few more days or a few more weeks.'

Despite his Irish passport, Britain still rightly regarded Daniel as its own. He was only the fourteenth home-grown Best Actor in sixty-two years of Oscars, only the fifth to win the great prize in a British-financed film, which, of course, it was in large part. It would take Hollywood time to come to terms with the complexities of its new star. Back in Britain, wiser heads knew that unpredictability was all that could be predicted.

Stephen Frears wondered whether the win would send his friend even deeper into depression than *Hamlet* had done. 'I know Daniel. He will be in a terrible state – utter depression,' he told the theatre critic Jack Tinker in the *Daily Mail*. 'He will find all the attention quite awful and people will be offering him film roles he won't want. He doesn't want to be a movie star and never will.'

Others predicted a smooth transition into the stratosphere. 'What the Oscar will do for Day-Lewis – apart from the silly offers from Hollywood agents to package him for millions of dollars in his next movie or find him a vehicle to star in alongside Eddie Murphy – is to give him choice, and the most luxurious aspect of that choice is the opportunity to work with first-division film directors such as Lawrence Kasdan, Martin Scorsese or Woody Allen,' Iain Johnstone, the respected *Sunday Times* film critic, wrote.

On both sides of the Atlantic suggestions about what the new Oscar winner would move on to appeared with sublime to ridiculous relentlessness. There was talk of a return to British television in a lavish costume drama, *Pride and Prejudice*. Daniel would take the part of Jane Austen's darkly handsome Darcy. There were already rumours of a collaboration with Martin Scorsese on an adaptation of Edith Wharton's period romance, *The Age of Innocence*. Somewhere there probably was talk of a 'vehicle' with Eddie Murphy.

Daniel would remain 'particular and somewhat idiosyncratic' about whom he worked with, Parseghian said in Holly-

Hamlet, National Theatre, London, March 1989. (*Donald Cooper*)

Facing page: With Tamasin at the BAFTA awards, London 1989. (*Alpha*)

Right: With his half-brother Sean, 1993. (*Richard Waite/Katz*)

Below: 'The most on-off relationship in the world.' Shying away from the cameras with Isabelle Adjani (left) in Los Angeles, March 1990.

Above: The longest night. In the grip of Oscar-mania, Los Angeles, March 1990. (*Alpha*)

Facing page: At ease with a disabled child on a visit to a centre for the disabled in Athens, Greece, May 1990. (*Rex*)

A matinée idol is born. Stripped to reveal the results of his months of training on *The Last of the Mohicans.*

The master's voice. At work with Martin Scorsese on the set of *The Age of Innocence.* (*Katz*)

The polite public figure. Dealing with autograph hunters in Manhattan, July 1993.
(*Marcel Thomas/Sipa/Rex*)

Right: Love requited? As Newland Archer with Winona Ryder as May Welland in *The Age of Innocence*.

Below: The boys are back in town. With Jim Sheridan and Pete Postlethwaite in New York for the Première of *In the Name of the Father*, December 1993. (*Rex*)

wood. 'He now has a wider range of material and a greater range of choices,' he told *Variety*. His client's asking price had 'significantly increased', he added.

Even the disappointment surrounding *Eversmile New Jersey* could not now harm him. Given a limited release in America, the reaction to Sorin's film was so uninspiring that Medusa Pictures, its UK distributors, shelved plans to screen the film theatrically. The brave attempt to transmute allegorically an American road movie to the magical landscape of Patagonia had not come off. It had ended up a mish-mash; the Anglo-Argentinian venture had fallen between cross-cultural stools. Daniel's first post-Oscar performance became the first film of his to suffer that shaming fate, 'straight to video'.

For Daniel, however, the landscape had changed for ever. In the split second it had taken to open an envelope, he had been transformed.

Perhaps the greatest luxury of all now was that he could take time between his roles and treat himself a little better than he had in the past. So as he reached his thirty-fourth birthday, he left the world to kick down the Brook Green barricades, sent Oscar off to the engraver, told his agents to leave him in peace, and went cycling alone in the hills of Enniskerry. As he left, Irish journalists asked whether he had any plans. 'None at all.' Time, once more, to travel light, unencumbered by the past . . . or the future, for that matter.

CHAPTER THIRTEEN

LOVE IN A WAR ZONE

'I tend to be drawn to characters who are totally outside
my own experience, whose motivations I don't
understand. Anyone who isn't like me. God, yes, as
unlike me as possible!'

DANIEL DAY-LEWIS, *Arena*, 1989

O NCE MORE America – and the world – had to double-
take. A year ago he had walked on to the stage of the
Dorothy Chandler Pavilion, tall, haunted, rail-thin.
His frail looks screamed out for a hearty supper, and Irish stew
and dumplings rather than canapés and caviar terrine.

Tonight, as the sixty-third Academy Awards moved with
Gil Cates's usual ergonomic efficiency towards its climax, he
had the well-fed appearance of a grid-iron line-backer or a
rugby loose forward. There were bulging neck muscles, stone-
carved shoulders, an extra, impressive bulk. Now he was on a
five-meal, 5000-calorie-a-day diet. Effete dandyism had given
way to sinewy machismo.

In March 1991 Daniel Day-Lewis was finally ready to re-
emerge from the post-*Hamlet*, post-Oscar wilderness. Another
Academy Awards night provided the first glimpse of an actor
now being remodelled to fit the 165-year-old vision of American writer James Fenimore Cooper: a man whose 'every nerve
and muscle appeared strung and indurated by unremitting
exposure and toil' – Hawkeye, the frontiersman hero of *The Last
of the Mohicans*.

For the first months that followed the tenth and most visible acting prize for *My Left Foot* – in all there were four American prizes, two Irish, three English and one Canadian – Daniel
had resisted the deluge of offers. 'I don't want to be in any big
films without any share of artistic control,' he had said in his

few post-Oscar utterings. Instead he wanted small-scale movies, work with 'people sharing the same secret'.

One shared secret was Sally Potter's ambitious project, *Orlando*. In early summer 1990 reports began to appear that Daniel had signed up to star in Potter's long-planned story based on a Virginia Woolf novel. Tilda Swinton had been cast in the title-role, an immortal poet whose journey through time and history also brings with it a change of gender.

Unlike the many other stories circulating about Daniel's first post-Oscar project, this one was partly true. He had become involved, but as associate producer rather than a member of the cast.

Potter had already been battling to get her movie made for two years. The challenging complexities of Woolf's story and Potter's script terrified many potential investors. 'They thought it was a film that was never going to get made, that it was impossible,' Potter's producer Christopher Sheppard said.

Daniel had heard of *Orlando* through Swinton. He was so impressed by Potter's screenplay that he agreed to help. 'I'm just trying to help Sally out with getting it set up,' he told Michael Dwyer of the *Irish Times* in May 1990. 'I am using whatever contacts I have to help get the film made.'

Daniel heaped praise on Potter. Her film 'transports you into a world you've never been before', he said. 'She has done a remarkable job on the script. It's about mortality and immortality, gender and class and it's got this whole historical sweep which makes you feel like you're travelling through time.'

Flitting between London and Paris, where he and Adjani were able to continue their relationship unobtrusively, Daniel spent much of the summer helping Potter raise the cash. By early 1991 five partners from France, Italy, the Netherlands, Britain and Russia had agreed to finance the £2.5-million movie. When *Orlando* was released to worldwide critical acclaim in 1992, however, Daniel shied away from taking credit. Five associate producers are listed. His name is not among them.

As doors opened so they closed, however. For every potential film investor now eager to speak to Britain's Oscar winner, there were also a hundred reporters. In their desperation for stories on the enigmatic new hero in their midst, newspapers scouted his every move. When, in July 1990, at the height of the news-starved 'silly season', he was sighted visiting Madonna at her London hotel, there was only one possible tabloid conclusion: the couple were enjoying what *Today* newspaper euphemistically referred to as a 'close friendship'. Daniel dealt with the rumour with his usual politeness. 'Goodbye, goodbye,' he told the paper's reporter when he called for a comment.

'The Madonna story is one of my favourites,' said his half-brother Sean. 'I'm sure it would have been fun seeing her introduced to Jill Balcon.'

The humorous side of Daniel's predicament, the intrusive price of fame, was lost on the subject of all this speculation. 'They say that when you become famous, you must know what you are letting yourself in for. But Daniel can't lead his own life,' Tamasin protested on his behalf. 'He can't step out of his front door without people wanting bits of him. No one can warn you about that.'

The Oscar-winning images, Byronic and beaming, had been reproduced around the planet. His handsome features had been engraved on a billion memories. Gone was the pleasure of walking a city's streets unnoticed, gone was the right to do or say anything without a greater significance being drawn, gone – and perhaps missed most of all – was the joy of sitting in the corner of a café, indulging in acts of actorly theft. Now the observer had become the observed. The toolbox of Daniel's craft had been half-emptied. It was not quite Nowhere to Hide. Not quite, but almost.

London became an almost unbearable burden. His dislike of his home city had already taken root. He was far more comfortable strolling the boulevards of the Left Bank of Paris and the streets off St Stephen's Green, Dublin. In both cities he felt some sense of liberty. In London all was uneasiness.

On a steely-skied October afternoon in 1990, however, as he left the fashionable haven of L'Escargot restaurant in Greek Street, Soho and walked down Shaftesbury Avenue in the heart of theatreland, Daniel had been oblivious to the prodding, pointing fingers, the stares and the whispers. The rasping Chicago accent of director Michael Mann had held him in its spell for four long hours over lunch. As the theatre billboards lit up the deepening gloom, Daniel had finally been persuaded to emerge from the shadows.

When he had first been shown the script for Twentieth Century Fox's adaptation of *The Last of the Mohicans* it seemed precisely to define the sort of film he had vowed he would not make. A $40-million budget. An epic-scale production. A studio's Great White Hope for the year.

The film had been brought to the cinema screen twice before, the first more than fifty years earlier in 1936. Randolph Scott played the part of Hawkeye in George B. Seitz's black and white western. Jon Hall took the part eleven years later in a lacklustre remake called *Last of the Redmen*, directed by George Sherman.

Writer-director Mann, who had made his name as the creator of the seminal designer-violence TV series, *Miami Vice*, had produced a screenplay that was more faithful to the flash of Don Johnson's one-man war against the drug trade than Seitz and Sherman's sturdy tales of Indians and settlers caught up in the Anglo-French frontier war in 1750s America. It was clear his film would be visceral and visually stylish. It was also clear that the burden of being 'the money' would be greater than anything Daniel had experienced before.

Yet as he read and then re-read the story he became fascinated by it. First his attention was drawn to the opening human image in Mann and co-writer Christopher Crowe's script. It was of a foot, not this time the sole functioning limb of a man, but the first visible part of a perfectly tuned athlete, effortlessly gliding through the backwoods. As he read on he became intrigued by the story's hero, Hawkeye or Nathaniel Poe, the white orphan of Scots–Irish settler parents, raised as his son by Chingachgook, father of Uncas, the Last of the Mohicans. His was a life dictated by the laws of nature, he was a wanderer, a man who when asked whether his allegiance is with the English or the French, says, 'I do not call myself subject to much at all.' Every other character Daniel had been drawn to had been inarticulate, uncertain, hemmed in. Here was a character who had no such neuroses.

He admired Mann's script and his ambition. Initially, however, he followed his instincts and said no. Michael Mann, whose last major movie had been the 1986 thriller *Manhunter*, the first screen incarnation of crime writer Thomas Harris's chilling Hannibal 'The Cannibal' Lecter, had come too far to be put off, however. 'Daniel Day-Lewis is the only man who can play Hawkeye,' he had told the heads of Twentieth Century Fox. He persisted.

Mann cannily enlisted the help of veteran agent Sam Cohn, whose client list included Daniel's friend and fellow *Stars and Bars* survivor, Pat O'Connor. The voice of the devil on his shoulder was suddenly drowned out by a chorus of friends advising him otherwise. O'Connor and others he trusted told him they believed the film was right for him.

As Daniel agonized, Mann kept up the pressure by pony-expressing research material and advance design ideas from his Los Angeles office to London and Paris. It included snatches of music, historical notes on the life of the real frontiersmen and images of how he perceived Hawkeye.

Sensing he might finally have his man within his sights, Mann flew across the Atlantic, met Daniel for the L'Escargot lunch and let the magical spell of his story do the rest.

The then forty-seven-year-old Mann knew London well. He had studied at the London International Film School in the late 1960s. It had been in Paris, however, that he had won his big break. As a student he had filmed civil rights riots in Chicago. As the French capital erupted in 1968, the abrasive son of a Ukrainian-born grocer headed for the action. Using contacts within the student movement in France, he shot some of the most remarkable footage of the street demonstrations. He took it back to America and was given his first job in television as a result.

Over lunch Mann, known in Hollywood for his perfectionism, overwhelmed Daniel with his encyclopaedic knowledge of the period in which Cooper's book is set. 'One of the things I find very attractive in people is when they know enough of the worth of what they are doing not to try and sell it to anybody else. Michael knew a great deal,' Daniel said later.

Daniel claimed he connected with Mann as they talked about the French general in Cooper's story, Montcalm. He said he told Mann that Montcalm had died at the battle of Quebec, the same spot where a distant ancestor of his, General Wolfe, famously perished. The unofficial Day-Lewis family historian, Sean, makes no mention of his family's links with the ill-fated English soldier in his biography of their father. Perhaps Daniel was privy to information Sean was not. Or perhaps, in an amnesic echo of his father, Daniel was using 'selective knowledge' to ensure the facts did not get in the way of a rather romantic lunch-time story. Either way, the two men left the restaurant with a shared sense that they would soon be working together. 'I think by the time we were walking down Shaftesbury Avenue we knew we were going to do the movie together,' Mann said later.

Daniel agreed to sign up for the picture within days. He knew that his first film since *My Left Foot* and his Oscar success would be crucial. In many ways he would have one shot. So why not entrust it to a character whose legend was built around his ability to kill with one bullet? And why not entrust himself to the first character he had played who displayed a burning sense of direction? 'For once in my life I was fascinated by someone who knew how to read the signs.'

James Fenimore Cooper's novel exerts a mythic hold over the minds of many Americans. Yet, as Daniel discovered as he pored over Mann's copious research, his writing style was unremittingly boring. Mark Twain once wrote a damning essay on the writer's 'literary offenses'. 'Cooper's word sense was singularly dull,' he wrote. Passages of dialogue like 'Come friends let us move our station, and in such a fashion too, as will throw the cunning of a Mingo on the wrong scent, or our scalps will be drying in the wind in front of Montcalm's marquee, ag'in this hour tomorrow' rather prove Twain's point.

The revisionist image Mann and his design team had in mind might have made the stoic novelist spin in his grave. The success of Kevin Costner's *Dances with Wolves* – an $18-million 'folly' that had gone on to break the magical $100-million barrier at the box office and was destined for even greater things at the March 1991 Oscars – had breathed new life into Hollywood's favourite film genre, the western. Mann wanted to summon up the spirit of that unconquered America in all its magnificent savagery. The director, who had made *Miami Vice* a worldwide success by populating the screen with glamorous, soft-lensed good looks, also wanted to fill his film with strikingly beautiful and heroic central characters. Daniel's Hawkeye should be the first great romantic screen hero of the 1990s.

Daniel was Mann's man. In the winter of 1990 he was not physically the embodiment of Cooper's 'strong and indurated' athlete, however. Continuing to adhere to the diet Tamasin had recommended to him, Daniel was still the 'long drink of water' he had been eight years earlier during auditions for *Another Country*.

It was agreed that his physique would need to be reshaped. Daniel also – enthusiastically – agreed to travel to America to learn the survival skills that were second nature to the eighteenth-century inhabitants of the frontiers. 'We designed a nine-month curriculum for his becoming Hawkeye,' Mann recalled.

English fitness trainer Richard Smedley saw through the first part of the curriculum. After a lengthy telephone conversation with the director, the ex-Parachute Regiment officer agreed to take on the job of transforming Daniel into the sleek, sinewed backwoodsman of Fenimore Cooper's imagination. The transformation he needed to undergo was not quite the grotesque ballooning act that Robert De Niro had been through for his performance in *Raging Bull*, the film and the role of the 1980s. To portray the bloated, bitter, older Jake La Motta, De Niro had binged on ice-cream to put on an extra sixty pounds. Smedley's brief was to put twenty pounds of muscle on to his charge's body within four months.

Daniel placed himself in Smedley's care, beginning by telling him all he could about his eating habits and fitness regime. The ex-soldier discovered a fit but unmuscular thirty-three-year-old who admitted to often eating only one meal a day.

'He was very slight but not unfit, just very wiry,' Smedley recalled. 'They didn't want any fat. They just wanted him to look incredibly strong and fit but with an animal grace. After seeing him I had the exact picture of what he could look like.'

Daniel assured Smedley of his commitment to whatever programme he wanted to plan for him. The two men went to work. Smedley's task was to transform a 'narrow, straight torso' into a classical V-shape. To do this he would need to thicken Daniel's neck and add definition to muscle groupings in his arms, shoulders and back.

The trainer designed a programme combining weight-training, running and sparring. He also put Daniel on a strict diet. 'He had to eat five times a day, good, wholesome, well-balanced meals like pasta with plenty of vegetables, lots of fresh fruit and a high-calorie drink every day,' he explained. The daily target was 5000 calories.

Daniel had little trouble losing the fat that built up. The Irish–Jewish genes he had inherited had always protected him from putting on the weight his father added to his sturdy frame. Daniel had the 'big feller' frame of his father and the nervous metabolism of his mother. Man and boy, he had remained the 'long drink'.

By the end of the sixteen-week programme, Daniel was barely recognizable. 'His whole body had been transformed and you could see the muscles there. His torso looked brilliant and his arms and back were perfectly defined. He was thrilled with the way he looked – so were the studio guys,' Smedley recalled later.

By the Academy Awards of March 1991 the transformation was already strikingly apparent. Oscar etiquette has it that the reigning Best Actor presents the Best Actress prize the following year. Daniel arrived to put four quaking actresses – Meryl Streep for *Postcards from the Edge*, Anjelica Huston for *The Grifters*, Joanne Woodward for *Mr and Mrs Bridge*, and Julia Roberts for *Pretty Woman* – out of their misery: 'And the Oscar goes to Kathy Bates.'

Daniel handed the statuette to the star of Rob Reiner's adaptation of Stephen King's novel with a broad, knowing smile. In the time it had taken him to open the envelope, the forty-two-year-old Bates, until now better known for her stage work, had undergone the same mutation he had experienced himself. 'All of us practise our Academy Award speech in the shower, but it seemed like something that would not happen to me,' said the stunned actress before she was led off stage by her dashing, newly muscle-bound 'backstage husband'.

There were familiar faces at the post-awards parties. Stephen Frears, nominated for Best Director for *The Grifters*, was there, as were 'Shay' Sheridan and Noël Pearson, whose follow-up to *My Left Foot*, *The Field*, had brought a nomination for the veteran Richard Harris. Both had lost, Frears to Kevin Costner, director of the night's big winner, *Dances with Wolves*, Harris to another Briton, Jeremy Irons, for his ice-cool portrayal of Claus von Bulow in *Reversal of Fortune*. All were impressed by the pumped-up new Daniel.

His London agent Julian Belfrage suffered the same shock over dinner before his star client travelled off for the next stage of his training in the summer. 'I had dinner with him before he left and hardly recognized him. He has put on so much weight and all of it is muscle, it was like sitting across the table from a Red Indian,' he confided to the London *Evening Standard*.

Filming was due to begin at the end of July 1991. For the final weeks before shooting Daniel completed Mann's curriculum under the watchful eyes of American experts. In Pittsview, Alabama he learned how to handle firearms. Fenimore Cooper's Hawkeye derives his nickname from his ability with a long rifle. While under Richard Smedley's wing Daniel had carried a heavy staff around with him wherever he went. The staff had simulated the twelve-pound gun he would have to carry everywhere with him as Hawkeye. At Pittsview's Special Operations Center, a private counter-terrorist and law-enforcement training centre, he would learn to fire an authentic frontier-period rifle.

David Webster, the Center's director, recalled afterwards a pupil with an insatiable interest. 'He soaked up information.

He didn't want Hawkeye to do anything that really wasn't feasible. He was going to find this character and he did.'

From there Daniel retreated to the woods of North Carolina, where Mann was to shoot the film. There he prepared to spend a month living as an eighteenth-century frontiersman would have done. Two decades after he had mischievously taken pot-shots at pigeons with an air pistol and fly-fished on the Thames, Daniel was forced to rely on advanced versions of both skills for his survival. He spent weeks learning how to trap and skin animals, to build canoes, fight with tomahawks and fire authentic twelve-pound flintlock rifles, even if reloading and on the run. Of all the escape acts he had performed, this was perhaps the most complete. He was living a lifestyle that civilization had left behind more than 200 years ago. And he was exhilarated by it.

He was joined by his director and briefly by the actress chosen to play the leading female role of Cora Munro, Madeleine Stowe. The love affair between Hawkeye and Cora would be the heart of the movie. Mann and Twentieth Century Fox sensed that the devastatingly beautiful Stowe, one of the few to emerge with any credit from *The Two Jakes*, Jack Nicholson's woeful sequel to the classic *Chinatown*, was at the same point in her career as the film's leading man. She was an A-lister-in-waiting too.

By the time Daniel arrived on Mann's set to meet the Indian members of the cast he had assembled they were willing to welcome him as one of their own. The part of Chingachgook was being played by Russell Means, a leading American Indian activist. Means was sufficiently impressed by the dignified way Daniel approached the part of the half-British, half-Indian Hawkeye to say: 'Daniel is the embodiment of someone I would adopt as a non-Indian.'

Mann's determination to deliver an accurate evocation of the raw reality of a new world in the making was as complete as his leading man's. The statistics mounting in his production office were impressive. He had ordered a reconstruction of Fort William Henry, the colonial outpost at the centre of the action, based on the archive plans of an actual eighteenth-century building. A 20-acre area of forest was cleared and 138 carpenters built the fort. Its cost was an estimated $3 million. Mann also hired 200 mainly Iroquois-speaking Indians from New York State.

Cameras rolled at the end of June to begin a scheduled eighty-day shoot. Mann's experience amid the flying bricks and teargas canisters of Paris and Chicago was soon serving him well. The film he had pitched to Fox as 'a love story in a war zone' proved exactly that. Life quickly became a battlefield mined with problems ranging from 'artistic differences' to a full-scale strike by the crew.

Mann's perfectionist eye for detail placed huge demands on many of his crew members. English costume designer James Acheson, responsible for *The Last Emperor*, left before shooting started, to be replaced by *Dances with Wolves'* Elsa Zamparelli. Then hair-stylist Vera Mitchell resigned, frustrated by what she saw as the epic film's lack of organization and poor pay. The final major casualty was cinematographer Douglas Milsome. He had arrived from Costner's *Robin Hood, Prince of Thieves* in England. Reports from the set suggest that the look he had served up for Mann was not what the pernickety director wanted. After five weeks Milsome left, to be replaced by Mann's *Manhunter* colleague, Dante Spinotti.

While the departure of the cinematographer, costume designer and hairdresser did not deal a mortal blow to the production, the situation that arose towards the end of July threatened to kill the film with the precision of a well-aimed long-rifle shot. Mann and his senior crew members arrived at the location to face the potential loss of their entire 100-plus crew and as many Indian extras. They were all complaining about working conditions, the then non-union crew led by an official of the American union IATSE, the extras by Russell Means.

Producer Hunt Lowry had little room for manoeuvre. *The Last of the Mohicans* became an officially unionized film within days and the Indians were given an improved deal too.

The oasis of calm and uncomplaining loyalty amidst all this was the production's most expensive single component, 'the money'. Once more, Daniel was self-contained and enigmatic throughout the shoot. And while he politely declined to give interviews during filming, it was left to other production members to circulate the latest examples of his obsessional discipline to his roles.

His affection for his long rifle – nicknamed Killdeer – provided much of the material. 'Daniel would carry his gun around all the time,' Stowe revealed. 'When he went to lunch he'd have the gun with him, when he went to the bathroom he'd have that gun with him.' Others went one step further and claimed he slept with Killdeer.

As he had done during *My Left Foot*, he stayed in character as Hawkeye throughout his time on the set. Colleagues told how he stood, still and waist-deep in water, while cameras were reloaded between takes, how he would roll his own cigarettes rather than take the 1990s Marlboros on offer from other crew and cast members.

There were stories of occasional flashes of darkness. One day Stowe found him sitting alone in a car on a sweltering hot day. She recalled later how, when asked whether he was too hot, Hawkeye had replied, 'I like misery.'

English actor Steven Waddington, starring in the part of Hawkeye's rival for the affections of Cora, Major Heyward, admitted he was confused by his fellow Briton. 'I thought at first he was always angry at something. Like, "What's wrong with Daniel? Is he okay?"' Soon, however, he realized that it was simply '100 per cent concentration'.

'He tends to close himself off a little bit, walks around looking at the ground,' Waddington told *Premiere* magazine. 'His concentrating 100 per cent all the time makes you work twice as hard.'

Daniel and Smedley, who travelled to America with his pupil, even landing himself a small part in the film, continued their sparring sessions during filming. Waddington joined in the sessions. He found Daniel a relentless fighter. 'He would hit you and hit you until you couldn't go on. He just has this thing within him, an amazing driving force.'

That animalistic energy was on display each day before the

cameras, too. Mann's persistence in chasing the elusive Anglo-Irishman was rewarded in take after take. As he filmed the movie's most spectacular battle scene, in which the retreating English army is ambushed by a party of Huron braves, the entire crew was dumbfounded by the drive on display. Mann's tableau, appropriately re-created in a remote, wooded tract of North Carolina's Burke County called Massacre Valley, was a sea of red and white bodies, flailing knives and exploding muskets. The eye of the storm was the captured Cora and her protector Hawkeye. At the moment she was about to be put under the Huron knife, he would appear, tomahawk poised, to save her. It was to be the film's triumphal moment. Daniel charged towards his Indian adversary with such focus and force that he was oblivious to a steady-cam camera. He ploughed into it, sending the camera's operator hurtling through the air.

Another moment impressed Mann even more. It came as Hawkeye discovered the bodies of a settler family, massacred by the Hurons. Cora, unaware they are Hawkeye's friends, is disgusted at the barbarism of his decision not to bury the dead strangers. Mann wanted Daniel to turn and walk towards Stowe, a look of anger on his face.

'I could take any number of trained actors and say, "Do contained rage", but he goes beyond,' the director enthused later. 'There's rhythm, breathing, gaps – it lives on a higher plane. He looks like he's gonna whack her, then he says, "They are not strangers – they stay as they lay." The genius of Daniel is he takes those moments and he makes them live.'

As the shoot drew to an end, the entire cast and crew were near exhaustion. Hawkeye's batteries, however, seemed super-charged. At one point he was even to be seen applying Stowe's make-up while everyone else was collapsed around them.

For all the Celtic gloom, however, there were moments of levity. Stowe and Daniel would race each other home in cars every night. Stowe's driver was faster than Daniel's. One night Daniel and his driver headed off ahead of their rivals. When Stowe and her driver turned a corner, they discovered their racing rivals' car off the road and the blood-soaked body of Daniel's driver lying in the middle of the dusty road. For a split second the actress was terrified that the high jinks had ended in tragedy. She soon spotted false blood, however. The 'accident' was a typically bleak piece of Daniel Day-Lewis humour.

By the end of the shoot Stowe and Mann had nothing but praise for their leading man. 'It was hard for Daniel but he never complained once,' praised Stowe. 'He is immensely concentrated and he's fearless. He will do and try anything,' said Mann.

As the trio and the rest of the crew left the remote locations, they took part in a communal ritual. Every member of the army which had survived the making of *The Last of the Mohicans* piled their hiking boots high. Mann doused the shoe mountain in gasolene and set it ablaze. They could not have known it as the flames licked the serene Carolina skyline. Soon Mann and the Hawkeye he had tracked halfway across the world would put a match to the American box office too.

CHAPTER FOURTEEN

THE FIRST AMERICAN HERO

'If I can't marry him I will stay single for the rest of my life.'

Unnamed female American cinema-goer,
September 1992

B ACK IN sleepy Somerset it would go down as 'Wicked Uncle Daniel's' most memorable present.

She had gently nagged her brother about letting her join him on set with the man they both revered as a hero. When she had been invited over to America, swept into New York in a stretch limousine, she assumed she would be allowed to hide in some darkened corner, watch, listen and learn from the master. Who knew, perhaps there might even be a chance for a brief conversation, on editing, directing, anything?

Tamasin Day-Lewis did not expect to be 'trussed up like a turkey' in authentic nineteenth-century finery, placed 'like a pot plant' next to Michelle Pfeiffer and Winona Ryder and hear Martin Scorsese's choir-boy voice coax 'action' out of her.

Tamasin flew over to New York in June 1992 for two days as her younger brother worked on Scorsese's long-awaited adaptation of Edith Wharton's tale of repressed romance, *The Age of Innocence*. Back in England, she was preparing to finish work on the BBC *Everyman* film on the Labèque sisters to whom Isabelle Adjani had introduced her. A carefree weekend in New York, 'some totally irresponsible fun', was just what she needed.

She had walked into her hotel suite to find her bed strewn with flowers, perfume, chocolates and a new pair of shoes. The shower of presents came complete with a card signed in her brother's distinctive scrawl. The ultimate gift came hours later when she was eased into a period dress and ushered with the other extras to take their places for a ball as splendid as any New York had seen since Wharton was a girl, growing up amidst the splendour of the Gilded Age of the late 1800s.

As children they had rummaged through dressing-up boxes at Greenwich and Litton Cheney. Once more they were indulging in make-believe together. For Tamasin the submersion was fascinating yet fleeting. No sooner had Scorsese called 'cut' than her eyes were darting around the set, a magpie stealing every memory she could for her husband and children back home. For her brother, however, there was no such escape. Straight-backed, starched, impeccably attired, he had settled perfectly into the ornate landscape. Scorsese, *petit* Napoleonic, precise, benignly orchestrated affairs. 'Daniel looks of the period, he behaves of the period,' he would say with a disbelieving smile.

Hours later, the ball scene complete, brother and sister danced to Irish music in Daniel's off-set caravan, their giggles and shrieks drawing bewildered looks outside. 'If anybody had seen us they would have thought we were insane,' said Tamasin later. After her first taste of her brother's world there was one madness she knew she did not share, however. For all the complicity, the shared secrets, the common dedication to work, there was a distance here between brother and sister. Back in England soon after her memorable moments with Martin Scorsese she admitted it. 'I could never do what Dan does, pretend to be someone else.'

The process of becoming 'someone else' had begun once more early in 1992. After returning to Europe at the end of the *Last of the Mohicans* shoot in October 1991, Daniel had turned his attention to the project he had cherished since before his Oscar win of almost two years earlier.

For years he had wanted to work with Scorsese, the Italian-American properly regarded as his country's finest director. When Scorsese had approached him on the night before the Oscars about his plan to bring Wharton's book to the screen, he had instantly expressed his interest. He admitted later, 'I would have done the Yellow Pages with him. I could actually say that it was a dream of mine, like a fantasy, that someday I might work with Martin.'

The Age of Innocence's journey to the cinema screen had been long and tortuous. Wharton's book, set in the stultified polite society of 1870s' New York, had been admired by many, all of whom would like to lay claim for having first spotted its potential. David Puttnam attempted to secure the film rights during his brief reign at Columbia. In *Enigma*, Andrew Yule's biography of Puttnam, his wife Patsy claims that she and her husband had been talking about making *The Age of Innocence* 'for years'. It was only when they moved to buy the rights that others responded. 'Nobody had even heard of Edith Wharton until then,' she said.

Scorsese had been given the book in 1980. As he completed *Raging Bull*, he had been handed it over dinner with his friend, *Time* journalist Jay Cocks. 'When you do that romantic piece, this one is you,' Cocks had told him. It was only in January 1987, however, during a visit to England and Scotland, that he had read the book. Instantly he had told himself, 'I have got to make this picture.' Scorsese beat Puttnam to the punch to acquire the rights.

Having won the sprint, the marathon of raising finance began. For all his acknowledged genius, Scorsese's career had suffered its troubles during the 1980s. After *Raging Bull* built on the success of his seminal *Mean Streets* and *Taxi Driver*, Scorsese turned in a commercial failure in the critically adored *The King of Comedy* and then ran up a $4 million tab on his controversial *The Last Temptation of Christ* before the film was scrapped. 'There was no more career. I was gone,' he now says of that time.

By 1989, however, *The Colour of Money* and *Goodfellas* had restored his reputation, and *The Last Temptation of Christ* was finally completed and released. After a $32-million deal with Twentieth Century Fox fell through, Columbia agreed to make *The Age of Innocence*.

Daniel was Scorsese's first choice for the part of Newland

Archer, a successful lawyer, engaged to marry a beautiful heiress, May Welland, whose ordered world is thrown into chaos when he falls in love with a scandalous older woman, the Countess Ellen Olenska. Scorsese had admired the way Tomas moved in *The Unbearable Lightness of Being*: 'It was kinda choreographed.' When he saw *My Left Foot* he saw an actor with the same sort of tunnel vision his friend and collaborator Robert De Niro had: 'He had a kind of dedication which I like.'

After their initial conversation in Los Angeles, Daniel met Scorsese in London again shortly before he was due to fly off to begin filming on *The Last of the Mohicans*. He admitted later that the book in itself was not the attraction. 'Had anyone else proposed to me the idea of making a film about that particular subject, I don't think I'd have done it. It was the only time I took on a film solely because of the opportunity to work with the director.'

As Michael Mann had done, Scorsese returned to America with the elusive Anglo-Irishman on board. By then the director had also secured the two women at the top of his list: Michelle Pfeiffer for Olenska, Winona Ryder for May Welland. Scorsese hoped to start shooting in February 1992, in New York and Philadelphia. With *Mohicans* due to end in October, Daniel would have three or four months to prepare.

As he reached the end of 1991, however, he once more found himself physically reduced to 'dog meat'. His months in the remote backwoods of Alabama and then North Carolina had left him disoriented. The 'decompression' problems he had suffered before afflicted him again. On the last day of filming, Michael Mann later revealed, his star had said to him, 'I don't know how not to be Hawkeye.'

Before heading to New York he spent time in Los Angeles, giving a few advance interviews in readiness for the release of *The Last of the Mohicans*, scheduled at that time for July 1992. Holed up at the Bel-Air Hotel, he admitted that the months of exposure to the open spaces had left him with a feeling of claustrophobia. Like his father before him, he confessed, he disliked being cooped up. 'I find it difficult to be in rooms now for a long time. I can take it for about an hour. Then I stride

233

out,' he told Richard Woodward of the *New York Times*. The punishment of the *Mohicans* schedule had left him exhausted, he admitted.

The groundwork for his portrayal of Newland Archer began in the Bel-Air Hotel. There he began reading the research material that Scorsese and Cocks, his co-writer on the movie, had provided. The society Wharton described in her books lived its life according to an etiquette and rigid order that made Daniel's own Croom's Hill childhood seem anarchic. Scorsese, if anything an even more fastidious director than Michael Mann, had gone so far as to hire an 'etiquette' teacher for the production. Even Daniel's impeccable manners would need adapting.

To feel his way into the part of Newland Archer, Daniel asked Cocks for copies of books he would have read at the time, in their original editions if possible. 'He knew old books are like little time machines; they have a way of taking you back,' Cocks said.

His preparation under way, Daniel returned to Europe for the New Year. It was a New Year and a new conundrum, romantically at least. Despite the months of separation during the making of *The Last of the Mohicans*, Isabelle Adjani was still an important part of his life. In March the *Daily Mail* reported that she had moved to London to share Daniel's Brook Green home. According to Baz Bamigboye, she had dismissed her agent, rented out her apartment and moved across the English Channel. Opinion among 'friends' was divided on her motives. Some suggested she had tired of being 'persecuted' over her outspoken interest in Algerian politics, others – more intriguingly – suggested she had moved to London to 'watch' Daniel. If the rumours flying around Dublin were to be believed, she had cause for concern. Daniel and the Irish rock star Sinead O'Connor had been spotted together several times. Weeks before Adjani's suitcases arrived in west London, the *Daily Mirror* reported its conclusion that O'Connor had 'fallen head over heels in love'. The couple were seen at two parties, one at the County Kildare mansion of *My Left Foot* investor Billy Gaff, and then at one of Dublin's most fashionable nightclubs,

Lillie's Bordello, on Grafton Street. The owner of the latter, Robbie Fox, was quoted as saying, 'Let's just say they came in – and left – together.'

The O'Connor story was the first in a series of sightings and tantalizingly unsubstantiated gossip items that would crop up that year. Daniel would, as was now his established custom, say absolutely nothing about any of them.

Isabelle Adjani, however, was a different matter. As he arrived in New York ready to begin final preparations for *The Age of Innocence*, her influence on Daniel was no secret. Interviewed in the *New Yorker* magazine, Daniel revealed that the French actress had been helping him research the finer details he needed to arrive at a convincing portrayal of the sophisticated Newland Archer.

Daniel had arrived in New York with most of Hawkeye's flowing black mane still intact. He booked himself into a small, old-world hotel and began the slow process of slipping into another skin. First he removed the backwoodsman's hair. Then he grew long, Bismarck-like sideburns, later trimmed to fashionable 1870s length. Within weeks he had exchanged his usual scruffy black clothes for an impeccable period suit, Killdeer had been replaced by an elegant walking cane, and a wide-rimmed Homburg hat completed the ensemble. Hawkeye's 5000-calorie diet was dropped and his physique returned to its former wiriness. The final stage of the transformation began when he booked out of the hotel as Mr D. Day-Lewis and then re-registered as Mr N. Archer.

The only missing piece in the chameleonic jigsaw, he decided, was the correct cologne. The *New Yorker* reported that Adjani, the public face of the Dior fashion house in France, had dispatched a selection of perfumes for him to choose from. Writer Joan Juliet Buck told how she witnessed Daniel producing fourteen small bottles of cologne, including Blenheim Bouquet and Floris's Stephanotis. 'He was concerned, in a playful yet serious way, with finding Archer's scent. The surfeit of odours made one giddy,' Buck wrote.

She found a Daniel Day-Lewis set in period surroundings. His hotel was one of the few remaining in the city that dated back to Wharton's *Age of Innocence*. He had taken a suite of two rooms. Dark and compact, they were furnished in turn-of-the-century style. The writer noted that the atmosphere was 'wilfully lugubrious'. A mournful piece of music played in the background. It was Fauré's *Requiem*, his father's favourite piece. 'The suite seemed to be the chambers of the faintly aesthetic and very stiff gentleman of Old New York,' she observed.

Daniel spent time with Scorsese at his brownstone house in the SoHo area of Manhattan. They had dinner and then watched 35-mm movies in the private screening room the cineholic director had had specially installed. Staple in their screen diet was *The Heiress*, William Wyler's Oscar-winning 1949 adaptation of a Henry James story. The film featured Montgomery Clift as a fortune-seeking young socialite, transformed from hunter to hunted when a wealthy but plain heiress, played by Olivia de Havilland, sees through her suitor's mask. Scorsese had seen the film when he was nine years old and had never forgotten it. 'That such brutality could occur in a household, in a family, and the household is so beautiful, and the manners are so good, and yet you have such cold brutality. It was overwhelming to me,' he explained later.

Daniel had for many years been a devotee of Montgomery Clift, the dark, brooding, ultimately tragic American star of the 1940s and 1950s, who died, aged just forty-five, in July 1966. His portrayals of victimized young men – the sort of 'damaged goods' Daniel himself had often been drawn to – made a lasting impression. Asked by the magazine *US Film Comment* in 1988 to name his favourite actor it had been Clift that he had volunteered. 'Everyone has been influenced by Brando; fewer by Clift. But for me he was an extraordinary actor,' he explained. 'Not because he covered a big range, but because he was different. Clift contained within him a vision of some kind, which I found absolutely riveting. Clift had a spiritual quality of some kind.'

After the escapism of Hawkeye, Archer was a return to the suppressive grindstone in many ways. As he had studied the script and listened to Scorsese's views, he discovered another trapped soul. In Newland's case he was caged by a combination of his own inadequacy and the social structure of his day. His love for Olenska would never be consummated. He was a man too weak to follow his heart and to risk the shame of his social circle.

There were reminders of a previous life. Newland often displayed all the snobbery of Cecil Vyse. Cecil dreamed of taking his and Lucy Honeychurch's children to Italy 'for subtlety'; Newland wanted to take May to the Italian Lakes 'to read Faust'. To both men there is nothing more awful than offences against 'good taste'.

'All the details build up, almost like a building, a wall, brick by brick, around Newland Archer, so that he couldn't escape,' Scorsese said of his leading character. 'It's like a prison. Imagine living like that every day, and each hour you stay, it's harder to make that break.'

As filming got underway Daniel and fellow-Britons, including Miriam Margolyes, an old friend of Jill Balcon, and Richard E. Grant, had to undergo etiquette instruction from Scorsese's special adviser, Lily Hodge. Much of the action in the film would centre on dinner parties. The British had to learn table manners – American-style. 'In England you use a knife and fork together, you don't just eat with a fork,' explained Hodge. 'I had to teach them to cut meat with the knife and fork, then put the knife down, move the fork to the right hand, and eat like that – the way we eat in America.'

Scorsese's dinner parties, now extended to include Pfeiffer and Winona Ryder, provided the perfect training ground. Daniel and Ryder, who since her breakthrough in *Heathers* had gone on to have a series of box-office successes, including *Beetlejuice* and *Dracula*, with Francis Coppola, struck up a larkish friendship. Daniel later revealed how they would sing together. Ryder's most impressive number, he told the *New York Post*, was 'I'm just a girl who can't say no'. Inevitably there were soon headlines suggesting as much and when the film was finally released some critics couldn't resist commenting on the 'chemistry' between the two.

By the time filming on *The Age of Innocence* was complete in June, however, the distant storm clouds of another unwanted set of headlines were gathering back in England. Confusion and what was either the pique or perfectionism of Hollywood's favourite pretty woman would combine to create the *cause célèbre* that was *Shakespeare in Love*.

During his time in Los Angeles Daniel's American agent Gene Parseghian had briefed him on a short-list of projects on offer. One, set to be directed for TriStar by the Oscar-winning Jonathan '*Silence of the Lambs*' Demme, called at various times *Probable Cause* or *At Risk*, was perceived as Hollywood's first attempt at a mainstream AIDS movie. The story of a lawyer who sues his WASPish company after he is fired for being HIV positive was already being talked of as a potential Oscar vehicle.

Another was the movie Universal hoped would signal the return of the mercurial Julia Roberts to the screen after a two-year lay-off. *Shakespeare in Love*, being produced by Edward Zwick, co-producer of TV's *Thirtysomething* and the Oscar-winning *Glory*, was a 'romantic comedy' based on a script by Marc Norman. The story had a young Will Shakespeare falling for the actor playing Romeo in a production of his new play. To his relief the playwright learns that Romeo is in fact a woman disguised as a man.

During June and July Daniel's name was consistently linked with both films. *Screen International*, the reliable trade magazine, tracked the to-ing and fro-ing, reporting first that Daniel was considering playing the smitten Will Shakespeare in the Universal film. According to the 12 June report, by columnist Leonard Klady, *Robin Hood, Prince of Thieves* director Kevin Reynolds was in line to direct him and Roberts.

Two weeks later, however, Klady reported that *Shakespeare in Love* was being held up because Roberts had not committed herself. As a result Daniel was set to star in *Probable Cause/At Risk* instead. Within one week of that report, however, Klady was writing that Roberts had now committed herself and that 'Day-Lewis is back on board as the Bard of Avon'.

If there was confusion elsewhere about what was going on, there was none at Pinewood Studios where, through the autumn, work went ahead with planning the production and building sets for the film, reportedly budgeted at £20 million.

In mid-September, in Los Angeles, the also reliable *Hollywood Reporter* ran a front-page story finally confirming that Roberts would be making her 'comeback' in *Shakespeare in Love*. Despite the fact that the actress was asking a 'king's ransom' of $4 million for the part, Universal now seemed confident the film would go ahead. A source close to Roberts said the actress 'loved the script' and was now waiting for 'the word' from Universal. *The Hollywood Reporter* also revealed that Daniel had been approached to play the leading role.

Within just over a month, however, the entire production would go up in flames as it emerged that 'the word' Roberts was waiting for was a 'yes' from the lips of Daniel Day-Lewis. In fact it emerged that Daniel did not receive a firm offer to play the part until the beginning of October. He turned it down within three days. On 6 October, Gene Parseghian told *Daily Variety* in Los Angeles that Daniel was committed once more to working with Jim Sheridan. He had agreed to star in a movie based on the memoirs of Gerry Conlon, a member of the Guildford Four, imprisoned wrongly for an IRA bombing.

By now Roberts, according to reports at the time, had arrived in London and begun costume and wig fittings. As she learned of Daniel's decision, producer Zwick and casting director Celestia Fox desperately searched for a replacement. Sean Bean, a diamond-in-the-rough Yorkshireman whose star was in the ascendant, Ralph Fiennes, star of a recent version of *Wuthering Heights* with Juliette Binoche, and Colin Firth, who like Daniel had graduated from *Another Country* to film success in movies like *A Month in the Country* and *Valmont*, were among those considered.

Roberts's divinity in the eyes of Hollywood provided her with the ultimate say over her leading man. She said no to all the suggested replacements.

At 10.30 a.m. on 20 October, line producer Terry Clegg gathered the 200-strong crew at Pinewood Studios' 'B' Stage to break the news that *Shakespeare in Love* was closing down. Roberts, it transpired, had left London and flown back to Los Angeles. Her departure was a body blow for the perennially vulnerable British film industry. A bleak winter was predicted for the casualties. The hunt for a scapegoat began.

Daniel's London agent Julian Belfrage and others connected with the production swiftly moved to defend the role he had played. They told the London *Evening Standard* that Daniel's behaviour had been impeccable. 'They had been pursuing him since July, lunches, and meetings and so on. They only came up with a firm offer three weeks ago. Daniel turned it down three days later. He has behaved entirely honourably,' said an unnamed casting agent connected with the production.

Julian Belfrage offered an interesting, alternative view: 'Julia's reason for not doing it is that she adores Daniel and doesn't want to do it without him,' the agent told the *Standard*. 'I think she thought that by leaving she might persuade him to reconsider. But now that Hollywood is blaming Daniel he will never do the film.'

In Los Angeles Roberts's public relations machinery launched its damage limitation exercise. The day after the *Standard* comments, Roberts's agent Elaine Goldsmith told *Daily Variety*: 'I think the frustration comes with everyone wanting to go forward with this project and not being able to find the right person once Daniel Day-Lewis passed.' Roberts's press agent Nancy Seltzer claimed her client had 'never been committed' to the film in the first place.

As the dust settled on the extraordinary *Shakespeare in Love* affair, the losers were clearly the 200 individuals forced once more to face the chill wind of a recession-ravaged industry. For Julia Roberts the fall-out was minimal: within six months she would pick up the threads of her career with another box-office success in *The Pelican Brief*. Within another year she would end years of disparity between male and female pay in Hollywood by being offered a staggering $15 million to make a movie.

For Daniel too there would be no discernible damage. He would work with Universal within months. He would even go on to form a close friendship with the 'adoring' Julia Roberts. Even before the *Shakespeare in Love* saga had been fully played out, his stock had begun to rise to unparalleled peaks. As the recriminatory crossfire died away, the release of *The Last of the*

Mohicans had been relegating the non-movie to non-story status.

Twentieth Century Fox, ironically headed by one of Julia Roberts's mentors, Joe Roth, had held back release of the film until late September. Backbiting Hollywood rumours that the film was ill-equipped to compete with the summer's block-buster, *Batman Returns*, soon disappeared, however. *The Last of the Mohicans* quickly became America's surprise fall season hit. Fox had poured money into a vast marketing campaign with posters of a charging Hawkeye and the single line 'The First American Hero'. A massive TV advertising campaign was booked for the opening weekend. The contrast between the treatment this movie and Daniel's last American-made release, *Stars and Bars*, had received could not have been greater. In one night Fox spent $2.5 million, twice the entire budget of *My Beautiful Laundrette*, on air time.

The reviews provided the final push, however. From the moment Daniel emerged in the verdant shadows of the Carolina woods, Killdeer on his back, hair flowing, Richard Smedley's muscular remodelling clearly visible through his thin veil of buckskin, American critics realized that a new romantic screen hero had been born. If Tomas had made Daniel a sex symbol for the cine-literate, Hawkeye was about to transform him into an object of unbridled lust for the masses.

The cerebral *New York Times*'s Janet Maslin was a breathless barometer for the reaction that would follow worldwide. 'On screen Hawkeye is defined less by what he has to say – not much – than by the viscerally powerful presence of Mr Day-Lewis, whose fierce and graceful body language speaks much louder than words,' she salivated. 'Does Mr Day-Lewis have the wherewithal to give this figure a matinee-idol magnetism? What a silly question.'

'It is to the credit of Mr Day-Lewis's performance that a character best known for his tracking skills and derring-do will now be thought of, first and foremost, as a hot-blooded leading man,' she concluded.

The rest of America was in agreement. *Time* magazine called it 'Grandly scaled – deliriously energetic'; *Sixty Second*

Preview said, 'The Oscar race begins with *The Last of the Mohicans*.'

In its first weekend *Mohicans* took $12 million at the US box office. Within the first month it had reached $50 million. Fox's confidence was rewarded. Daniel could open and act. The world was at Hawkeye's moccasined feet.

When the film opened in Britain weeks later the emergence of the first serious, home-grown contender for 'Hollywood Heart-throb' clichédom in a generation was celebrated in full.

Shaun Usher in the *Daily Mail* proclaimed *Mohicans* 'among the finest adventure films I have ever seen'. The 'sinewy, laconic, watchful' Day-Lewis was, he wrote, 'Mann's ace in a handful of trumps'.

Anne Billson in the *Sunday Telegraph* led the oestrogen-charged female appreciation. 'You know he means business because even before the opening credits have finished rolling he has slipped out of his buckskin shirt to expose a nicely developed deltoid arrangement,' she wrote. 'We have just been introduced to one of the all-time great action heroes. And this is the actor I always used to think was England's answer to Meryl Streep.'

There was no dissent. 'Daniel Day-Lewis makes an extraordinarily fine job,' said Adam Mars-Jones of the *Independent*. 'Day-Lewis is the only actor of his generation whose move to Hollywood seems to involve no compromise.'

Alexander Walker in the *Evening Standard* hailed 'the chameleon man of the movies' as 'the only heir to Caine and Connery that's come from these shores in the last decade'.

Women on both sides of the Atlantic wondered how one man had managed to cast such a mesmeric hold over an entire gender. For some it was his impassioned plea to Cora: 'Stay alive, and I will find you.' Here was a man who would track the earth for love. For others it was the muscular directness when Cora wonders what he is looking at: 'Why, you, miss.' No quaking 1990s correctness there. For others it was less what he said than what he stood for. Rootlessness, adventure, danger, a man 'subject to not very much at all', a man prepared to take his woman to the frontier – and beyond. Hawkeye was the perfect antidote to the sterile security of marriage. He was everything a husband was not. The more they read about Daniel Day-Lewis, the more they realized he was in part a modern-day Hawkeye.

The New York magazine *Glamour*'s books editor Laura Mathews later took the beating pulse of a nation and at least half a planet. 'I owe a lot to this man. I'm convinced I got pregnant after seeing *The Last of the Mohicans* three times.'

In London, before the release of *Mohicans*, Daniel admitted that dealing with the recognition *My Left Foot* had brought him had been problematic enough. 'I do have a resistance to fame, and the problem is that that probably makes things harder,' he said. 'But privacy is something you have to be very careful of: once you have given it away you can never get it back again.'

Half-heartedly re-introducing himself to the British public after the *Hamlet* hiatus, he did little to discourage the already established image of a rootless drifter, a dark-souled Byronic outsider, a Hamlet in hiding. He admitted for instance that he had been so unsure where his correspondence should be sent that his bankers had suggested placing No Fixed Abode in his file. 'I don't think they'd had a customer of no fixed abode for 400 years.'

As 1992 drew to a close, however, he knew precisely where his next abode would be. In an interview with Iain Johnstone of the *Sunday Times*, he admitted that the lengths he was now going to to find each character had made him a 'prisoner of his parts'. He confirmed that his next project would be the Conlon project with his friend Jim Sheridan. 'So the imprisonment you referred to may actually be more literal this time.'

CHAPTER FIFTEEN

PLAYBOY OF THE WESTERN WORLD

'Anyone who has been to an English public school will
always feel comparatively at home in a prison. It is the
people brought up in the gay intimacy of the slums . . .
who find prison so soul-destroying.'

EVELYN WAUGH, *Decline and Fall*

I T HAD BEEN twenty-seven years since Cecil Day-Lewis had
visited Kilmainham Jail, watched a drab, Dublin sky broken
by a sun 'bursting' over its grim execution yard, and paid
his respects to the fallen of the Easter Uprising of 1916. In the
poem he had written to commemorate the fiftieth anniversary of
one of the great turning points in Irish history, he had wondered
whether the men who had been starved of sunlight in Kilmainham's cells could have known what would flower later from the
spilling of their blood and an incident he felt represented one of
England's darkest 'follies'.

In the spring of 1993 the late Poet Laureate's son stood in the
shadow of that same execution yard. The muscled bulk of
Hawkeye wasted to fierce flesh and bone, his hair a tinker's
tousled mop, Daniel had once more metamorphosed. A year
before he had assumed the upright gait of a nineteenth century
New York socialite. As he paced the perimeter wall of his Dublin
prison his walk was the shambling swagger of a backstreet
ragamuffin.

He was there to tell the story of another father, and another
bloody English folly. Controversy and further confirmation of
his genius would be the flowers of his time in Kilmainham's
light-starved cells.

It had been during a break in Ireland after the ending of *The*

Age of Innocence in the previous summer that he had first been drawn to the idea of playing Gerry Conlon. The bond he had formed with Jim 'Shay' Sheridan on *My Left Foot* had remained unbroken. He had become a regular house guest at the director's homes in prosperous Ballsbridge, Dublin and an hour or so outside the city in the Wicklow Mountains. Shay's only charge for a comfortable bed and generous helpings of his wife Fran's cooking was that his friend listen to the ideas perpetually buzzing around his head. 'Jim has a new one every week,' Daniel joked once.

As he sat 'knackered', needing another film 'like a hole in the head' after his exertions in America, the Sheridans' visitor had begun to hear the latest story to take hold in Shay's excitable imagination. 'Shay's not a bad storyteller at the best of times, so within a few minutes I remember thinking, "Please don't tell me any more of this story", because I could feel the nagging compulsion begin to drag me closer to it,' he recalled later. The story Sheridan told in his broad, northsider Dublin brogue was an adaptation of Conlon's autobiography, *Proved Innocent*.

Gerry Conlon had been released from prison in October 1989. He had spent almost fifteen years behind bars for the Guildford and Woolwich pub bombings of 1974, in which seven people had died. At an appeal at the Old Bailey in London the judge, Lord Justice Lane, declared the conviction of Conlon, Carole Richardson, Paul Hill and Paddy Armstrong, the so-called Guildford Four, 'unsafe and unsatisfactory'. The court upheld Conlon's claims that police had forced him to confess to a crime he had not committed.

Conlon's elation at his moment of release – pictures of him, his shirt-tails flapping in the autumn breeze, his building-site fists punching the air in triumph, were beamed around the world – had been tainted by the tragic death of his father Guiseppe in prison for a crime of which he too was innocent. A quiet bookmaker's assistant, only drawn to London from his Belfast home because his son had been arrested there, he was one of the so-called Maguire Seven jailed for manufacturing the bombs used in Guildford. The Seven's convictions were also quashed, but only after Conlon senior had died in prison in 1980.

Sheridan had come to the story through another of Ireland's successful American exports, the actor Gabriel Byrne. Byrne had met Conlon in New York. *Proved Innocent*, he thought, 'had the great makings of a movie'. After talking to Harold Pinter about adapting the book for the screen, Byrne commissioned Terry George, another New York-based Irishman, who knew Conlon, to write the screenplay. Sheridan, with whom Byrne had worked on the film *Into the West*, based on the director's own screenplay, was also recruited.

After reading Sheridan and George's screenplay, called *In the Name of the Father*, Daniel's initial reaction had been that he was too old to play Conlon, who had been twenty at the time of his wrongful arrest. Daniel would be thirty-six the following April, and felt sixty-six. 'Working on films seems to accelerate the ageing process, I felt like a very elderly person and Shay was telling me a story about a young man which fascinated me, but it seemed absolutely impossible that I would be able to squeeze enough drops of youth to be able to do that,' he recalled later. He was, however, sufficiently interested to read *Proved Innocent* and then, just a few days later, to meet Conlon himself.

By the autumn of 1992, as *Shakespeare in Love* and Jonathan Demme's AIDS drama, *Probable Cause/At Risk*, were offering him the potential for a massive pay-day, Daniel opted for a second film with Sheridan instead. Hollywood was waking up to his unpredictability. He was now worth $5 million a role, one producer claimed. 'But he probably settled for one tenth of that on *In the Name of the Father*. I think we are all getting the idea that money isn't the bottom line for this guy,' the producer said.

My Left Foot had earned Sheridan a two-picture 'first-look' deal with Universal Pictures. Negotiations with them quickly led to a green light. The studio's reaction to the idea of a drama based on one of the most emotive events in recent British history, at a time when IRA violence was still claiming the lives of innocents in Northern Ireland and on the British mainland, was a vivid testimony to the power Daniel could now exert in Hollywood. Sheridan later admitted that without Daniel the film might never have been made. 'Daniel's wanting to do it made it a bit easier. Once *Mohicans* was a big hit and everybody loved him, that made it easier still,' he conceded.

Sheridan pitched the film as the story of a father and a son. The core conflict of the movie he wanted to make was that between the quiet, wise Guiseppe and his angry, rootless son. Gerry, a petty thief, dope-smoker and drifter, had believed his taciturn, law-abiding father was a weak man. It had only been in prison that he had come to see his extraordinary strength. It was the stuff of classical Greek drama, a son first rebelling against, then becoming converted to, his father's beliefs, a prison epiphany. If *My Left Foot* had been a mother's story, now Sheridan was set to make a father's story.

The theme struck a chord in both the director and his leading man. 'Societies and religions are structured around father images. England became a kind of father-figure whom the Irish have been trying to confront for a long time,' Sheridan explained later. 'I wanted to do a story about a good father because there aren't any good fathers in Irish literature.

'Most people don't really know their parents, especially their fathers, because they are away from home so much. But if you're locked in a space with your father, eventually you'll have to talk to him. That doesn't happen in Ireland, fathers and sons never talk.'

Shay's ideas were ones with which Daniel, of course, was all too familiar. Throughout much of 1992, his relationship with his own late father had once more loomed large. He had re-read his father's poems, his verse on Kilmainham Jail no doubt included, in the spring of 1992. On the twentieth anniversary of his death, C. Day-Lewis's complete poems had been published for the first time. Years of lobbying by Jill Balcon had persuaded Sinclair-Stevenson to release them.

To coincide with the book's launch, Daniel had agreed to write an appreciation of his father's work for the *Observer* in London. The haunting, delicately written piece evoked his childhood memories of Cecil, a man he remembered for his 'bristly chin' and 'tobaccoey'-tasting kisses. He recalled his Christmas morning readings at Litton Cheney, his King Edward potato faces and his final, deathbed moments, 'the alienated, emotionless first encounter with the great scythe'. He admitted that his feelings for Cecil had 'grown steadily', particularly as he had come to recognize more and more 'the invisible writing', the inevitable inheritances of the 'sack of genes I did not choose, though finally of which I am immensely proud'. He shared, he wrote, 'a melancholic inclination', 'the ability to smile attentively while not listening to a word' and 'an irrevocable sense of decay'. 'I still crave his wisdom and lyrical delicacy,' he said poignantly. He also explained his father's part in his Hamlet, the constant conversations with him, and the words that were – that night – 'particularly hard to bear'.

Months later, as he prepared to start work on his latest film, Terry George's climactic words in the *In the Name of the Father* screenplay must have seemed familiar terrain. 'I will fight on ... in the name of my father and of the truth.' Here was another avenging son, a Hamlet with a broad West Belfast accent.

Daniel had worked with Scorsese because he admired his perfectionism. He was working with Sheridan once more because he admired his madness. Sheridan was someone who would let him 'dangle upside down from a hundred-foot crane for a couple of hours to get some blood into my brain'. All had not been roses for the *My Left Foot* team since their rocket-ride to first division status in 1990, however. In the wake of their Oscar triumphs, Pearson, Sheridan and company had talked down any hopes of huge profits. 'Even if it makes $20 million it may still be in debt. If we get anything we will be lucky,' Pearson said then. In the weekend following its Oscar win alone, however, *My Left Foot* took in $1.5 million in America. It went on to make tens of millions more worldwide, producing a profit of £50 million, Pearson later claimed.

By January 1993, however, neither the producer nor his star had seen their share of the profits. A suit was launched at the Dublin High Court in pursuit of their money. The court papers confirmed that Daniel had been paid £70,000 for playing Christy but that he had been promised 10 per cent of the profits. At the time he had received just £20,000 extra. 'Daniel is owed an awful lot of money,' Julian Belfrage told the *Mail on Sunday* in London as they ran a report on the case under the headline 'My Lost Loot'. 'The film was a huge success and he has seen nothing,' he added, seemingly forgetting the advance payment.

Pearson accused Granada of failing to collect the profits and box office receipts properly. The court reserved judgment, leaving both sides' accountants to pore over the figures. As Daniel and Sheridan once more planned to work together, the acrimonious mess was still being tidied up.

Daniel helped Sheridan in the early stages of casting in Dublin. Camped at the Westbury Hotel with casting directors Nuala Moiselle and Patsy Pollock, he sat in on interviews. Sheridan's most problematic part was Guiseppe. Daniel suggested his Bristol Old Vic colleague Pete Postlethwaite.

Postlethwaite's reputation as one of the finest actors in England had not been translated into popular success. His nuggety, 'stone arch' features had typecast him as a television villain; his only significant success in movies had come in the acclaimed *Distant Voices Still Lives* by Terence Davies.

When Sheridan first saw Postlethwaite he was concerned that he was too young for the part. By the time he saw him a second time a week later, however, Postlethwaite had performed the sort of chameleonic act his former understudy had become famous for. Dressed in Oxfam cast-offs, he announced his arrival at the Grosvenor House Hotel, Sheridan's London base, in a Belfast accent: 'Guiseppe Conlon here to see Jim Sheridan.' It turned out to be the most inspirational casting of the movie.

Postlethwaite drew on memories of his own late father to build up the part of Guiseppe. Daniel, playing a living person for the first time in his film career, began to spend time with the former builder's mate and house burglar who had become a symbol of British injustice.

Daniel had still been at school at the time of the Guildford and Woolwich pub bombings. The blasts were among the IRA's most hurtful strikes, their targets two communities Daniel's own childhood had straddled, the white-collar, gin-and-tonic Home Counties, the blue-collar, light-and-bitter London. Woolwich was just a few miles away from the Croom's Hill home his mother still owned at the time. Millwall territory.

In 1974, while Dan Day-Pinup had continued adding to his Bedalian legend, the rest of England had demanded the murderers' blood. Under pressure the police wilted, Conlon and company had been rounded up, a case constructed to fit their 'crimes'.

As he travelled to Belfast, Daniel got to know the man who had spent fifteen years paying for simply having the wrong accent in the wrong place at the wrong time. He became a regular visitor to Conlon's home. 'When he started getting interested he wanted to study me,' Conlon recalled later. He remembered how Daniel would arrive on his doorstep at 7 a.m. As if that were not bad enough, he arrived 'with no milk, no coffee, and no bread'. 'But we got on, he was a sweet guy.'

'I couldn't have worked on the film if we hadn't spent that time together,' Daniel said later, praising Conlon's honesty and openness.

As the March start date for the beginning of principal photography approached, however, Daniel disappeared from Conlon's kitchen. The most important scenes of the movie demanded that he once more go to extraordinary lengths to understand the emotions involved.

Ardmore studios were familiar with the process, and so were Sheridan and other *My Left Foot* veterans like co-producer Arthur Lappin. For those who had never worked with Daniel before, however, the scenes at Ardmore and then at a disused hospital in Dublin were like nothing they had seen before. As Daniel again banned journalists from talking to him on set, it was left to others to describe what went on.

Rumours of how Daniel had gone on a prison diet before shooting so as to portray a scarecrow-thin Conlon had begun circulating in March. His emaciated, dishevelled appearance outside Liverpool's St George's Hall, scene of the reconstruction of Conlon's emotional emergence from the Old Bailey, would later lead two attractive women extras to pull at his sleeve and fret, 'Are you all right? What's happened to you? You were so handsome in *Last of the Mohicans.*'

In Dublin, as he prepared for the scenes in which Conlon is interrogated and psychologically tortured by police, Daniel, under Sheridan's watchful eye, was subjected to the same sort of cruelty that the Guildford Four had endured. In a report in Dublin's *Sunday Tribune* one of the actors who took part in the scene described his bewilderment at what he saw.

Martin Murphy, hired to play one of the policemen who extract Conlon's confession, received his first surprise when he arrived for work. Any ideas the Dublin-based actor might have had of talking to Ireland's favourite adopted son were dashed by Sheridan's greeting. 'Now when Daniel's around I don't want anyone talking to him, ignore him. Completely,' he was told. 'He has got to feel this is the loneliest place on earth.'

Murphy and fellow-actor Richard Graham were told that Daniel had been confined to a cell for forty-eight hours, had been living off slops, deprived of sleep, occasionally by having buckets of ice-cold water thrown over him. Whenever he had left his cell to visit the toilet he had done so covered in a blanket. In addition he had been interrogated by real members of the Gardai's Serious Crimes Squad. The actors were shown videos of the grilling.

When it came to the moment when he and Graham had to physically manhandle 'Gerry', Murphy feared the realism had gone too far. Murphy and Graham were playing police officers involved in the breaking down of Conlon. Their main scene with 'Gerry' involved them forcing him to look at photographs of the bodies of the Guildford bomb victims.

Murphy described how 'Gerry' had kept wriggling free and throwing himself into a corner, 'screaming and kicking'. An assistant director told him this must not happen. 'Get him back to his mark as quickly as possible. Forget the acting,' he had been told. Seconds later 'Gerry' tried to break free again. 'He nearly gets away from me, but I just manage to hold on. He's going berserk, trying to wriggle away,' Murphy said. 'For a split second my film career hangs by a thread and suddenly it's not acting any more. The chair goes flying, I slam his arm against the edge of the table. Hard. He screams. We force his head down on to the table on top of the photographs.'

Murphy admitted that both he and Graham had been concerned they had hurt their celestial cellmate. 'In another scene Richard goes to slap him but he turns at the wrong moment and there's a very real crunch of bone against bone. We freeze in horror but "Gerry" stares back. Afterwards Richard is quite shaken. He thinks Daniel did it deliberately.'

Murphy's job had been to create an us-and-them situation within the make-believe police cell. He was left with the impression that there was a similar divide between Daniel and the rest of the production. 'I can't help thinking there will always be a gap between us and Him,' he wrote.

A similar divide was already forming between Sheridan and company and Establishment England. It came as no surprise: the case of the Guildford Four, described by some as 'the worst miscarriage of justice of the century', had exposed a raw nerve. The production's most prominent English member was the subject of the first skirmish. Emma Thompson, the London *Evening Standard* suggested before she had even arrived on set to play Gareth Pierce, the solicitor who played a key role in freeing the Four, was 'being naïve in taking on such a provocative role'. Thompson, who had collected an Oscar for her role in *Howards End* in March, was risking the wrath of the British public in the wake of renewed bombing from the IRA. 'Given the prevailing mood in Britain, it is likely to turn her from darling to rebel overnight,' the *Evening Standard* said.

There had been rumblings of discontent about Daniel's involvement too. As criticism of his 'zealous devotion to all things Irish' surfaced, the unlikely figure of Stephen Frears stirred the pot. 'I knew Daniel before he was Irish,' he was quoted as saying.

A shoot whose only mishap had been the brief disappearance of some guns during filming of a Belfast-style riot in Sheridan's old stamping ground, Sherriff Street – 'the Special Branch were not too happy but we put the word out and they came back pretty rapid,' the director explained later – came to an end in May. Only as parties were held inside the walls of Kilmainham Jail and at nightclubs like Lillie's Bordello did Daniel finally begin to break free from the shackles of being 'Gerry'. He had been happy to share a jar or two of Guinness with cast and crew during filming. 'But sometimes he does prefer that you call him Gerry,' Arthur Lappin had confided.

A high-spirited Julia Roberts was in Dublin to share the celebrations. Speculation about Roberts and Daniel had been rife since the *Shakespeare in Love* débâcle. After Julian Belfrage's remark that Julia 'adored' Daniel, newspapers on both sides of the Atlantic had been fanning the flames, suggesting that Roberts had left her current lover, Jason Patric, for Daniel. In mid-December the respectable *USA Today* repeated the question the country's tabloids had been asking for weeks: 'Has Jason Patric become the "Last of the Mohicans" on the trail of Julia Roberts? Are Roberts and Daniel Day-Lewis a new twosome?' Days earlier the *New York Post* had alleged that Roberts had 'dumped her boyfriend' for the 'hawkeyed playboy' that was Daniel Day-Lewis. Roberts's press agent Nancy Seltzer did not deny the two had become friends. 'To make more out of it is not fair,' she added.

Early in the New Year an American biography of Roberts claimed her romance with Patric had ended in an ugly and very public slanging match. According to author Aileen Joyce, a drunken argument in the street outside Patric's Los Angeles home had ended with the actor accusing Roberts of sleeping with Daniel Day-Lewis. 'You fucked him. I know you fucked him!' neighbours heard Patric scream. 'I can fuck anyone I want to,' Roberts had replied.

Back in London in March the *Daily Express* reported that Roberts had 'spent a fortune on flights from Hollywood to Ireland'.

As had been the case with other of Daniel's supposed romances, the one commodity the newspapers lacked during all this speculation was a firm sighting of the two together. If they had joined the Sunday afternoon drinkers at the historic Wren's Nest in the Strawberry Beds pub on 30 May 1993, they would have found their elusive prey. The diary behind the bar of the centuries-old pub in the Chapelizod area, near

253

Kilmainham, records that was the day two of Hollywood's superstars spent three intimate hours together there.

'They were having great crack, she was all over yer man,' remembered one of the pub's barmen, Francis Heffernan. The two, Daniel dressed in a dark jumper and jeans, Roberts in jeans too, arrived in a red Mercedes and were joined by a driver throughout their visit to the pub. 'He was drinking Guinness and she was drinking lager,' recalled Heffernan. 'If you did not know them you would have thought they were boyfriend and girlfriend. There was a lot of laughing and whispering going on.'

Within just under four weeks of that afternoon drinking session the rumours surrounding the couple were over. On 27 June Roberts and country singer Lyle Lovett married in the town of Marion, Indiana. Drinkers in the Wren's Nest read the reports with surprise. 'She did not look like she was about to get married that day,' said Francis Heffernan with a smile.

By now Dublin was offering Daniel the nearest he had had to a home since his Greenwich childhood. The lack of intrusion in the city and the warmth of the welcome he received everywhere he went contrasted with London, a city which by now he had almost grown out of. 'I think a part of me has quite irrevocably moved away from the city in a spiritual way,' he said. Dublin had almost become a place he could call by that four-letter-word home.

Acts of generosity like that of 4 June that year only served to endear Dublin and Dubliners to him even more. Daniel's grey, BMW convertible car had been parked in the Sandymount district of the city when it had been stolen. When locals discovered what had happened a search was launched. Within two hours the car had been reclaimed from joyriders and returned to its owner.

As a soft Irish summer wore on, Daniel made a significant step towards ending his nomadic, 'no fixed abode' lifestyle. He had asked Grafton Street estate agents Jackson, Stops and McCabe to look for properties in his old childhood heartland of western Ireland. Tamasin was spending more and more of her time at her home in Mayo. She was in the process of making a film on an anchorite nun who lived under the shadow of a favourite haunt, Croagh Patrick, and was able to use her home as a base.

While Daniel sifted through the estate agent's suggestions, however, he learned that one of the outstanding properties in County Wicklow, an area he knew well through Sheridan, was on the market. Castlekevin, a five-bedroomed Georgian house in the shadow of the great mass of the Wicklow Mountains, near the village of Annamoe, had been the home of one of Ireland's greatest playwrights, John Millington Synge. Synge's most famous play, *The Playboy of the Western World*, remains one of the most enduring and popular pieces of Irish theatre. Castlekevin's owners, Dublin solicitor Jonathan Brooks and his wife, had given the go-ahead for an auction of their famous home. Daniel travelled out to Annamoe and instantly fell in love with the property, with its stables and 105 acres of rolling land. An agent involved in the negotiations revealed that he registered for the upcoming auction but then put in a 'very generous' offer of £500,000. It was accepted by the Brookses. By July, Castlekevin was his. Soon he was hinting that he would be living in his beautiful home 'for many years to come'. At last part of him had found a place to lay down roots.

During the late summer he set about furnishing and refurbishing the house. The former cabinet-maker no longer felt confident enough to make his own fittings; local craftsmen were called in instead. Only a brief visit to the Venice Film Festival, where Scorsese's *The Age of Innocence* was being shown, distracted him. He had agreed to attend a press conference for Scorsese. His response to the by now boring old question of Hamlet seemed a measure of his happiness and growing self-confidence. 'The first time I played Hamlet I had some personal difficulties. Oddly enough though, I would quite like to play Hamlet again,' he told gathered journalists. 'I don't know where or when and I don't think it would be for some time, but I will play it again.'

As he returned to Ireland and the work on Castlekevin, however, his composure was dented by Sheridan. The director broke the news that he would need to re-shoot a scene from *In the Name of the Father*. As he worked with editor Gerry Hambling on assembling the film, Sheridan had realized that the climactic scenes he had shot in Liverpool were not all he had hoped. Sheridan's plans to spend $200,000 on a 2000-strong crowd of professional extras for Conlon's triumphal release had been blocked by Universal in a rare intervention. The locals he had used instead had not given him the drama he had wanted for the film's climactic moment.

The decision caused the first serious rift between the two men. Daniel, having once more gone through the difficult process of readjusting to normal life, felt anger at having to slip into Conlon's skin again. After talking the problems through with the director, however, he understood Sheridan's arguments. 'I had to acknowledge with total humility to Shay that the re-shoot was completely justified,' he said.

At the end of September the moment when Conlon emerges from his fifteen-year nightmare at the hands of the English judiciary was re-shot. Days earlier Daniel had faced his own brief appointment with a judge. He had been caught speeding on his 900-cc Triumph motor-bike in the West Country.

If his father's speed-fixation had been fed by his beloved Mercedes, Daniel's desire to fly was satisfied by his passion for powerful motor-cycles. He had first been smitten in Los Angeles during post-production work on *The Unbearable Lightness of Being* back in 1987. A friend offered him a trial run on a Harley Davidson. 'I would lie awake thinking, "Where will the bike take me tomorrow?" I'd invent any excuse to get on it. It's something you never get over.'

Daniel had been travelling from Tamasin's Somerset home to catch a ferry to Roscoff in northern France, from Plymouth, Devon. Police had timed his flying, yellow-leathered figure at 102.56 mph. He dutifully appeared at Cullompton Magistrates in Devon, Tamasin – as ever in a time of crisis – at his side as he faced photographers, to be chastised by court chairman Cyril Williams. 'We are not worried about your safety and well-being, but other road users',' he told a solemn, silent Daniel. 'It was a powerful motor-cycle and his speed unfortunately crept up. He had no excuse. It has caused embarrassment and he is very sorry,' his counsel John Smith told the court. Smith asked for leniency as a long ban would cause 'considerable difficulties'. The court smiled kindly and banned Daniel for just one week, fining him £210 plus £35 costs. He travelled on to Liverpool by train.

The year of Conlon became the year of living dangerously. Weeks later, Daniel was once more brought to heel by authority, no less a power than the United Nations this time.

Along with Jeremy Irons, his mother's old friend Vanessa Redgrave and Sheridan, he had attempted to enter the besieged Bosnian city of Sarajevo. With press passes obtained from the United Nations Protection Forces the four planned to attend a film festival being held in the city. *In the Name of the Father* and Irons and Redgrave's new film, *The House of the Spirits*, were being shown, and their stars had been invited to lift the gloom. In Italy, however, the group had been turned away from the UN aid flights into Sarajevo. The UN High Commission for Refugees said that the actors had been warned there were strict guidelines on who could and could not board aid flights.

News of the abortive journey provoked the most bitter response among journalists, who had seen thirty-seven bona fide colleagues killed in the conflict. 'It is an insult to these people for Vanessa Redgrave and her "luvvies" to use press credentials as a means of furthering what appears to be little more than a stunt for their own publicity,' Britain's National Union of Journalists complained.

Daniel later explained that they had planned to board after aid workers and genuine press people had taken their seats. 'We didn't feel in that respect that we were abusing the system, but it became a bit of a fiasco, unfortunately,' he said. 'It was important primarily because we were invited. Unfortunately the idea of culture seems to be associated with frivolity. It's the last thing that human beings need to survive. If I really believed that, I doubt I'd be doing this work.'

Universal quickly smelled Oscar potential for *In the Name of the Father* and had given Sheridan until late October to deliver. He made his deadline. In December he and his leading man travelled to New York for a charity premiere. *The Age of Innocence* had already opened there, in October, to generally ecstatic notices.

The *New Yorker's* new film critic, Anthony Lane, picked up where Pauline Kael had left off in praising Daniel. He thought his Newland Archer evoked more emotion even than Edith Wharton's tragic portrait. 'If anything he improves on Wharton's original,' he wrote. 'There is huge devastation in his eyes, which are wet not with tears but with pure pain, as if somebody were chewing his leg off under the table.'

'Daniel Day-Lewis's superb performance also helps us to enter Newland's mind and experience the ambivalence that leaves him tragically paralyzed,' wrote Stephen Farber in *Movieline*.

His portrayal was not universally liked, however. Stanley Kauffmann in the *New Republic* thought Daniel 'the biggest disappointment' in a 'thin' film. 'On the basis of Day-Lewis's past work, forceful and graphic in *A Room with a View*, *My Beautiful Laundrette* and *My Left Foot*, he seemed very likely to inhabit the role, to vitalize it. He doesn't. He merely moves through it. There is never a spark to sting us: he leaves us cold, observant.'

There were few cold observers at the post-screening party for *In the Name of the Father*, however. Once again Daniel's effect on members of the opposite sex generated a percentage of the publicity.

In the Name of the Father was premiered at the Museum of Modern Art. Party guests included Spike Lee, Carly Simon and a clutch of so-called supermodels, including Naomi Campbell, Linda Evangelista and Kate Moss. Newspapers in New York, Dublin and London alleged that the models spent the party 'drooling' over the star of the evening's entertainment and that the waif-like Moss penned a 'love poem' for him. The papers then alleged that the couple spent the party 'totally oblivious to everyone and everything' and then 'disappeared' never to reappear, while Sheridan and company headed off for 'a few' at a favourite Irish haunt, Eamon Dornas.

The story by now conformed to a familiar pattern. Neither

Daniel nor his supposed conquest would say a word about events. And within days Isabelle Adjani's striking presence re-emerged. In mid-December according to Dublin newspapers, she was ensconced at Castlekevin. The 'most on–off relationship in the world' had continued to live up to its billing. Within months of Adjani arriving in London in 1992 she had moved back to Paris. In November of that year, on her way back to the French capital, she talked of Daniel in the past tense. 'He has great Irish charm and used to give me the most poetic gifts,' she was quoted as saying.

Early in 1994, however, it appeared that all was lost for the couple. The *Daily Express* in London carried an interview with Adjani which confirmed she had finally given up on the relationship. It seemed as if her attempt at pinning down Daniel had brought the same sacrifices as the only other woman to have a long-running romance with him. 'I am one of those actresses who, when they are in love, forget everything else,' she said. Her commitment had brought the same results as Sarah Campbell's years of devotion. Ultimately the price was disappointment.

Adjani looked back on the affair with happy memories. 'With Daniel, I never noticed that the time was passing by,' she said. 'I'm leaving a mirage. It was painful ... but it was delicious.'

CHAPTER SIXTEEN

WAITING FOR THE WINDS

'The poet knows that spirit is a wind which "bloweth where it listeth". He cannot command its presence. If he is lucky it may whirl him aloft for a few years or a few weeks of his life and then it drops him, it may be, for ever.'

CECIL DAY-LEWIS, speech at Bedales School,
Autumn 1970

B
Y MARCH 1994 the verdict was near enough unanimous. On the downtown Los Angeles newsstands his hawkish, hatchet-jawed face stared out from the cover of *Time* magazine – the preserve of presidents and prime ministers, a cover and seven pages of analysis and interview devoted to the actor they were now calling The Chameleon. Hollywood backed it up with a tsunami of statistics: one of the twenty most powerful actors in the world, the ninetieth most influential figure in the entire film business, a $5-million-and-up movie man, an instant green light for $30 million budgets and upwards.

Even inside the Dorothy Chandler Pavilion, as they applauded Tom Hanks and his Best Actor Oscar, everyone knew Daniel Day-Lewis had passed on the role now giving the American the most emotional moment of his life. Four years on from the triumph of *My Left Foot*, Daniel enjoyed a defeat filled with all manner of victories. Inside and outside the Oscar pavilion almost everyone was now saying it. As *Time* put it: 'probably the most accomplished actor of his generation'.

Typically, Daniel had not been near a telephone on 9 February as his second Oscar nomination had been announced before dawn in Los Angeles. As Academy President Arthur Hiller and actress Christine Lahti listed his name along with those of Hanks, Sir Anthony Hopkins for *The Remains of the Day*, Laurence Fishburne for *What's Love Got to Do with It?*, and Liam Neeson for *Schindler's List*, he had been walking in the Wicklow Mountains. Hard and fast, as usual, oblivious to the fuss.

He picked up the news back at Castlekevin and headed up to join 'Shay' Sheridan, Gerry Conlon, Bono and a party of others at the Clarence Hotel in Temple Bar, Dublin. U2 were about to open a new nightspot, the Kitchen Club, there two nights later. There was no reason why the celebrations should not start immediately.

In the Name of the Father had gone two better than *My Left Foot*, racking up seven nominations. As producer-director, Sheridan had been nominated for Best Picture and Best Director, Postlethwaite for Best Supporting Actor, Emma Thompson for Best Supporting Actress. There were also nominations for soundtrack and screenplay.

Daniel roared up to town on his bike. The forty-five-minute ride from Annamoe to Dublin had become a trial during a sharp Irish winter. Between the mountains and the city the picturesque had become the perilous. At one point, where a stream crossed the road, his Triumph 350 had slalomed off in a heap. He was lucky to have two knees left, he admitted afterwards. Little wonder that film insurance companies now banned him from riding while he was shooting movies they underwrote. Little wonder either that he arrived late for the Oscar party pints at the Clarence Hotel.

After returning from the New York opening of *In the Name of the Father* Daniel had pulled up the Castlekevin drawbridge. Life there was now an echo of the sort of Anglo-Irish past that had, a dozen years earlier, provided the backdrop for *How Many Miles to Babylon?* Brendan Behan called the Anglo-Irishman 'a Protestant with a horse'. Daniel's links with the Church his grandfather had served were tenuous. During his time with Isabelle Adjani he had taken an interest in her chosen religion, Buddhism. He did now, however, have horses. Tamasin, a

261

passionate horsewoman since the Carrowniskey strand race days, helped him choose the stock for his stables. Together brother and sister charged around the Wicklow countryside.

Daniel was not Annamoe's sole celebrity. The director John Boorman and Paddy Moloney, leader of Ireland's most famous traditional band, The Chieftains, also lived there. A mutual friend told Daniel that Boorman believed Castlekevin was haunted.

Throughout December and January, however, Dublin had demanded his occasional presence. It started with a premiere for *In the Name of the Father*, on 16 December 1993. Once more the Savoy Cinema on O'Connell Street wore a feather in its cap. Daniel arrived arm in arm with Emma Thompson. TV crews and reporters from both sides of the Irish Sea were there. In the run-up to its Irish and British releases the controversy over the movie had, predictably, intensified.

First three policemen accused of fabricating the evidence that put the Guildford Four away were acquitted of the charges at the Old Bailey. They had objected to their portrayal as intimidatory bully boys. Then members of the Maguire family expressed their unhappiness at factual inaccuracies in the film. Sheridan had compressed the trial of the Guildford Four and the Maguires into one court-room. In fact they had been held separately. He had also placed one of the family, Annie Maguire, at an appeal she did not attend. 'Playing fast and loose with the facts', the *Daily Telegraph* called it.

Finally it had emerged that Terry George, eventually nominated for an Oscar with Sheridan for his screenplay, had served three years in prison on firearms charges and had connections with the Irish National Liberation Army, the group responsible for one of the most shocking terrorist killings, that of Tory MP Airey Neave at the Houses of Parliament.

The publicity had done the film little harm in America. Thousands of miles from the bloody reality of it all, untouched audiences were being moved to tears by Sheridan's 'good father' story. That angered British critics even more. They said Sheridan's loyalty was to the world's biggest film audience rather than the truth. He had played on the misty-eyed romance of the politically naïve.

The sheer, screaming intensity of Daniel's performance had provided him with almost complete immunity from the political fall-out, however. His portrayal of Conlon had been as electric and vivid as Sheridan and the studio had hoped. To many seeing it for the first time it was his finest role yet, an ultimate expression of the fire within him.

(Sean Day-Lewis and his wife Anna saw something else too. 'In one scene he blows out his cheeks just like Cecil used to do,' says Sean. The King Edward potato had made it on to celluloid.)

In the Name of the Father was not due out in Britain until February. Alexander Walker of the London *Evening Standard* had aided the Sheridan cause greatly in December 1993 by writing a review that dampened some of the furore. The critic did not even think it was a political film. The only storm he felt it deserved was a 'storm of compassion'. 'It is one of the few good things to come out of the Troubles.' Gerry Conlon was a *tour de force*, he thought. 'Daniel Day-Lewis adds one more astonishing change of shape, looks and accent to his storehouse of chameleon roles.'

In the reception at the Savoy, Daniel faced the firing squad and politely backed his decision to make the movie. The film was not anti-English, he said. 'I don't find it so. I think it encourages the British judiciary to subject itself to more rigorous self-examination, but I don't perceive it as anti-English. I was quite overwhelmed by the story,' he told the blanket of reporters. 'It wasn't a case of me choosing the film, more the sense of it choosing me.'

Afterwards Tamasin, a guest at Castlekevin, sat at her brother's side for the official dinner at Dublin Castle. Julian Belfrage and Gene Parseghian were also there, as was Paul Smith, the London clothes designer. Daniel and Smith had met at a Royal Academy of Arts dinner years earlier and had discovered a shared passion for powerful motor-bikes and the cathedral calm of the workshop. They had become close friends.

The next night, with Sheridan, Thompson, Postlethwaite and company, Daniel appeared on *The Late, Late Show*, descending into his mists as the question about his method came up. Daniel revealed that he had no plans for the future. He told Gay Byrne that he was working on his new home and enjoying his new motor-cycle. Over a drink afterwards the two men were lost in a world of their own as they discussed their shared passion for two-wheel speed. 'In that situation Daniel is fine, you see, he loves that sort of conversation,' says a Dublin colleague.

Journalists from England and America travelled to Dublin to see him during the coming weeks. Every editor with his eyes open wanted an interview. Once more Daniel was forced to become the observed rather than the observer. 'Interviews are God's great joke on me,' he confessed. By now, however, there were 'misconceptions' about him which he felt had gone beyond a joke.

Hollywood has always invented stories for its stars. The dream factory demands icons with eye-catching stories. If they do not exist, then make them up. Some, Brando and Burton famously, embellished their biographies themselves. Brando, an insecticide manufacturer's son from Omaha, Nebraska, used to claim he was born in Bangkok or sometimes Rangoon, the son of an eminent etymologist. Burton, who never denied he came from Pontrhydyfen, Wales, once recounted his friend and fellow Welshman Stanley Baker's childhood rather than his own.

Daniel, however, had never wanted any part of that game. He preferred to keep silent on subjects like his love life, his acting method and his time away from the cinema. In the void of his silence, a mythology had grown.

'It pleases people to think I am a kind of roaming maverick on the edge of either committing suicide or killing somebody else and popping all sorts of strange things into my mouth and homeless and unpredictable,' he told Lisa Schwarzbaum of the American magazine *Entertainment Weekly* over tea at 'Shay' Sheridan's Ballsbridge house. 'And I suppose all those things sound quite appealing. And even if all of them at some time in one's life may have a certain degree of truth, it doesn't begin to describe me.'

In interviews with magazines and newspapers including *Time* and *Entertainment Weekly* from America, *Time Out*, the *Guardian* and the *Independent on Sunday* from London, he attempted to slay parts of his own legend. He did not deny the role his father had played in his Hamlet collapse.

'It is true that during that time because of the work I was doing I did preoccupy myself with the relationship of a father and a son and dwell on the aspects of that relationship that I had no protection against when I was very tired,' he told Steve Grant of *Time Out*. Like Hamlet, however, he had now made an accommodation with his father's death. 'I think I've over-stressed in my own mind the degree to which he must only have ever felt I was a source of frustration, someone he was always getting out of trouble,' he told Simon Garfield in the *Independent on Sunday*. 'But parents aren't like that, I can see that now. Parents have problems with their kids, and they get them out of it, and that's life. I don't think my father feared for me in the future, or thought that I was going to end up as a total waster.'

The peace he had now made with his father did not, how-ever, mean he would be left with a peaceful life. Cecil's imprimatur is indelible on his work. The drive and the danger are an inheritance from him, he said. Fear was the key for the poet, and so it is for his son. 'I share with my late father a capacity for running full-tilt towards the things that scare me most, rather than away from them,' he told Simon Garfield. 'That may not necessarily be a very healthy thing to do.'

He had been angered, however, at suggestions that he would be forever haunted by his Hamlet, that he had been 'scarred forever by his encounter with theatre's fiery hoop'. 'Archaic and snooty', he called that view. 'I still look back on it as an interesting experience,' he told *Time Out*.

The distance between Daniel and the English theatre seemed wider than ever before. He was now 'bored to distrac-tion' whenever he went to the theatre and angrier than ever that making movies was still regarded by some as the 'great

Faustian sell-out'. 'I personally think there are works in cinema history which have as much to say to us as any great piece of theatre,' he told *Time*.

As for suggestions that he had re-invented himself as an Irishman, he had a simple reply to Stephen Frears's 'I knew Daniel before he was Irish' remark. 'I never knew Frears before he was a facetious slob.'

In return for the platform to clear up his current bugbears, however, Daniel offered little other than his best angelic smile. Any inquiries about the present state of his relationship with Isabelle Adjani were met with a furrowed brow. When *Entertainment Weekly* asked whether he was in love, he said, 'It's good you saved that question. If it had been the first I might have got back on my bike.' 'The Unbearable Politeness of Being Daniel Day-Lewis', the magazine called the experience of trying to extract something new and unwanted from him.

To his new extended Dublin family, however, Daniel was far more available. Through the rest of the winter they had given him good and bad times.

Since the day he walked into Sandymount Clinic in 1988, he had unobtrusively helped the school and its connected charities. He had carried on writing to one young girl he met there, Clare Louise Creedon. Clare has Friedrich's Ataxia, a genetic disorder which affects her balance and co-ordination. She had written to Daniel late in the year inviting him to an exhibition of her paintings in Dublin. He turned up, made a speech in her honour and helped her sell twenty-nine of her thirty pictures within a day. 'We kept in touch and I knew he'd come tonight if he could,' she told Irish newspapers. 'I was afraid that he might be tied up somewhere else.' 'I never saw her pictures before,' he said. 'They are absolutely beautiful. I am very proud of her.'

In January there had been sadness. Shay's theatrical producer father Peter, who had taken a small role in his son's latest film as the manager of Guiseppe's betting shop, died, aged seventy-one. During the long nights when he and Sheridan had talked about *In the Name of the Father*, Shay had shared the secrets of his filial guilt with Daniel. 'Jim once said to me that a son can't talk to a father unless he's dying, and I know what he means,' he said. At least Sheridan had been able to bridge the gap before the end, however. In the last days of filming in Dublin, Daniel explained in his interview with *Time Out*'s Steve Grant, Sheridan senior had leaned on Sheridan junior on the set. 'I think we all realized that this hadn't happened before in their life.'

During the same week he had helped Bono and The Edge of U2 work on a video to be released with *In the Name of the Father*. The musicians, along with Daniel and Sheridan, had ended up singing in Tosca's restaurant. It was not the first time his light tenor voice had been heard in public. During filming of *In the Name of the Father* he had burst into song at Dobbin's, a popular Dublin eaterie. Years earlier he had also been persuaded to perform at an AIDS benefit concert in London.

At the end of January *In the Name of the Father* and *The Age of Innocence* opened within a fortnight of each other across Britain. Eight years after Johnny and Cecil presented his chameleon credentials to New York, Gerry and Newland offered two more enigma variations. There was division on which was the better role, harmony on what the latest pair of performances proved beyond question.

'I really think, with this performance, that we should all stop pretending that there is any actor on earth who is even in the same league as Lover Boy: he makes De Niro, Oldman, Malkovich, Roth all look like Roger Moore on a bad hair day,' Julie Burchill said in the *Sunday Times*, reviewing *In the Name of the Father*.

Christopher Tookey in the *Daily Mail* had arrived at the same opinion, writing about *The Age of Innocence*. 'He is the most versatile young screen actor in the world today, and the finest by an embarrassingly large margin,' he wrote.

By now every major movie in Hollywood wanted Daniel on board. He had leap-frogged over Tom Cruise, the reigning number one box-office banker, as the name at the top of some most wanted lists. When, the year before, he had been approached to play the lead in an adaptation of the first of Anne Rice's Gothic-chic vampire books, *Interview with the*

Vampire, it had been Cruise who had picked the crumbs off the rich man's table. He read the part of Lestat, but Daniel, twice a distinguished Dracula on stage, did not bite. Anne Rice publicly mourned his decision, also questioning the casting of Cruise and Brad Pitt. 'It is like casting Huck Finn and Tom Sawyer,' she had been quoted as saying. According to Hollywood, Daniel would have been able to ask $5 million and more to play Lestat. In the court-rooms of London, however, there were reminders once more of the days when his value had been a fraction of that.

While the *My Left Foot* court case still rumbled on, another action was being launched by Daniel and his *A Room with a View* co-stars, Helena Bonham-Carter and Julian Sands. In March it was revealed that the trio of actors were suing for their share of the profits of the Merchant–Ivory movie. It emerged that the three, then little known, had signed back-ended deals, which gave them modest up-front payments of around £20,000 each and a share of profits later on.

A Room with a View had become the box-office phenomenon of 1986 in America. Without raising their voices, let alone their fists, Cecil, Lucy and the rest of E. M. Forster's genteel set had eclipsed Sylvester Stallone's Cobra and every other all-action hero Hollywood could bring to the front line to become the most unlikely hit of the spring and summer. Boosted by eight Oscar nominations and three wins (for art direction, adapted screenplay and costumes) the 'art house' film, which had cost a mere £2 million to make, had grossed £20 million at the box office and, according to lawyers, made an £8 million profit. As with *My Left Foot*, however, Daniel, like Bonham-Carter and Sands, claimed he had not seen the 1 per cent share of the profit he was due under his contract. The stars' suit was launched against Goldcrest, the British film company which had subsequently folded.

While lawyers continued to fret over both his cases, Daniel headed off to Los Angeles, to join in the bizarre bingo game that is the Oscars once more. 'It's not about deserving to win – because no one deserves to lose. I thought I might win for *The Apartment* until Elizabeth Taylor had her tracheotomy,' Shirley

MacLaine once said. Long before the end of March, Daniel and the rest of the world sensed that Tom Hanks's character's demise through AIDS meant the other four nominees would be the undeserving losers. Daniel himself had benefited from the Academy's weakness for actors playing the afflicted. Now he would suffer from its sympathy syndrome.

Hanks's performance in *Philadelphia* had undoubtedly enabled him to make the comic-goes-straight transition in one impressive bound. But there was common consensus that both Daniel's performance and Hopkins's, in Merchant–Ivory's lush adaptation of Kazuo Ishiguro's novel *The Remains of the Day*, were finer and subtler.

The sixty-sixth Oscars were to be as predictable as the sixty-second had been unpredictable, however. It was to be the year Steven Spielberg was finally recognized – his Holocaust epic, *Schindler's List*, was to hoover up – and Hollywood was to congratulate itself on making a responsible, popular success on AIDS. There would have been years when a provocative pot-boiler like *In the Name of the Father* might have built up momentum. This was not to be that year, however.

Daniel replaced the sweeping locks and Byronic dress-coat of 1990 with a pixie short haircut and a traditional tuxedo. He sat, more relaxed than before, even managing a smile as his clip was shown.

He was within an envelope's width of Oscar immortality. A win would have made him just the sixth recipient of two Best Actor awards, the first to do so from his first two nominations. At the age of thirty-six, he would have been the youngest double winner in the history of the Oscars. Only Fredric March, Spencer Tracy, Gary Cooper, Marlon Brando, Dustin Hoffman had done it. De Niro had not, nor had Jack Nicholson. It would have been fine company to keep. Instead, the prize went to Hanks.

This time the Irish army returned to Dublin empty-handed. Sheridan could only applaud as *Schindler*'s sweep brought Spielberg long-overdue recognition with Best Picture and Best Director awards. Tommy Lee Jones beat Postlethwaite, Anna Paquin in *The Piano* beat Emma Thompson.

As he headed back to Ireland, Daniel found himself on Hollywood's annual high-roller register – *Premiere* magazine's 100 Most Powerful People in Hollywood list. He is as familiar in Hollywood, County Wicklow, a village a dozen or so miles from Annamoe, through the Wicklow Gap, as he is in Hollywood, California. At least the other nineteen actors on the list, from Kevin Costner (ranked sixth) to Eddie Murphy (ranked eighty-fifth), lived in the right country, if not LA itself. Yet according to *Premiere*, Daniel's absence was only making Hollywood's heart beat stronger. 'Powerful performances in *The Age of Innocence* and *In the Name of the Father* keep him ahead of the acting line, but what will it take to get him into another *Mohicans*-esque audience pleaser?' *Premiere* asked. 'Everyone wants him.'

Daniel's ninetieth place on the 'power list' bore testimony to the sure-footedness he had shown over the past four years. While other actors had stained their reputations with bad choices, Daniel – in Hollywood terms – had made nothing but right moves. He had got his disasters out of the way early in his career. Now he could do no wrong.

Julia Roberts still felt that way too. For months there had been speculation that the ill-fated lovers from *Shakespeare in Love* would work together in *Mary Reilly*, a reworking of the story of *Dr Jekyll and Mr Hyde*. Roberts had once more placed Daniel at the top of her list of leading men. The presence of Stephen Frears as director was seen as an extra attraction. Once more, however, Daniel politely declined.

The fantasy casting continued throughout the spring and early summer. There was talk of a Nathaniel Hawthorne costume drama, *'A' The Scarlet Letter*, a lavish adaptation of Dickens's *A Tale of Two Cities*, to be directed by Terry Gilliam of Monty Python, *Brazil* and *The Fisher King*, and a biopic of Dennis Nilsen, one of Britain's most notorious mass murderers, who killed and mutilated fifteen homosexuals in his north London home. Daniel, it emerged later, was also considered for the lead role of Vince Vega, the hapless hitman, in American wunderkind Quentin Tarantino's second feature, *Pulp Fiction*. Instead the role went to John Travolta, revitalizing in one stroke a career that had seemed becalmed.

There were also whispers of a version of Michael Ondaatje's *The English Patient*, to be produced by Saul Zaentz, an ardent admirer of Daniel since working with him on *The Unbearable Lightness of Being*. If it ever did come to pass the Ondaatje role would further frustrate Hollywood and its yearning for another display of Mohicanesque machismo – the character remains swathed in bandages throughout the story.

Most far-fetched of all, however, Daniel was briefly installed as a 7–1 shot to slip into the dinner jacket of cinema's most enduring secret agent, James Bond. Timothy Dalton's departure late in the spring created a berth that names from Mel Gibson to emerging Englishmen Hugh Grant and Ralph Fiennes were touted for. By June, however, Pierce Brosnan had been given the licence to kill.

Daniel had at least provided his answer to the possibility of him playing Bond years earlier. Asked about the role as he had promoted *My Left Foot*, he had replied: 'Never say never.' No doubt he had done so from behind a cheesy, Cheshire Cat smile.

Isabelle Adjani was, it seemed, another name to defy any attempts at the definitive. As if to prove that the world could also never say never about its most on-off relationship, she resurfaced at Daniel's side in August. Photographs of the two – motorbike helmets swinging in their arms – relaxing in a secluded, southern French town called Saint-Rémy-de-Provence, once more stirred the gossip pot. There were even rumours in French magazines that she was pregnant.

As the summer wore on, however, Daniel remained committed to non-commitment – at least in a professional sense. And so he stands today.

Only he holds the clues to what lies ahead, but it is safe to guess how it will go. There will be days when he will think of never acting again, weeks when he will want nothing more than to enjoy the bog and the breeze, see the foggy dew rise over the Wicklow Mounains, race his bike around the tracks on The Scalp near Enniskerry.

There will be days when he will feel the burden of a part taking over. Then he will emerge again, summoned from his exile by fear and fascination, taken, as his father promised

271

him he would, by 'a wind that bloweth where it listeth'.

It is safe to guess it will be a brief and blazing passion, the sort of romance his father was inspired by too. It will begin with a falling in love and end with an infidelity. It will be a marriage of sorts, and it will end like the rest of them. 'Great at starting affairs but not so good at marriage.'

It is safe to guess it will be an experience filled with pleasure and pain. It will take him into a life far removed from his own. He will selflessly, perhaps selfishly at times, inflict the pain on himself. The pleasure he will leave to the rest of us, the watching, waiting world.

What is certain is that he will remain consistent in his contradictions, an enigma, like Hamlet, a Prince of insoluble opposites.

In a sense, that leaves him no different from the rest of us. He said it himself, of Hamlet: 'He's kind, he's cruel, he's in love, he isn't, he's elated, he's depressed. In other words, he's a human being!'

But of course he is different, he is one of the most compellingly different human beings of our age.

On the day he was born his father called him a 'mannikin' newly broken free from prison, destined from that moment on to step into his own unique identity. A speck of unshaped clay.

The irony is that he has been breaking prison ever since, stepping free, often gratefully, into the comfort of gaols other than the one that is his own identity. Travelling light, unencumbered by his past, the mannikin has chosen to hide behind an iron-barred mask.

Like so many actors, he remains rooted in his childhood. The boy in love with the dressing-up box, the brilliant, barb-tongued sixth former, the kid showing off in the drama school classroom, the pyrotechnic chameleon, each has been moulded from that same atom of clay. 'Scratch an actor and you find a child,' they say. Then scratch Daniel Day-Lewis and you find the most extraordinary of all the boy-men at play in the land of movie make-believe.

The mannikin and his masks, blazing away in the skins of others, keeping his own fires hidden within. Watch him burn.

AFTERWORD

As this book was being readied for publication, Daniel Day-Lewis's life was once more being overwhelmed by the cold and confining realities of life. Once more these forces were leading him to some form of escape. But at what price?

The new year had hardly been ushered in when the first hammer blow struck. Julian Belfrage, his agent and guiding light since his Bristol Old Vic apprenticeship, died of cancer at the age of sixty. Daniel was sorely wounded by the loss of the abrasive Belfrage, the man who had, certainly in a profesional sense, become a surrogate father. The great scythe had removed another paternal influence—a great weight to bear.

Adding to the strain, his relationship with Isabelle Adjani then entered its most acrimonious and public phase. By now Adjani had confirmed that Daniel was the father of the child—a son—she was expecting in the early spring. She had also hinted in the press, however, that he was less happy than she about the impending birth of the baby, apparently conceived in St.-Rémy-de-Provence the previous summer.

The press on both sides of the English Channel worked themselves into a frantic lather as they tracked each twist in the drama, reporting on a series of rows about the pregnancy. The final shot in the war of words came when, according to the press, Daniel contacted Adjani long-distance, breaking off their relationship permanently.

Speculation abounded as to what had happened. As Daniel maintained a monastic silence, only one thing seemed clear: his life was once more entering a phase of renewal, a time to again "travel light."

The question is whether he will be able to do so unencumbered by a past that will soon, all being well, have firm roots in the future? As I have argued in this book, the story of Daniel Day-Lewis is fundamentally one of a father and a son. How will he now fare as a father? Will he repeat his own father's experience, thereby fulfilling his own prediction that "human beings are constantly making the same mistakes from generation to generation"? How will his newest experiences reflect themselves in his work? Time alone will tell.

Los Angeles, March 1995

ACKNOWLEDGEMENTS

There is much that is mysterious about Daniel Day-Lewis. His enigmatic unreachability is, of course, part of his irresistible appeal. Of one thing we can be sure, however. He would rather that this book had not come to be written. I approached him at the very outset of my research, asking for his co-operation and an interview.

During a lengthy, impeccably polite telephone conversation with my editor Helen Gummer a few weeks later he made it clear that he was uncomfortable with the idea of a biography. He repeated his oft-expressed dislike of public scrutiny and concluded that he would prefer not to meet with me.

His decision was, in many ways, a great help, and I would like to thank him for that. In responding in such a straight-forward, uncomplicated way – any other star of his magnitude, I feel sure, would have unleashed publicists and pitbull lawyers – he clarified my task. He did not actually need to do so.

Forced to work harder than an 'official' biographer might, I was led to a disparate group of people who have known him at various stages of his life. They provided a new and, I hope, illuminating view of him. Some of them were happy to be identified, many, particularly those with ongoing professional relationships with him, were not. I owe a debt to each of them.

Of those I can name I am most deeply grateful to Daniel's half-brother Sean Day-Lewis. His permission to draw on his excellent biography of their father Cecil Day-Lewis (*C. Day-Lewis: An English Literary Life*, Weidenfeld & Nicolson/Unwin Books) allied with the advice and the insights he provided during the interviews I conducted with him proved priceless. (It is his view that the Day-Lewis name should always be hyphenated. I have presented it that way even in instances where

Daniel's screen credit, as it often did early in his career, fails to include the hyphen. However I have, for the sake of accuracy, omitted it in direct quotations from other writers where they have presented it in its hyphenless form.)

Special thanks are also due to: Janet Stone, a rare and inspiring woman, for her kindness and in particular her permission to use her wonderfully evocative photographs of Daniel at Greenwich and Litton Cheney, Jenny Passmore and Ann Broadbent, twin guides to the Greenwich of Daniel's childhood, Brian Scragg for permission to draw on his exhaustive history of Sevenoaks School, and Brian and Elizabeth Townend for taking precious time to see me.

For contributions great and small I would also like to thank: Tom Broadbent, Brenda Firminger, Dolly Lyddall, Margot Gair, Ian Saunders, Hugh Pullen, Anne Archer at Bedales, John Makepeace, Rudi Shelley, Simon Dunstan, Penelope Dening, Tony Jordan, Francis Heffernan, Jeremy Northam, Janet Maw, Paul Rossiter at the Associated Newspapers reference library, the staff at the British Film Institute Library, the National Theatre press office, the National Library in Dublin, the Press Association, Pamela Dear at Channel Four, Sylvia Morris at the Shakespeare Birthplace Trust, Michael Daly at Independent Newspapers, Dublin, Mick Brunton at Time Inc., London, Mary McLaughlin at the ILAC Centre, Dublin, Stephen D'Arcy at RTE, Janet Birkett at the Theatre Museum, and Tracy Cronin at the Bristol Old Vic.

A debt is also due to the writers who kindly gave me permission to refer to their interviews with Daniel Day-Lewis. I am particularly grateful to Richard Mayne, Deirdre Purcell, Aileen Joyce and Angela Brooks.

The task of researching and writing this book was a solitary and sometimes maddening experience. To my eager, ever persistent researcher Colin O'Toole I owe thanks for lightening not just the workload but, with wit and wisdom beyond his years, the occasional gloom as well.

In the same vein, heartfelt thanks are also due to Bart, Tina, Lucy, Martyn, Daphne, Steve and Fiona – supporters, soul-savers and encouragers all.

Finally I would also like to thank my editor Helen Gummer for her quiet, calming stewardship of this biography. I look forward to collaborating with her again.

THEATRE, TELEVISION AND FILM 1979–94

THEATRE

The Recruiting Officer (September/October 1979)
Bristol Old Vic
Role: Member of a group of townspeople, soldiers and servants
Director: Adrian Noble   Writer: George Farquhar
Cast: James Cairncross, Andrew Hilton, Albie Woodington, William
    Hoyland, Miles Anderson,. Neil Stacy, Peter Postlethwaite, Lind-
    say Duncan.

Troilus and Cressida (October/November 1979)
Bristol Old Vic
Role: Deiphobus and one of Greek/Trojan soldiers
Director: Richard Cottrell   Writer: William Shakespeare
Cast: Robert O'Mahoney, Meg Davies, Pete Postlethwaite, Jonathan
    Kent, James Cairncross, Andrew Hilton, Patrick Connor.

Funny Peculiar (November/December 1979)
Bristol Old Vic
Role: Stanley Baldry
Director: Peter Postlethwaite   Writer: Mike Stott
Cast: David Neilson, Caroline Holdaway, Nigel Cooke, Mark Lambert,
    Brenda Peters, Sian Thomas, Gregory Martin, Albie Woodington.

Old King Cole (December 1979/February 1980)
Bristol Old Vic
Role: Faz
Director: Bob Crowley   Writer: Ken Campbell
Cast: David Foxxe, Caroline Holdaway, Ian Mackenzie, Robert
    Reynolds, Nigel Cooke, Mark Lambert.

Class Enemy (March/April 1980)
Bristol Old Vic

Role: Iron
Director: David Rome   Writer: Nigel Williams
Cast: Richard Willis, Paul McCleary, John Fowler, Richard Speight, Kelvin Omard, David Foxxe.

Edward II (May/June 1980)
Bristol Old Vic

Role: Leicester
Director: Richard Cottrell   Writer: Christopher Marlowe
Cast: John Boswall, Meg Davies, David Foxxe, Andrew Hilton, Gregory Martin, Paul McCleary, Robert Oates, Robert O'Mahoney, Brian Southwood, Ian Reddington, Stuart Wilson, Clive Wood, Clive Wouters.

Oh, What a Lovely War! (May/June 1980)
Bristol Old Vic

Role: Uncredited
Director: David Tucker   Writer: Joan Littlewood
Cast: Richenda Carey, Sue Aldred, June Barrie, John Boswall, John Telfer, Brian Southwood, Andrew Hilton, Lynne Pearson, Jenny Galloway, Ian Reddington.

A Midsummer Night's Dream (August/September 1980)
Bristol Old Vic

Role: Philostrate, Master of the Revels to Theseus
Director: Richard Cottrell   Writer: William Shakespeare
Cast: Robert O'Mahoney, Nickolas Grace, Louise Jameson, Andrew Bicknell, Julia Hills, Alan Coveney, Carl Halling, Mark Buffery.

Look Back in Anger (January 1981)
Little Theatre, Bristol

Role: Jimmy Porter
Director/Producer: George Costigan   Writer: John Osborne
Cast: Nigel Cooke, Rosalind March, Sally Baxter.

Dracula (February/March 1981)
Little Theatre, Bristol

Role: The Count
Directors: George Costigan, Colin Butler   Writer: Christopher Bond
Cast: Albie Woodington.

Another Country (September 1982/May 1983)
Queen's Theatre, Shaftesbury Avenue

Role: Guy Bennett
Director: Stuart Burge   Writer: Julian Mitchell
Cast: John Dougall, Anthony Calf, Philip Goodhew, Michael Park-
house, Paul Pennington, Simon Roberts, Guy Henry.

Romeo & Juliet/A Midsummer Night's Dream (October 1983/January 1984)
Royal Shakespeare Company 'little tour'

Role: Romeo/Flute
Directors: John Caird, Sheila Hancock   Writer: William Shakespeare
Cast: Amanda Root, Philip Jackson, Penny Downie, Robert Eddison.

Dracula (November/December 1984)
Half Moon, Mile End Road

Role: The Count
Director/Writer: Christopher Bond
Cast: Peter Capaldi, Judy Holt, Richard Ireson, Bob Mason, Victoria
Hardcastle, Erica Shorrnoid.

Futurists (March 1986)
National Theatre

Role: Mayakovsky
Director: Richard Eyre   Writer: Dusty Hughes
Cast: Charlotte Cornwell, Roger Lloyd-Pack, Jack Shepherd, David
Calder, Julian Fellowes.

Hamlet (March/September 1989)
National Theatre

Role: Prince Hamlet

Director: Richard Eyre   Writer: William Shakespeare

Cast: Judi Dench, Michael Bryant, John Castle, Stella Gonet, David Burke, Jeremy Northam.

TELEVISION
(leading roles, UK transmission dates)

Frost in May (1982)
BBC TV

Role: Archie Hughes-Follett

Director: Ronnie Wilson   Producer: Anne Head

Adapted screenplay: Alan Seymour

Cast: Janet Maw, John Carson, Elizabeth Shepherd, Imogen Boorman, Patsy Kensit, Charles Dance.

How Many Miles to Babylon? (1982)
BBC TV

Role: Alexander Moore

Director: Moira Armstrong   Producer: Innes Lloyd

Cast: Christopher Fairbanks, Sian Phillips, Barry Foster.

My Brother Jonathan (1985)
BBC TV

Role: Jonathan Dakers

Director: Tony Garner   Producer: Joe Waters

Cast: Benedict Taylor, Mark Kingston, Helen Ryan, Caroline Bliss, T. P. McKenna.

The Insurance Man (1986)
BBC TV

Role: Mr Kafka

Director: Richard Eyre Producer: Innes Lloyd Screenplay: Alan Bennett

Cast: Robert Hines, Jim Broadbent, Hugh Fraser, Tony Haygarth, Ona Kirsch, Diana Rayworth, Tessa Wojtczak, Ralph Hammond, Roger Hammond, Alan McNaughtan, Geoffrey Palmer, Trevor Peacock.

FILMS

(UK year of release)

Sunday, Bloody Sunday (1971)
UA/Vectia

Role: Delinquent boy

Director: John Schlesinger Producer: Joseph Janni Screenplay: Penelope Gilliatt

Cast: Glenda Jackson, Peter Finch, Murray Head, Peggy Ashcroft, Maurice Denham.

Gandhi (1982)
Columbia/Goldcrest/Indo-British/International Film Investors/National Film Development Corporation of India

Role: Colin, a South African thug

Director/Producer: Richard Attenborough Screenplay: John Briley

Cast: Ben Kingsley, John Mills, John Gielgud, Candice Bergen, Ian Charleson, Trevor Howard, Martin Sheen.

The Bounty (1984)
Dino De Laurentiis/Orion–EMI

Role: Mr Fryer

Director: Roger Donaldson Producer: Bernard Williams Screenplay: Robert Bolt

Cast: Anthony Hopkins, Mel Gibson, Liam Neeson, Laurence Olivier.

281

My Beautiful Laundrette (1985)
Working Title/SAF/Channel Four

Role: Johnny

Director: Stephen Frears   Producers: Sarah Radclyffe, Tim Bevan

Screenplay: Hanif Kureishi

Cast: Saeed Jaffrey, Gordon Warnecke, Shirley Anne Field, Roshan Seth, Derrick Branche.

A Room with a View (1985)
Merchant–Ivory/Goldcrest

Role: Cecil Vyse

Director: James Ivory   Producer: Ismail Merchant   Screenplay: Ruth Prawer Jhabvala

Cast: Maggie Smith, Denholm Elliott, Helena Bonham-Carter, Julian Sands, Judi Dench, Simon Callow.

Nanou (1986)
Umbrella–Caulfield/Arion

Role: Max

Director/Screenplay: Conny Templeman   Producer: Andrew Mollo

Cast: Imogen Stubbs, Jean-Philippe Ecoffey.

The Unbearable Lightness of Being (1987)
Saul Zaentz

Role: Tomas

Director: Philip Kaufman   Producer: Saul Zaentz   Screenplay: Jean-Claude Carrière, Philip Kaufman

Cast: Lena Olin, Juliette Binoche, Erland Josephson, Daniel Olbrychski.

Stars and Bars (1988)
Columbia Pictures

Role: Henderson Dores

Director: Pat O'Connor   Producer: Sandy Lieberson   Screenplay: William Boyd

Cast: Harry Dean Stanton, Martha Plimpton, Joan Cusack.

My Left Foot (1989)
Palace/Ferndale Films/Granada/Radio Telefis Eireann
Role: Christy Brown
Director: Jim Sheridan   Producer: Noël Pearson   Screenplay: Shane Connaughton, Jim Sheridan
Cast: Brenda Fricker, Ray McAnally, Fiona Shaw, Ruth McCabe, Hugh O'Conor.

Eversmile New Jersey (1989)
J & M Entertainment/Los Films Del Camino
Role: Fergus O'Connell
Director: Carlos Sorin   Producer: Oscar Kramer   Screenplay: Jorge Goldenberg, Roberto Shever, Carlos Sorin
Cast: Mirjana Jokovic, Gabriela Acher, Alesandro Escudero.

The Last of the Mohicans (1992)
Twentieth Century Fox
Role: Nathaniel/Hawkeye
Director: Michael Mann   Producers: Michael Mann, Hunt Lowry   Screenplay: Michael Mann, Christopher Crowe
Cast: Madeleine Stowe, Russell Means, Eric Schweig, Jodhi May, Steven Waddington, Wes Studi, Maurice Roeves, Patrice Chereau.

The Age of Innocence (1994)
Cappa/Columbia Pictures
Role: Newland Archer
Director: Martin Scorsese   Producer: Barbara DeFina   Screenplay: Martin Scorsese, Jay Cocks
Cast: Michelle Pfeiffer, Winona Ryder, Miriam Margolyes, Richard E. Grant, Geraldine Chaplin, Sian Phillips, Alec McCowen.

In the Name of the Father (1994)
Universal Pictures
Role: Gerry Conlon
Director/Producer: Jim Sheridan   Screenplay: Terry George, Jim Sheridan
Cast: Emma Thompson, Pete Postlethwaite, John Lynch, Beatie Edney, Corin Redgrave.

283

INDEX

285

286